The Case of Sherlock Holmes

The Case of Sherlock Holmes

Secrets and Lies in Conan Doyle's
Detective Fiction

Andrew Glazzard

EDINBURGH
University Press

Edinburgh University Press is one of the leading university presses in the UK. We publish academic books and journals in our selected subject areas across the humanities and social sciences, combining cutting-edge scholarship with high editorial and production values to produce academic works of lasting importance. For more information visit our website: edinburghuniversitypress.com

© Andrew Glazzard, 2018

Edinburgh University Press Ltd
The Tun – Holyrood Road,
12(2f) Jackson's Entry,
Edinburgh EH8 8PJ

Typeset in 11/13 Adobe Sabon by
IDSUK (DataConnection) Ltd

A CIP record for this book is available from the British Library

ISBN 978 1 4744 3129 3 (hardback)
ISBN 978 1 4744 3132 3 (webready PDF)
ISBN 978 1 4744 3131 6 (epub)

The right of Andrew Glazzard to be identified as the author of this work has been asserted in accordance with the Copyright, Designs and Patents Act 1988, and the Copyright and Related Rights Regulations 2003 (SI No. 2498).

Contents

List of Illustrations vii
Acknowledgements ix
Texts and References xi

Introduction: The Art of Deduction   1

Part I: Finance
1. Stone into Money   11
2. The Roylotts of Stoke Moran   20
3. The Guardians of Securities   30

Part II: Class
4. The Pick of a Bad Lot   39
5. The Fall of the House of Musgrave   50
6. A Scandal in East Yorkshire   61

Part III: Family
7. Singular Occurrence at a Wedding   73
8. The Rock of Gibraltar   83
9. The Discreetly Shadowed Corners   91

Part IV: Sex
10. The Worst Man in London   103
11. The Whole Queer Business of Wisteria Lodge   112

Part V: Race
12. Nice, Amiable People!   125
13. A Nobler Man Never Walked the Earth   138
14. The Heat of the Amazon Was Always in her Blood   147

Part VI: War

15. This Circle of Misery and Violence and Fear   159
16. Do We Progress?   169
17. The East Wind   179

Part VII: Secrecy

18. That Secret History of a Nation   195
19. Oaths and Secrets   206
20. The Giant Rat of Sumatra   218

Conclusion: The Problem of Finality   229

Bibliography   237
Index   245

List of Illustrations

Figure 1 'A very seedy hard felt hat.' Illustration by Sidney Paget, *Strand Magazine*, January 1892.   16

Figure 2 'Which of you is Holmes?' Illustration by Sidney Paget, *Strand Magazine*, February 1892.   22

Figure 3 '"Mr. Hall Pycroft, I believe?" said he.' Illustration by Sidney Paget, *Strand Magazine*, March 1893.   32

Figure 4 'He examined with his glass the word upon the wall, going over every letter of it with the most minute exactitude.' Illustration by D. H. Friston for *A Study in Scarlet*, in *Beeton's Christmas Annual*, 1887.   40

Figure 5 'Reginald Musgrave'. Illustration by Sidney Paget, *Strand Magazine*, May 1893.   57

Figure 6 'Colonel Moran sprang forward, with a snarl of rage.' Illustration by Sidney Paget, *Strand Magazine*, October 1903.   66

Figure 7 'As we approached, the lady staggered against the trunk of the tree.' Illustration by Sidney Paget, *Strand Magazine*, January 1904.   80

Figure 8 'It was the body of a tall, well-made man, about forty years of age.' Illustration by Sidney Paget, *Strand Magazine*, September 1904.   87

Figure 9 'Beside him stood a very young man.' Illustration by Sidney Paget, *Strand Magazine*, February 1904.   95

Figure 10 '*You couldn't come any other time–eh?*' Illustration by Sidney Paget, *Strand Magazine*, April 1904.   105

Figure 11 'This is awful! You don't mean – you don't mean that I am suspected?' Illustration by Arthur Twidle, *Strand Magazine*, September 1908.   115

Figure 12 'I shall reward you, young Sahib, and your governor also, if he will give me the shelter I seek.' Illustration by Herbert Denman in *Lippincott's Magazine*, February 1890.   130

Figure 13 'There was a little coal-black negress.' Illustration by Sidney Paget, *Strand Magazine*, February 1893.   143

Figure 14 'She poured her whole wild fury out in burning and horrible words –' Illustration by Alfred Gilbert, *Strand Magazine*, March 1922.   153

Figure 15 Illustration by Sidney Paget, *Strand Magazine*, January 1893.   163

Figure 16 '"Good heavens!" I cried, in amazement.' Illustration by Sidney Paget, *Strand Magazine*, March 1902.   171

Figure 17 'He was gripped at the back of his neck by a grasp of iron, and a chloroformed sponge was held in front of his writhing face.' Illustration by Arthur Gilbert, *Strand Magazine*, September 1917.   189

Figure 18 'Do you mean to say that anyone holding these three papers, and without the seven others, could construct a Bruce-Partington submarine?' Illustration by Arthur Twidle, *Strand Magazine*, December 1908.   199

Figure 19 'He nearly fainted at the sudden shock of it, but he bit his lip and clenched his hands to hide his agony. "I can take more of that," said he.' Detail from illustration by Frank Wiles, *Strand Magazine*, March 1915.   211

Figure 20 'He did not rise, but sat upon a floor like some strange Buddha.' Illustration by Frank Wiles, *Strand Magazine*, February 1927.   222

Figure 21 'The death of Sherlock Holmes.' Illustration by Sidney Paget, *Strand Magazine*, December 1893.   228

Acknowledgements

Like many others, I first encountered Sherlock Holmes in childhood – in the series of films from the 1930s and 1940s starring the incomparable Basil Rathbone (shown in the 1970s on BBC2, as I recall), and then in an abridged audiobook of *The Hound of the Baskervilles* narrated by Hugh Burden. Several decades later, I have been fortunate to have an opportunity to return to the stories as a part-time academic rather than a childish enthusiast: this book is the result.

There are many people to thank. Douglas Kerr, author of a brilliant monograph on Conan Doyle and now general editor of the forthcoming Edinburgh Edition of the Works of Arthur Conan Doyle, contributed both knowledge and support; most importantly, if he had not employed me as his post-doctoral research assistant for his work on George Orwell, there is a very good chance that this book would not have been written. Robert Hampson, who supervised my PhD on Conrad, was an invaluable source of advice as I embarked on this project. Other members of the board of the Edinburgh Edition have been supportive in different ways, in particular Jonathan Cranfield, Linda Dryden, Anthony Mandal, Jonathan Wild, and, at Edinburgh University Press, Michelle Houston and Adela Rauchova. Two anonymous readers of the sample material I supplied to EUP provided perceptive and helpful comments.

I have benefited greatly from the generosity and friendship of the Edwardian Culture Network (ECN), especially two of its founding members, Samuel and Sarah Shaw, and Harry Wood; I presented a version of Chapter 16 ('Do We Progress?') at the ECN's conference at Lancaster University in 2017. I should also thank the organisers of the 2016 conference of the British Association of Victorian Studies (BAVS) at Cardiff University at which I presented a version of Chapter 1 ('Stone into Money'). I would particularly like to thank Adam Green, editor of the excellent *Public Domain Review*, whose acceptance of an essay on 'The Empty House' in 2013 enabled me to make my first step towards a sceptical reading of the Holmes saga, which eventually became this book. I draw on the material from this essay at various points, especially in Chapter 6 ('A Scandal in East Yorkshire').

Much of this book was written in the British Library and the incomparable London Library, and I would like to thank the expert librarians and other staff at both institutions, which, in their different ways, provide an invaluable service to literary scholars.

Most importantly, I would like to thank Sarah Mitchell, for reading and commenting on the manuscript, for tolerating my frequent absences, but most importantly for her love and support.

Texts and References

Unless otherwise stated, all quotations from the Sherlock Holmes stories are taken from the Oxford Sherlock Holmes (general editor Owen Dudley Edwards), first published in 1993. (Details of each volume can be found in the bibliography.) To spare the reader an excess of endnotes, page references for quotations from the Holmes stories are in parentheses in the text; all other works are referenced by endnotes. Shortened titles (*Adventures*, *Hound*, *Last Bow*, etc.) have been used for the first quotation from a volume in each chapter.

Introduction

The Art of Deduction

'You know my methods. Apply them, and it will be instructive to compare results.'
Arthur Conan Doyle, *The Sign of Four* (1890)

'A Case of Identity' (1891) opens, like so many stories in the Sherlock Holmes saga, in 221B Baker Street, where Holmes and Dr Watson receive a new client who bears a problem that is also a story. Watson is both Holmes's pupil in the science of detection and, crucially, the story's narrator. Both roles give him the scope to observe and record the client, Miss Mary Sutherland: his description for the reader of her 'preposterous hat', 'vacuous face' and 'general air of being fairly well to do, in a vulgar, comfortable, easy-going way' (*Adventures*, 39–40) suggests that she is bourgeois ordinariness personified. However, in this instance as in many others, Watson is a conventional but somewhat limited narrator – he reports accurately enough, but also superficially. Holmes sees beyond her appearance and detects her uniqueness as a human being: she is 'an interesting study ... more interesting than her little problem, which, by the way, is rather a trite one' (39). Her problem, of course, turns out to be anything but trite, but Holmes's message is that no one is as ordinary as they might appear. Put on the spot by Holmes, Watson succeeds in identifying only the outward and obvious features of her appearance, particularly the colours and cuts of her apparel. Holmes's response is crushing: 'It is true that you have missed everything of importance, but you have hit upon the method.' Holmes upbraids Watson for failing 'to realize the importance of sleeves, the suggestiveness of thumb-nails, or the great issues that may hang from a bootlace' (40). 'It has long been an axiom of mine that the little things are infinitely the most important' (36), Holmes tells Miss Sutherland. Watson has trusted to 'general impressions' but missed the details: the traces left in the plush of her sleeve by habitually leaning on a table reveal her to be a typist; her nose bears the dint of a pince-nez, indicating shortsight; her boots are odd, not a pair, and incorrectly buttoned, so she put them on in a hurry; an ink-stain on her glove and finger shows she had written a note in haste. 'You appear to read a good deal upon her which is invisible to me', is Watson's response. Holmes corrects him: 'Not invisible, but unnoticed' (40).

The Case of Sherlock Holmes examines the 'little things' in the Holmes saga in order to detect stories that are present but which are concealed or obscured and which are, therefore, usually unnoticed. Some of these stories are implied but overlooked or not examined by Watson. Some are deliberately concealed by Holmes. Others are invisible to us because we have lost touch with the contemporary context that would have been familiar to Doyle's readers. As 'A Case of Identity' exemplifies, Watson's limited insight is one of Doyle's principal techniques of obfuscation. Watson may not be wilfully mendacious, but he frequently gets things wrong or overlooks them because, while he succeeds as a reporter, he fails *as a reader*. Holmes, by contrast, skilfully reads not only people like Mary Sutherland, but also objects, such as Watson's watch in *The Sign of Four* or Dr Mortimer's stick in *The Hound of the Baskervilles* (1902). He is also a careful and sophisticated reader of texts. In *A Study in Scarlet* (1887), for example, he correctly reads '*Rache*', written in blood at the crime scene, as the German word for 'revenge' whereas the police assume it to be an abbreviated attempt to write 'Rachel'; in 'The Adventure of The Three Gables' (1926) he unlocks the case through an interpretation of Douglas Maberley's agonised prose and deduces from its inconsistent use of pronouns that it must be autobiographical. What Holmes calls 'the Science of Deduction' (*Study*, 19) is, then, a method of reading, and one that Holmes implicitly teaches to the reader as well as to Watson. The 'solutions' that Holmes reveals almost invariably hinge on what appear to others as trivialities – as he says in 'The Adventure of The Red Circle' (1911), the 'smallest point may be the most essential' (*Last Bow*, 96). And yet there are other details in the narratives which escape incorporation into the plot but which remain obstinately present, and frequently unexplained.

Holmes, we should remember, also acts as a narrator, and not just in the two late stories from 1926, 'The Adventure of the Blanched Soldier' and 'The Adventure of the Lion's Mane', which he rather than Watson narrates from the outset. Holmes is very frequently an internal narrator, reporting to Watson his activities and deductions. In 'A Scandal in Bohemia' (1891), for instance, he tells Watson in some detail how he carried out surveillance of Irene Adler in disguise, what he discovered and how he became an accidental witness at her wedding. In 'The Adventure of the Gloria Scott' and 'The Adventure of the Musgrave Ritual' (both 1893), Holmes digs out old cases from his archive and retells them to Watson. But some of Holmes's accounts are highly problematic, including a strikingly contradictory account of his first meeting with Professor Moriarty in 'The Adventure of the Final Problem' (1893), which will be discussed in this book's conclusion.

More generally, Holmes may be infinitely more perceptive than Watson but he is also – often by his own admission – rather less honest. In addition to adopting disguises and false identities, gaining entry to premises through subterfuge, and obtaining information through trickery, Holmes is capable of spinning elaborate fictions to save the reputations of others or to ensure that the public have a satisfactory explanation for disturbing events. In 'The Adventure of the Speckled Band' (1892), for example, he colludes with the authorities to ensure that Dr Grimesby Roylott's death is recorded as accidental at the inquest – whereas Roylott was the victim of his own murderous plot (and with Holmes's own actions contributing significantly to his death). 'The Adventure of the Abbey Grange' (1904) goes further, and offers a sustained and sceptical examination of the reliability, credibility and accuracy of apparently authoritative accounts. In his investigation of the death of Sir Eustace Brackenstall, Holmes initially accepts the explanation, offered by Lady Brackenstall and confirmed by her maid, of a burglary gone wrong. When, however, he realises the significance of a detail at the crime scene – the presence of beeswing in a wine glass – he announces to Watson that Lady Brackenstall's plausibility, charm and social status do not automatically make her a reliable witness: 'dismiss from your mind the idea that anything which the maid or her mistress may have said must necessarily be true' (277). But when Holmes discovers Lord Brackenstall to be a treacherous, serial abuser of his wife, and the real killer to be Lady Brackenstall's former lover who was acting in self-defence, he agrees to keep silent and allow the fabricated cover story to remain the 'official' explanation.

As Tzvetan Todorov has pointed out, the form of the detective story requires two stories – the story of the investigation (what narratologists call 'subject'), told chronologically, and the story of the crime (the 'fable'), told in reverse.[1] 'The Abbey Grange', though, is more complex: it has two fables – the official solution (a burglary, a glass of wine, a violent death), and what we are told actually occurred (a love affair, a betrayal, an abusive relationship, a return, an accident). 'Truth' in the Holmes canon is multiple and variable, not fixed or absolute, and so stories multiply too. For this reason the sceptical reader is frequently dissatisfied by Holmes's apparently definitive explanations. This was noticed as early as 1945 by Edmund Wilson, who pointed out in a classic essay that the brilliantly surreal *mise en scène* of 'The Adventure of the Greek Interpreter' (1893) is insufficiently explained in the story's conclusion:

> [A] professional interpreter of Greek finds himself suddenly shanghaied in a cab and taken to a stuffy London house with velvet furniture, a high white marble mantelpiece and a suit of Japanese armour, where a man who wears glasses and has a giggling laugh compels him to put questions in Greek to a pale and emaciated captive, whose face is crisscrossed with sticking plaster. . . . The way of accounting for the sticking plaster seems, indeed, entirely unsatisfactory, and since Watson tells us that this 'singular case' is 'still involved in some mystery,' we are almost inclined to suspect that the affair concealed something else which the detective had failed to penetrate[.][2]

Wilson had earlier assumed in his essay that the errors and loose ends of the Holmes stories can be attributed to Conan Doyle's carelessness in writing what Wilson considered to be superior potboilers, but here he acknowledges that more may be going on beneath the surface. 'The Greek Interpreter' is a good example of a story with numerous minor puzzles in which much is left open: the villains Harold Latimer and Wilson Kemp escape from their sinister house, taking their victim (Sophy Kratides) with them; months later Latimer and Kemp are found stabbed to death in Budapest, apparently after a fight, although Holmes appears to surmise that Sophy has had her revenge. But even this is expressed by Watson in a curiously provisional mode: 'Holmes, however, is, I fancy, of a different way of thinking, and he holds to this day that if one could find the Grecian girl one might learn how the wrongs of herself and her brother came to be avenged' (*Memoirs*, 212). The story is indeed 'still involved in some mystery' (211) – but exactly what kind of mystery is left only partially disclosed.

Some stories have become obscure not through Doyle's artistry, but simply because we do not tend to read them in their historical contexts, whereas Doyle's first readers would have recognised their frames of reference. For example, Holmes and Watson make numerous forays into the world of the aristocracy and landed gentry, where they often encounter folly, and sometimes find rampant criminality. In the late nineteenth and early twentieth centuries, readers would have been more attuned to at least some of the symptoms of the enormous and fundamental changes going on in British society, in which landowners were largely replaced at the pinnacle of British politics and society by a new elite, enriched by manufacturing, commerce or financial speculation, and accompanied by a new segment of the middle class which derived status and income from professional services.[3] As this book will show, the Holmes saga narrates the fall of the aristocracy and the rise of the middle class in stories such as 'The Speckled Band', 'The Musgrave Ritual', 'The Abbey Grange', 'The Adventure of the Priory School' (1904) and 'The Problem of Thor Bridge' (1922). Similarly, today's readers are likely to know less than Doyle's contemporaries about divorce law reform, the shenanigans of the Prince of Wales who became King Edward VII, and the great national self-examination that followed Britain's pyrrhic victory in the Second Boer War (1899–1902). All of these issues and many others are part of the texture of the Holmes saga, and this book aims to tease out these contexts, thereby showing the stories, to quite a surprising extent, to be socially and politically engaged.

When Holmes interprets and deciphers Douglas Maberley's writing in 'The Three Gables', he is engaging in a literary-critical practice called 'close reading'. Close reading – attending to the specific, individual, particular features of a text – has developed beyond the aesthetically focused 'practical criticism' which was in vogue in literary studies during the 1930s and 1940s, and which Terry Eagleton has dismissed as 'just a more rigorous form of wine-tasting'.[4] As Eagleton suggests, a drawback of this approach was in excluding from study anything outside a text, including its social and political contexts. But literary criticism has moved beyond this limitation, and it is now not unusual to find close reading techniques on display in works which bring in intellectual, social and political history. After all, context readily becomes text in that writers will often use their knowledge of the real world when constructing fiction, consciously or otherwise, and we can detect and interpret the relationship between text and context by focusing on textual details. As Holmes demonstrates, a textual detail such as a pronoun or a single word may be a sign of something truly important, such as a sexual relationship, or a murder. However, Holmes also demonstrates that close reading is necessary but not sufficient. He also brings two vital qualities to the science of deduction: knowledge and imagination.

Holmes's knowledge is formidable but, at least in the first story, *A Study in Scarlet*, very idiosyncratic. Early on in their friendship, Watson discovers that Holmes knows an enormous amount about chemistry and crime, but does not know that the earth orbits the sun. This leads Watson to assemble a summary of Holmes's strengths and limitations: 'Knows nothing of practical gardening . . . Has a good practical knowledge of British law' (16). Holmes's limitations might seem odd until we read his explanation of why he chooses to know some things and not others: 'the skilled workman is very careful indeed as to what he takes into his brain-attic' (15). Holmes's criterion for selection is criminological value: cosmology has no conceivable application in that field, so it is excluded. For Holmes, knowledge is valuable only in its application. As it happens, Holmes becomes considerably more knowledgeable about topics that he initially disdained. The most famous example is the Victorian sage Thomas Carlyle, whom Holmes quotes in *The Sign of Four* despite not knowing a thing about him in *A Study in Scarlet*.[5] By 'The Adventure of the Bruce-Partington Plans' (1908), Holmes has become an expert on the polyphonic motets of the Renaissance composer Lassus, and in his retirement he becomes a published authority on bee-keeping. However, despite his apparent disdain for acquiring knowledge for its own sake, Holmes repeatedly demonstrates the value of general knowledge in solving crimes, on topics ranging from German vocabulary (*A Study in Scarlet*), tropical snakes ('The Speckled Band'), the behaviour of sediment in wine ('The Abbey Grange'), as well as more specialised matters such as bicycle tyres, tobacco ash and newspaper typefaces. Even more importantly, Holmes knows where to go to find out more. He keeps a formidable archive to record his own casework as well as newspaper reports about crimes and criminals, and – like a good academic researcher – is able to locate the relevant literature. In 'The Lion's Mane', for example, he uses a real book, John George Wood's *Out of Doors: A Selection of Original Articles on Practical Natural History* (1874), as the source of his knowledge of unusual jellyfish (*Case-Book*, 189).

Contextual knowledge is essential to decode the full meaning of a Sherlock Holmes story. As with Holmes's deductions, knowledge of what might seem to be irrelevant or arcane topics – the price of wheat, an obscure Victorian gambling scandal, the topography of a South African valley are just three instances I shall explore later – can illuminate a story and offer ways of reading it anew. As well as historical and social context, the knowledge drawn on in this book is also literary and biographical. Like many of his contemporaries,

Doyle was a voracious reader and he incorporated elements from many of his favourite works in the Holmes saga, in particular novels and short stories by Edgar Allan Poe, Robert Louis Stevenson and Wilkie Collins. It is well known that Doyle based Holmes in part on Poe's C. Auguste Dupin (as well as Émile Gaboriau's M. Lecoq), but Doyle's frequent allusions to Poe sometimes provide significant contexts which help us interpret stories more fully. Doyle's reading, partly documented in his memoir *Through the Magic Door* (1907), often provides an interpretative key to unlock their inner meaning. So too do the facts of Doyle's life. While using a writer's life to understand his or her work is fraught with theoretical and methodical risks – it is all to easy to read fiction simplistically as an expression of an author's opinions and experiences – Doyle's life provides some valuable clues that it makes sense to explore. His social and political campaigns – for divorce law reform, for more effective propaganda in time of war, and for the victims of miscarriages of justice – are just three of the issues which we can see influencing the Holmes saga.

The third element of the Holmesian approach is imagination. Holmes demonstrates the value of imagining what might have occurred in 'The Adventure of Silver Blaze' (1892), and criticises the otherwise capable Inspector Gregory for lacking an imaginative approach. He similarly takes Inspector Lestrade to task in 'The Adventure of the Norwood Builder' (1903). But the importance of imagination is implicit throughout the saga, and is the quality that most clearly separates Holmes from the far less successful police detectives who almost always follow the most obvious line of enquiry. Imagination allows Holmes to see the full range of possibilities, which can then be narrowed down by the patient collection of evidence and its analysis, leading to his most famous dictum: 'when you have eliminated the impossible, whatever remains, *however improbable*, must be the truth' (*Sign*, 41). Imagination is equally necessary in literary criticism, and not just because we are dealing with imaginative works in a very obvious sense. Literary criticism is interpretation as much as analysis, and thanks to the insights of theorists from the New Critics of the 1940s to the structuralists and post-structuralists from the 1960s onwards, there are few literary scholars today who assume that there is a single, correct interpretation of a literary text, or that the job of the reader is to simply deduce what lay in the author's mind when he or she was writing. All literary texts are open to a range of readings and the process of interpretation necessarily involves constructing as well as decoding meaning. One of the principal arguments of this book is that the Holmes stories – once dismissed by critics as simplistic crowd-pleasers, and not worthy of academic attention – invite and at times demand highly imaginative interpretations, and can be surprisingly open to a wide range of possible meanings.

The Case of Sherlock Holmes is an attempt to follow Holmes's own advice in 'A Case of Identity' and read what is '[n]ot invisible, but unnoticed' in the stories. Following this advice will lead to a wide range of readings and re-readings, examining the stories' preoccupation with unhappy marriages, the recurrence of plots involving stocks and shares, and the occasional hints that Sherlock as well as his brother Mycroft works for British Intelligence. Throughout, the apparently incidental will be shown to be highly significant to the themes and subtexts of the stories. I shall explain why the grisly and partly suppressed story 'The Adventure of the Cardboard Box' (1893) alludes to the death of General Gordon and the American Civil War, why blackmail is presented in 'The Adventure of Charles Augustus Milverton' (1904) as a crime worse than murder, and why 'The Adventure of Wisteria Lodge' (1908) and 'The Blanched Soldier' encode homosexual relationships into the text. I shall challenge the official accounts in stories such as 'The Adventure of the Empty House' (1903), showing that Holmes's preposterous explanation of the Hon. Ronald Adair's murder is a deception. *The Case of Sherlock Holmes* comprises twenty essays organised into seven parts – finance, class, family, sex, race, war and secrecy – plus a conclusion. Its primary aim is to show that, for all their lightness of touch, the Holmes stories are often implicated in the political and social circumstances in which they were written, and are deeper and more complex than they first appear.

Notes

1. See 'The Typology of Detective Fiction' in Todorov, *The Poetics of Prose*, pp. 42–52.
2. Edmund Wilson, '"Mr Holmes, They Were the Footprints of a Gigantic Hound"', p. 35.
3. For background to these developments, see Chapter 2 below.
4. Eagleton, *Literary Theory*, p. 38.
5. For a more detailed discussion of the selectiveness and inconsistency of Holmes's knowledge, see Douglas Kerr, *Conan Doyle*, pp. 71–6.

Part I: Finance

Chapter 1

Stone into Money

The Adventures of Sherlock Holmes, published in the bestselling *Strand Magazine* in 1891–2, shows Holmes investigating not just his clients' problems, but the hidden wiring of Victorian Britain. The wires were the social and economic relationships that connected cab drivers to kings, pawnbrokers to bankers, and hotel attendants to countesses. In these stories Holmes detects not only the physical traces of those relationships, such as the bruises on a woman's wrist or the shiny patch on a man's cuff, but also the financial traces. Usually overlooked by readers and critics, Holmes's skill as an economist is fundamental to his detective method, and fundamental to the social function of Conan Doyle's detective fiction.

We can see this demonstrated in the first of the stories, 'A Scandal in Bohemia' (1891). The story begins with Holmes receiving a letter, unsigned, asking for his assistance on a matter of profound importance to one of the royal houses of Europe. Holmes examines the paper and concludes that it is from Bohemia, and that it is expensive. 'Such paper could not be bought under half-a-crown. It is peculiarly strong and stiff' (9). Holmes then observes the author of the note arriving at Baker Street in a 'nice little brougham and a pair of beauties. A hundred and fifty guineas apiece. There's money in this case, Watson, if there is nothing else' (9–10). Holmes can read this particular client even before meeting him: the clues he identifies point not only to the wealth but also to the character of the client, whom we later discover to be the King of Bohemia. Although he employs a rather unsuccessful disguise, this is a man who wishes to demonstrate to the world that he is wealthy. The king's behaviour anticipates one of the period's most influential economic theories, 'conspicuous consumption', set out by the American economist Thorstein Veblen in *The Theory of the Leisure Class* (1899), his famous study of the lifestyles of the rich and famous. Veblen argued that those who do not need to work display their wealth so as to maintain their status: by encouraging those beneath them to envy and emulate them (rather than, as Karl Marx predicted, to rise up in revolt), they cement their positions at the top of the hierarchy.[1] Despite being incognito, the king cannot put aside his need to show off, behaviour that would not have surprised Veblen just as it does not surprise Holmes. But the king's ostentatious wealth is part of a broader examination of economic behaviour in the story, which suggests that Doyle was attuned to what economists had begun to claim about society – not just the plutocrats and aristocrats studied by Veblen, but everyone.

The most significant and influential British economist of the late Victorian period was Alfred Marshall. The first holder of the chair of economics at Cambridge University, by the 1890s Marshall was probably the world's leading thinker in neoclassical economics, a school of thought which sought to model economic behaviour through the application of mathematics and logic, and which focused on markets rather than whole economies. In his enormously influential *Principles of Economics*, published shortly before *The Adventures* in 1890, Marshall made a series of important claims which shaped the way that economics was understood, and how it was taught, for many decades. Three of his claims are relevant here. The first is that when we study markets – the buying and selling of goods – we are really studying mankind: 'Political economy or economics is a study of mankind in the ordinary business of life . . . Thus it is on the one side a study of wealth; and on the other and more important side, a part of the study of man.'[2] In other words, observing economic transactions helps us to understand people and how they interact in society. The second is the notion of consumption. The metaphor, one of the most fundamental in economics, is misleading: even when we consume something literally, like food or drink, Marshall claims – and here he was following his predecessor William Stanley Jevons who invented the economic concept of 'marginal utility' – that we are really consuming utilities, not the thing itself.[3] In other words, it is the pleasure or use that we gain from a good or service that we are enjoying: 'the "consumer" of pictures, of curtains, and even of a house or yacht does little to wear them out himself; but he uses them while time wastes them'.[4] This means that the value of a good or service is dependent on the demand for it, and demand is determined by how much pleasure or use we can get out of the good or service; 'marginal utility' means the additional pleasure we gain from an additional unit. The third claim is that utility is not the only factor at work in markets. There is production as well as consumption, and supply as well as demand. Marshall's conceptualisation of the relationship between supply and demand was probably his greatest single gift to economics. He envisaged supply and demand working together like two blades of a pair of scissors, and the point at which they cross is the price of a good or service. Prices go up or down in relation to changes in supply and demand: greater supply means lower prices; greater demand means higher prices.

It is perhaps unlikely that Conan Doyle actually read *Principles of Economics*, or took much interest in academic economics – although he was knowledgeable enough to identify 'the large questions of supply and demand which regulate the price of labour' in a letter to the *Daily Mail* in 1912 taking issue with the sociological speculations of H. G. Wells.[5] But stories such as 'A Scandal in Bohemia' demonstrate a high degree of interest in economic behaviour and how it can be detected, and there is a great deal of commonality between Doyle's assumptions and conclusions, and those of Marshall and his marginalist predecessors. Doyle was far from being alone in his interest: for instance, as Regenia Gagnier has shown, Oscar Wilde engages directly with neoclassical economics in works such as *The Picture of Dorian Gray* (1891), a work admired by Doyle and which the American publisher J. M. Stoddart commissioned for *Lippincott's* magazine at the same dinner at London's Langham Hotel during which he commissioned Doyle's *The Sign of Four* (1890).[6] But whereas Wilde was concerned to demonstrate the superiority of art to the quotidian reality of market transactions – 'All art is quite useless'; 'Nowadays people know the price of everything, and the value of nothing'[7] – Doyle is interested in what prices can reveal about the people transacting relationships and their values. This is evident in the attention paid in 'A Scandal in Bohemia' to the compromising photograph of the king with the American music-hall artist Irene Adler. Holmes assumes that Adler is merely a blackmailer, and tells the king that he has no option but to buy the photograph from her, but the king reports that she will not sell. Her reluctance to part with the photograph is presumably explained by the fact that it has sentimental value for Adler – and value is what this story is concerned with, as shown by the series of economic transactions that follow. The king pays Holmes a thousand pounds in gold and notes for his service; the man who turns out to be Adler's fiancé pays a cab half a guinea to get him to the church on time; Adler then does the same, paying half a sovereign; Holmes sets off in pursuit, and pays another cab half a sovereign also to get to the church; Holmes in disguise is then recruited to witness Adler's wedding, for which she pays him a whole sovereign. So in this world in which most things can be bought and premiums are paid for particularly good service, Irene Adler's refusal to sell stands out, and it becomes the focus of the story's climax and its finale. 'When a woman thinks that her house is on fire', Holmes tells us, 'her instinct is at once to rush to the thing which she values most', so he uses a smoke rocket to trick her into showing him the location of the photograph (25). But the value of the photograph turns out not to be sentimental, but entirely practical: Irene Adler needs it as a weapon to protect herself from the King's power. This in effect makes it priceless – or at least gives it a utility for Irene which is so high that the market cannot allocate a price to it.

The economic facts of this and other stories in *The Adventures* are plain enough, although easily overlooked by a modern reader uninterested in such apparently trivial details as how much it cost to hire a cab in Victorian London. Even more important in *The Adventures* is the method that Holmes uses to make deductions from financial data. We can see this illustrated in one of the most celebrated of the early stories, 'The Red-Headed League' (1891). This story is set, literally, in the centre of the Victorian economy: its main events take place in and near the fictional Saxe-Coburg Square, which Watson describes as being situated adjacent to 'one of the main arteries which convey the traffic of the City to the north and west', a 'roadway . . . blocked with the immense stream of commerce flowing in a double tide inwards and outwards' (64). The story begins with the narrative of the red-haired Jabez Wilson, a pawnbroker – someone who acts in effect as a banker using consumer goods as security for his loans. He answers a newspaper advertisement inviting applicants to join the Red-Headed League and earn 'a salary of four pounds a week for purely nominal services' (52) – which turns out to be copying out the *Encyclopaedia Britannica*. Wilson turns up to work at offices owned by an accountant. And the target of what turns out to be an elaborate plot to gain access to Wilson's cellar is the Coburg branch of the City and Suburban Bank, which is holding a loan from the Bank of France of thirty thousand Napoleons (gold coins).

Wilson's story contains two important clues that Holmes immediately notices. One is that Wilson is being paid quite handsomely to do something of very little importance; the other is that Wilson is paying his assistant, Vincent Spaulding, half of what the market would dictate. These are obviously financial clues, and Holmes's skill in detecting what they mean – that Spaulding is not who he says he is, and is part of a plot to get Wilson out of his shop – depends crucially on Holmes's knowledge of prices. In this case it is the price for labour, and Holmes's understanding of its market value enables him to appreciate variations from what supply and demand in theory should determine.

The significance of this was astutely noted by Franco Moretti in a classic essay on detective fiction, one of the few critical works to identify the importance of economics in the genre:

> The economic ideology of detective fiction rests entirely upon the idea that supply and demand tend quite naturally towards a perfect balance. Suspicion often originates from a violation of the law of exchange between equivalent values: anyone who pays more than a market price or accepts a low salary can only be spurred by criminal motives.[8]

Other stories in *The Adventures* feature similarly suspect wage rates: Victor Hatherley in 'The Adventure of the Engineer's Thumb' earns a mere twenty-seven pounds and ten shillings from two years' work as a consultant, but is then offered fifty guineas for a single night's work; Violet Hunter in 'The Adventure of the Copper Beeches' (1892), who previously earned four pounds a month, is offered £120 a year to act as governess to Jephro Rucastle's obnoxious son. In all of these cases, as Moretti observes, disproportionate wages are not evidence of labour market failure: when we know for example that the criminals in 'The Red-Headed league' are after a consignment of French gold, their willingness to pay over the odds to their employee and receive below-market wages is entirely rational and explicable. Rucastle and the counterfeiters of 'The Engineer's Thumb' have similarly pecuniary motivations.

The most sustained demonstration of Holmes's skill as an economist-detective comes in 'The Adventure of the Blue Carbuncle' (1892), the story of a Christmas goose found with a stolen gem in its crop. The story begins with a celebrated scene in which Holmes exercises his deductive method on a battered billycock hat, abandoned with the goose after an altercation on Christmas morning in Tottenham Court Road. After describing the circumstances of the incident, Holmes invites Watson to apply his method, who fails to see anything. Holmes then performs a master class in ratiocination, deducing that its owner is intelligent, sedentary, unfit, has 'fallen upon evil days', has regressed morally (possibly as a result of alcoholism) but retains a measure of self-respect, is married to a woman who no longer loves him, has grizzled hair 'which he anoints with lime-cream', and probably does not have 'gas laid on in his house' (152). Crucially, Holmes is able to deduce all this because

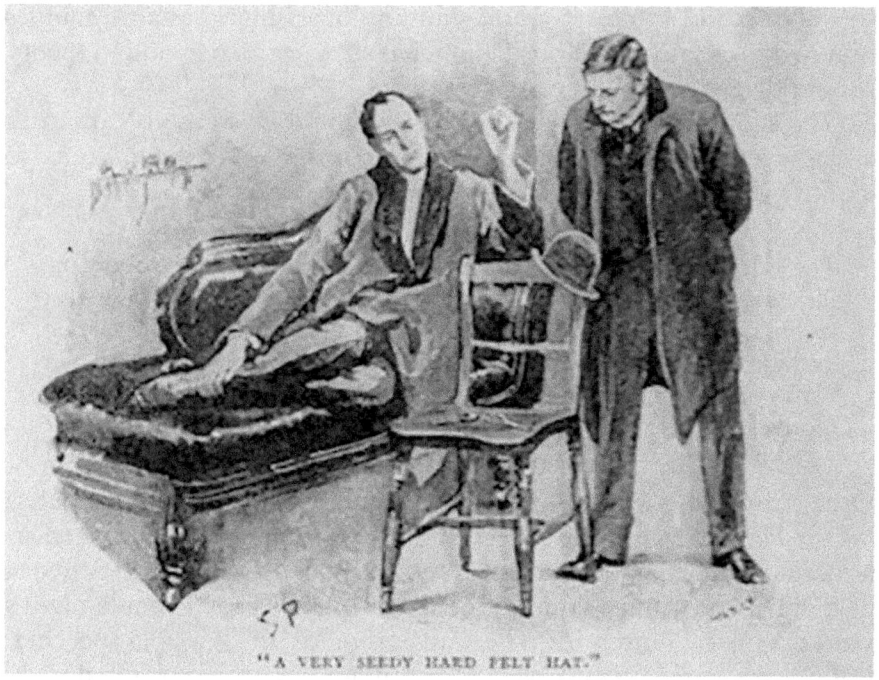

Figure 1 'A very seedy hard felt hat.' Illustration by Sidney Paget, *Strand Magazine*, January 1892.

the owner, in utilising the hat, has left telltale traces all over it: he has attached a hat-securer but the elastic has broken; he has concealed stains with ink; there are cut hairs, sweat marks and the odour of lime-cream on the hat's lining. Much of this evidence points also to other utilities he has or has not consumed (hair cream, gas lighting). One of the few economic theories which has been discovered by literary critics is Marx's theory of commodity fetishism, which states that because in a capitalist society we believe economic goods (commodities) to have intrinsic value, commodities conceal the labour that produced them: as a result, we perceive social relationships through the commodities themselves, rather than between people (such as workers, sellers, buyers), leaving people, particularly workers, alienated. But although the hat is a very good example of a commodity, Holmes's technique is Marshallian, not Marxian: by analysing the hat's consumption (in the economic sense), he recovers the owner's social relationships – even his relationship with his wife.

Holmes then applies his microeconomic method to the blue carbuncle: 'It is absolutely unique, and its value can only be conjectured, but the reward offered of a thousand pounds is certainly not within a twentieth part of the market price.' He adds: 'I have reason to know the there are sentimental considerations in the background which would induce the Countess to part with half of her fortune if she could but recover the gem' (155). This is another examination of economic utility, but quite a complex one. The gem might be said to have intrinsic value but only because its scarcity makes it seem valuable to the owner. After all, one cannot do anything with a blue carbuncle except own it, although the goose which starts the story's wild chase apparently has eaten it: we later learn that the thief concealed it in a live goose's crop by pushing it down its throat. Holmes himself comments on the mysterious effects of scarcity and perceived value: 'There have been two murders, a vitriol-throwing, a suicide, and several robberies brought about for the sake of this forty-grain weight of crystallised charcoal. Who would think that so pretty a toy would be a purveyor to the gallows and the prison?' (157) Holmes here clearly knows the price of everything, but does not share in the appreciation of the value of precious stones and metals: what he needs to be able to do is determine the value that others place on objects such as the carbuncle. But the carbuncle's rightful owner (the Countess) clearly attributes some other value to it, in addition to its scarcity value – it gives her pleasure because of its associations. Again, in Marshall's neoclassical economics this sentimental value is not irrational, merely yet another illustration of economic utility in action.

The story then becomes an exercise in economic analysis, as Holmes traces the lineage of the goose which apparently consumed the blue carbuncle. First, he discovers the man who bought the goose in the Alpha Inn, a public house near the British Museum. From the Alpha Inn, Holmes traces it to a stall in Covent Garden market, where through a stratagem (involving payment of a sovereign) he discovers not only the supplier but also the fact that another man is also asking about a particular goose. This man turns out to be James Ryder, the head attendant at the Hotel Cosmopolitan, who stole the gem from the Countess, and then hid the loot in the crop of one of the geese being fattened for market by his sister in Brixton, with the intention of taking the goose after its slaughter for himself. By mischance, however, the goose was sold on before Ryder could requisition it, leaving Brixton on a long journey that ended in 221B Baker Street. As a result, Ryder is following the goose's economic trail – as is Holmes, but from the opposite direction. It is therefore elegant and appropriate that the two investigators of the supply chain collide in the centre of a market, Covent Garden.

Throughout his investigations, Holmes detects each stage in the goose's journey from the farm to the dinner table and the price paid in each transaction. The Covent Garden dealer buys geese at 7s 6d and sells at 12s. The landlord of the Alpha Inn then sells the geese through a club scheme which requires members to contribute 'some few pence' (160) each week, suggesting that the price was somewhere around 13s: the landlord, Mr Windigate, is not making a significant profit from the scheme. Holmes's microeconomic analyses reveal the path the bird has taken back to its economic origin where it became an unwitting accessory to a crime. Why, though, is Ryder so determined to obtain the gem? Unlike the Countess, he has no interest in the object itself. Its utility for him lies in what economists call its exchange value – what it can buy in the marketplace. In his confession he tells Holmes he planned to take it to a fence in Kilburn who 'would show me how to turn the stone into money' (168). This, then, is a further aspect to the story's investigation of Victorian micro economies. To consume, someone first has to produce, but Marshall reminds us in *Principles of Economics* that we do not really create things from nothing: we produce utilities. A producer

> can produce services and other immaterial products, and he can consume them. But as his production of material products is really nothing more than the rearrangement of matter which gives it new utilities; so his consumption of them is nothing more than a disarrangement of matter, which diminishes or destroys its utilities.[9]

The transactions in 'The Blue Carbuncle' are a series of transformations or rearrangements designed to produce utility for one person or another.

The last word lies with Holmes who, as elsewhere in *The Adventures*, confides to us that for him utility comes from solving interesting problems, not from owning things. 'Chance has put in our way a most singular and whimsical problem, and its solution is its own reward' (170). There may not be a financial transaction here, but it is economic utility in action nonetheless. Holmes, proposing to dine upon a woodcock, then adds: 'we will begin another investigation in which also a bird will be the chief feature' (170). This comic elision of the criminal investigation and literal consumption reminds us finally of the interconnectedness of our social and economic lives: the story has revealed that birds do not simply fly onto our tables to be eaten, but pass through many hands, each one adding economic value to the last; and sometimes, by analysing the processes of consumption and production, we can detect the social relationships as well as the plots and stratagems that hold us together. Analysing the economic production and above all consumption of a goose, a hat and a precious stone shows the otherwise hidden connections between a countess, her maid, a detective, a plumber and his wife, a hotel attendant, a pub landlord, a poultry dealer and many others. 'The Blue Carbuncle' opens with a vision of

> four million human beings all jostling each other within the space of a few square miles. Amid the action and reaction of so dense a swarm of humanity, every possible combination of events may be expected to take place, and many a little problem will be presented which may be striking and bizarre without being criminal. (149)

This complex jostling is what Marshall called the 'ordinary business of life', and both he and Holmes suggest that following the money is one way of making sense of it all.

Notes

1. Thorstein Veblen, *The Theory of the Leisure Class*.
2. Alfred Marshall, *Principles of Economics: An Introductory Volume*, p. 1.
3. For Jevons and the impact of the theory of marginal utility on literary culture of the *fin de siècle*, see Regenia Gagnier, *The Insatiability of Human Wants*.
4. Marshall, *Principles of Economics: An Introductory Volume*, pp. 53–4.
5. Conan Doyle, *Letters to the Press*, p. 169.
6. For Wilde and marginalist economics, see Gagnier, *Insatiability of Human Wants*, Ch. 3. For the commissioning of *The Picture of Dorian Gray* and *The Sign of Four*, and Doyle's opinion of Wilde, see Peter D. McDonald, *British Literary Culture and Publishing Practice*, pp. 122, 135. Doyle's own account of his 'golden evening' at the Langham is in *Memories and Adventures*, p. 78.
7. Oscar Wilde, *The Picture of Dorian Gray*, pp. 4, 47. Wilde reused the latter line in *Lady Windermere's Fan* (1892).
8. Franco Moretti, 'Clues', in *Signs Taken for Wonders*, p. 139. Another valuable contribution is Clare Clarke's analysis of *The Adventures* in *Late Victorian Crime Fiction*, pp. 72–103. Clarke draws a different conclusion from Moretti, seeing the preoccupation with disproportionate wages as an examination of late Victorian work ethics, and evidence of Doyle's own unease at earning easy money for the Holmes stories.
9. Marshall, *Principles of Economics, An Introductory Volume*, pp. 53–4.

Chapter 2

The Roylotts of Stoke Moran

Dr Grimesby Roylott, the wicked stepfather in 'The Speckled Band', is one of Conan Doyle's most grotesque, gothic villains. Like several other evildoers in the Holmes stories – Jonathan Small in *The Sign of Four*, Colonel Barclay in 'The Adventure of the Crooked Man' (1893), Colonel Sebastian Moran in 'The Empty House' – Roylott has gone bad in the East. Having established a medical practice in Calcutta, he narrowly avoided execution after beating his servant to death in a fit of rage: his stepdaughter Helen Stoner tells Holmes that '[v]iolence of temper approaching to mania has been hereditary in the men of the family, and in my stepfather's case it had, I believe, been intensified by his long residence in the tropics' (175). After serving a prison sentence in India, he returned to England 'a morose and disappointed man' (175), and attempted to put his medical knowledge to good use by establishing a new medical practice in London. But following the death of his wife in a railway accident at Crewe – an event that the alert reader will surely suspect may not have been entirely accidental – he abandoned his business and retired with his two stepdaughters to the ancient family seat at Stoke Moran in Surrey. There, Roylott has inflicted his violent temper on his neighbours in a series of brawls, while creating a safari park among the decaying grounds and collapsing seventeenth-century mansion of his inherited estate: 'He has a passion also for Indian animals, which are sent over to him by a correspondent, and he has at this moment a cheetah and a baboon, which wander freely over his grounds, and are feared by the villagers almost as much as their master' (176). At the climax of the story, we discover that Roylott has another tropical creature in his collection: a swamp adder, the weapon used to murder Helen Stoner's twin-sister Julia two years before the story begins, and which Roylott intended to use against Helen – only to be fatally bitten himself after Holmes causes the snake to return back to its master's bedroom through the ventilator which was its route to the scene of the crime.

It is little wonder, then, that critical attention has focused on Roylott's oriental backstory, his gothic literary heritage, and the disturbing psycho-sexual implications of his behaviour. Along with Jephro Rucastle in 'The Copper Beeches' – another patriarch who hatches an elaborate scheme to obtain a daughter's money – he owes something to the fairy-tale figure of Bluebeard, murdering women in a rambling building in which locked rooms conceal hidden menace.[1] Like Small and his Andamanian accomplice Tonga in *The Sign of Four*, as well as the three Indian sages in Conan Doyle's *The Mystery of Cloomber* (1888), he represents both moral regression and a kind of reverse colonisation, bringing violence and horror from the East back to the West. Roylott thus exemplifies Doyle's persistent interest in what Patrick Brantlinger influentially labelled 'imperial gothic': the redeployment of the tropes of gothic fiction to explore the politics and cultural challenges brought about by Britain's empire.[2] Unsurprisingly, in a post-Freudian age Roylott's snake has attracted particular attention.[3] For Catherine Wynne, Roylott's zoo 'demonstrates the absurdity of the imperial enterprise' by removing tropical wildlife from their natural habitats for relocation to the Home Counties, thus inverting 'the process of patriarchal colonisation'. In Wynne's interesting but rather strained analysis, Roylott's swamp adder is both 'phallic and gynarchic, penetrative and consuming, rapacious and procreative, colonising and decolonizing', its decision to bite and kill its owner symbolising the threat to the coloniser from the colonised.[4] Similarly, Joseph Kestner reads the adder as a symbol that is simultaneously political and psychoanalytical: it 'condemns the colonial enterprise' and, in its nocturnal journeys into the beds of Julia and Helen Stoner, reminds us that masculine power is sexual as well as social.[5] Roylott's hypermasculine behaviour – throwing Stoke Moran's blacksmith over a ledge, bending a steel poker to demonstrate his physical strength to Holmes and Watson, and bruising Helen Stoner's wrist with the force of his grip – is, for Kestner, an expression of control from a patriarchal system under threat from increasing female independence. Suggestions of incest – Doyle initially conceived Helen and Julia to be Roylott's natural daughters – only add to this story's potent combination of the sexual and the political in its examination of power relationships.[6]

However, there is a more apparently mundane aspect of Roylott's domestic circumstances that has remained largely unexamined but is nonetheless of great significance to the social and economic background of this and other Holmes stories of the 1890s and early 1900s. Roylott is 'the last survivor of one of the oldest Saxon families in England' (174), and according to Helen Stoner has inherited a double legacy: an estate, and a dissolute character. She tells Holmes:

> The family was at one time among the richest in England, and the estate extended over the borders into Berkshire in the north, and Hampshire in the west. In the last century, however, four successive heirs were of a dissolute and wasteful disposition, and the family ruin was eventually completed by a gambler, in the days of the Regency. Nothing was left save a few acres of ground, and the two-hundred-year-old house, which is itself crushed under a heavy mortgage. The last squire dragged out his existence there, living the horrible life of an aristocratic pauper . . . (174)

Figure 2 'Which of you is Holmes?' Illustration by Sidney Paget, *Strand Magazine*, February 1892.

In Helen's telling, Roylott's genetic inheritance has partially destroyed his economic one, and this contradictory legacy explains both his decision to start a new life in India and his plot to murder his stepdaughters in order to claim their rather more healthy inheritance, left to them by the unfortunate Mrs Stoner. 'The Speckled Band' thus anticipates the malign inheritance represented by the Baskerville curse in *The Hound of the Baskervilles*, as well as the diminished legacy of 'The Musgrave Ritual', both of which will be examined in later chapters.[7] More generally, it illustrates the attention paid throughout the Holmes saga to landed property – one need only look at the titles of 'The Copper Beeches', 'The Abbey Grange', 'Wisteria Lodge', 'The Three Gables' and 'The Adventure of Shoscombe Old Place' (1927) to realise the importance of estate. But there is another factor at work here, without which we cannot fully understand why Roylott needs to kill in order to achieve financial security. Holmes himself identifies this as the crucial factor in breaking open the case when he triumphantly exclaims to Watson on returning from Doctor's Commons where he has consulted Mrs Stoner's will:[8]

> 'I have seen the will of the deceased wife,' said he. 'To determine its exact meaning I have been obliged to work out the present prices of the investments with which it is concerned. The total income, which at the time of the wife's death was little short of £1,100, is now through the fall in agricultural prices not more than £750. Each daughter can claim an income of £250, in case of marriage. It is evident, therefore, that if both girls had married, this beauty would have had a mere pittance, while even one of them would cripple him to a serious extent. My morning's work has not been wasted, since it has proved that he has the very strongest motives for standing in the way of anything of the sort. (184)

In summary, allowing his stepdaughters to live and marry would reduce Roylott's income from £1,100 per annum to a mere £250. In their approach to work and money, then, Roylott and Holmes are at opposite poles: Holmes is introduced to us in this story once again as motivated by the pleasure of work – 'Working as he did for the love of his art than for the acquirement of wealth' (171) – but Roylott wants a substantial income without having to work for it. No longer willing to support himself through his medical skills and knowledge, Roylott has abandoned the late nineteenth-century ethic of professionalism to become a classic rentier – and a particularly lazy one at that. Although his inherited property is much reduced from its seventeenth-century abundance, he still has a mansion with grounds considerable enough to include a plantation and in which a cheetah has space to roam. But it is clear that Roylott has inherited his ancestors' disdain for efficient land management. What is left of the estate is, according to Helen, a 'few acres of bramble-covered land' (176); the house is 'a picture of ruin', its roof 'partly caved in' and in one of the wings 'the windows were broken, and blocked with wooden boards' (186); the lawn is 'ill-trimmed' (186); inside Helen Stoner's temporary bedroom Watson observes 'the panelling of the walls were brown, worm-eaten oak, so old and discoloured that it may have dated from the original building of the house' (187). As we might infer from his atrocious relationship with his neighbours, Roylott is as far from being the responsible country squire as it is possible to be. But even if he had wished to make something of Stoke Moran, Holmes's discovery at Doctor's Commons should tell him that his estate, as well as his inheritance from his wife, is declining in value. The 'fall in agricultural prices' that has wiped over thirty per cent from the value of his wife's investments will have similarly devalued Stoke Moran. Roylott is in serious financial difficulties not only because of his own character but also because of what had happened to the rural economy of the late nineteenth century.

The great agricultural depression of 1875 to 1896 was the result of many forces – a succession of poor harvests, a glut in the supply of wheat, new technologies of storage and transport, Britain's antiquated estate system which stifled innovation and limited flexibility – and it led to a significant decline in the rural economy, especially in the arable regions of the south and east of England (its effect was far less severe in the pastoral regions of the north and west). Although historians now doubt whether it was quite as catastrophic as was once believed – G. M. Young in *Victorian England: Portrait of an Age* (1936) claimed that 'Great Wars have been less destructive of wealth than the calamity which stretched from 1879, the wettest, to 1894, the driest, year in memory'[9] – there is no doubt that late Victorians believed that rural England had undergone a fundamental decline. It was sufficiently serious to lead to two royal commissions, in 1879–82 and 1894–8.[10] Contemporary accounts are full of elegies to the once great agricultural lands of southern and eastern England, now – like Stoke Moran – left to brambles and gypsies. One of the investigators for the second royal commission wrote in 1893 that north-east Essex 'has suffered terribly by the agricultural depression . . . A considerable amount of land is altogether out of cultivation . . . A more melancholy sight from an agricultural point of view can scarcely be imagined than this part of the district presents.'[11] Conan Doyle's acquaintance, the popular novelist and Norfolk gentleman-farmer H. Rider Haggard, researched the problem for the *Daily Express* in 1901 and 1902 and concluded that:

> the agricultural industry in England is as steadily going down hill as the capital sums invested in it are wasting; that the owners of the soil are becoming impoverished; that the farmers are at best making no headway, and, owing partly to poverty and partly to the natural discouragement that results from continual non-success, are losing heart and enterprise.[12]

Of the three sections in the English estate system – landowner, tenant and labourer – Haggard wrote:

> the owner has suffered most. In many counties, such as Essex, Hertfordshire, Norfolk, and Suffolk, there is often nothing at all left for him after the various expenses have been met, whereas, if it is in any way encumbered, landed property is as a millstone around his neck.[13]

Others, notably the Liberal Unionist statesman, Joseph Chamberlain, blamed the landlords themselves for the depression for charging excessive rents and neglecting their responsibility to improve their land – an allegation that 'The Speckled Band' seems to endorse. But Haggard was by no means alone in diagnosing a fundamental collapse of a way of life: as one modern historian has put it, the depression 'was perceived as part of a much more worrying phenomenon, the loss of national momentum, and the surrender of technological leadership in many of the older industries, including agriculture', leading to an 'almost obsessive concern with decay and . . . resignation, loss of confidence, and a predilection for regarding the depression as retributive justice for the extravagance of former times'.[14] The cultural response to the depression can therefore be seen as both reflecting and influencing a more general sense of *fin de siècle* decline – the economic depression and perceptions of moral and physical degeneration were, thus, mutually reinforcing. In this sense, Roylott is an emblematic figure not just of imperialism and patriarchy, but also of the declining power of landlords, and what this meant for society and the national moral character.

Roylott will have suffered from the depression as both a landowner and as an investor. In this he is rather less fortunate than his near-contemporary, Jack Worthing in Oscar Wilde's *The Importance of Being Earnest* (1895), who tells Lady Bracknell that his income derives mostly from investments (securities) rather than land, to which Lady Bracknell replies:

> That is satisfactory. What between the duties expected of one during one's lifetime, and the duties exacted from one after one's death, land has ceased to be either a profit or a pleasure. It gives one position and presents one from keeping it up. That's all that can be said about land.[15]

The depression saw a twenty-five per cent fall in agricultural income and a forty per cent fall in agricultural rent – showing that the dwindling value of Mrs Stoner's investments was actually proportionate to the wider rural economy.[16] Despite getting so many things factually wrong in this story, Doyle was highly accurate in his estimate of the falling value of agricultural land.

There was another, perhaps even greater social effect of the depression: rural depopulation. Writing just over a decade after the depression's end, the Liberal politician and social critic C. F. G. Masterman claimed in *The Condition of England* (1909) that the last quarter of the nineteenth century experienced 'the largest secular change of a thousand years: from the life of the fields to the life of the city'.[17] Between 1871 and 1901, the population in England and Wales increased by forty-three per cent, but the rural population declined in the same period by more than thirty per cent.[18] Rural depopulation and its evil twin, urban overpopulation, were major sources of anxiety in the period, contributing to the widespread sense of social malaise while prompting a wide range of social campaigns and initiatives, from land nationalisation to the garden cities movement.[19] And it left its mark strongly on British fiction. H. G. Wells's great Edwardian condition-of-England novel *Tono-Bungay* (1909), for instance, vividly evokes an atmosphere of entropy in its portrait of the country house, Bladesover, situated in a rural economy losing both investment and labour to the cities ('The hand of change rests on it all, unfelt, unseen; resting for a while, as it were half reluctantly, before it grips and ends the thing forever.')[20] Conan Doyle acknowledges the same economic and social forces rather more obliquely than Wells in 'The Musgrave Ritual' (1893), but then more explicitly in 'The Adventure of the Dancing Men' (1903), which occupies similar ground to 'The Speckled Band' with its rural manor-house locale. Holmes's client in the story, Hilton Cubitt, is like Roylott landed gentry of ancient pedigree: he tells Holmes, 'my people have been at Ridling Thorpe for a matter of five centuries, and there is no better-known family in the county of Norfolk' (75). When Cubitt is killed, the stationmaster at North Walsham exclaims: 'Dear, dear! one of the oldest families in the county of Norfolk, and one of the most honoured' (84). Like Roylott, Cubitt is impoverished: 'I'm not a rich man', he tells Holmes (75). The explanation for his straitened circumstances becomes apparent when Holmes and Watson travel to Ridling Thorpe Manor:

> we were passing through as singular a country-side as any in England, where a few scattered cottages represented the population of today, while on every hand enormous square-towered churches bristled up from the flat, green landscape and told of the glory and prosperity of old East Anglia. (84)

The echo of the opening of Edgar Allan Poe's 'The Fall of the House of Usher' (1839), in which the narrator glimpses 'the melancholy House of Usher' after 'passing . . . through a singularly dreary tract of countryside' is significant: like Roderick Usher, Hilton is the last of the Cubitts, and has no heir.[21] But what matters more in a story which takes place a year after Victoria's 1897 jubilee is Watson's clear reference to the consequences of the great depression that was, by that date, coming to its end. Like Cubitt himself, East Anglia – the region most severely affected – had fallen on hard times. Unlike Roylott, though, Cubitt is not in any way responsible for his own misfortunes. He is 'a tall, ruddy, clean-shaven gentleman, whose clear eyes and florid cheeks told of a life led far from the fogs of Baker Street' (74). Watson then presses the point: 'He was a fine creature, this man of the old English soil, simple, straight and gentle, with his great, earnest, blue eyes and broad, comely face' (77). His marriage is also more to his credit than other matches involving the landed gentry. 'The Adventure of the Noble Bachelor' (1892), for instance, explicitly acknowledges the contemporary trend for impoverished aristocrats to marry American heiresses as a way of keeping their devalued estates intact: 'One by one the management of the noble houses of Great Britain is passing into the hands of our fair cousins from across the Atlantic' (224). Lord St Simon's father, the Duke of Balmoral, 'has been compelled to sell his pictures within the last few years' and 'Lord St Simon has no property of his own, save the small estate at Birchmoor' (224), so it makes sense for the noble bachelor to marry the daughter of an American millionaire.[22] However, Cubitt's marriage to the American Elsie (who turns out to be the daughter of a Chicago gangster) is not motivated by gain: 'His love for his wife and his trust in her shone in his features' (77). He is, then, morally and socially a most upstanding figure, as far removed from the evil Roylott as it is possible to imagine. But both are equally victims of impersonal, economic forces that swept southern and eastern England in the late nineteenth century, transforming the landscape both literally and metaphorically. Their responses to the crisis could not be more different, but their fates are strikingly similar: a violent death in the manor houses to which they were born. The forces unleashed by the great agricultural depression treated hero and villain much the same.

Notes

1. For the influence of 'Bluebeard' on 'The Copper Beeches', see Michael Atkinson, *The Secret Marriage of Sherlock Holmes*, pp. 129–35.
2. Patrick Brantlinger, *Rule of Darkness*, pp. 227–54. *The Mystery of Cloomber* anticipates *The Sign of Four* in plot and its orientalist tropes, and both novels are plainly descended from one of Doyle's favourite novels, Wilkie Collins's *The Moonstone* (1868).
3. Several critics have pointed out that the snake is also evidence of Conan Doyle's ignorance of natural history: snakes are deaf, do not drink milk and cannot climb ropes, and yet Roylott has trained his swamp adder by whistling and feeding with milk to climb and descend a bell pull. See for example Atkinson, *The Secret Marriage*, p. 28.
4. Catherine Wynne, *The Colonial Conan Doyle*, pp. 129–30.
5. Joseph A. Kestner, *Sherlock's Men*, p. 90.
6. For Doyle's original conception of Helen and Julia as Roylott's daughters, see *The New Annotated Sherlock Holmes*, vol. I, p. 246.
7. For more on Doyle's interest in cursed legacies in 'The Speckled Band' and other stories, see Peter Thomas, *Detection and its Designs*, p. 134, and Barry McCrea, *In the Company of Strangers*, pp. 71–5.
8. Doctor's Commons was the home of a society of lawyers in London who worked on civil cases. It effectively ceased in 1865, and the buildings were demolished shortly afterwards. Doyle presumably derived his knowledge of the institution from fiction rather than fact, as it is where Lady Verinder's will is examined by solicitors working on behalf of Godfrey Ablewhite in *The Moonstone*. In narrating this part of the novel, the solicitor Matthew Bruff observes: 'the law allows all wills to be examined at Doctor's Commons by anybody who applies, on payment of a shilling fee'. Wilkie Collins, *The Moonstone*, p. 315.
9. Quoted in E. J. T. Collins, 'The Great Depression', p. 141.
10. See E. J. T. Collins, 'Introduction', p. 18.
11. Quoted in Alun Howkins, *Reshaping Rural England*, pp. 140–1.

12. H. Rider Haggard, *Rural England*, vol. II, p. 563.
13. Ibid., p. 543.
14. Collins, 'Introduction', p. 16.
15. Oscar Wilde, *The Importance of Being Earnest*, Act I, 686–91.
16. Collins, 'The Great Depression', p. 140.
17. C. F. G. Masterman, *The Condition of England*, p. 96. Masterman would later co-opt Doyle into propaganda work during the First World War: see Chapter 17 below.
18. R. C. K. Ensor, *England 1870–1914*, pp. 285–6.
19. Collins, 'Introduction', pp. 17–18.
20. H. G. Wells, *Tono-Bungay*, pp. 8–9. Conan Doyle met Wells in 1898 on holiday in Rome with E. W. Hornung and George Gissing – Lycett (*Conan Doyle*, p. 240) speculates they may have met in Southsea in the early 1880s, where Wells was a draper's assistant and Doyle a general practitioner – and they remained in occasional contact for the rest of their long careers. The influence of Wells's science fiction is evident in Doyle's Professor Challenger stories, especially *The Lost World* (1912), which is clearly indebted to *The Time Machine* (1895), and *The Poison Belt* (1913), which resembles both *The War of the Worlds* (1898) and *In The Days of the Comet* (1906).
21. Edgar Allan Poe, *Selected Writings*, p. 138.
22. One historian estimates that more than 130 Americans married into the British aristocracy between 1870 and 1914 (Charles S. Campbell, *Anglo-American Understanding*, p. 9). Among the most famous matches were Consuelo Vanderbilt's to the Duke of Marlborough in 1895, which enabled the Duke to preserve Blenheim Palace, and Nancy Shaw's to Waldorf Astor in 1906.

Chapter 3

The Guardians of Securities

Wealth, or capital, tends to be represented in the earliest Holmes stories in the reassuringly familiar form of specie (coins and notes), or precious stones or metals. The Agra treasure in *The Sign of Four*, the French gold in 'The Red-Headed League', the Australian gold mines of 'The Boscombe Valley Mystery' (1891) and the American gold mine of Hatty Moran's father in 'The Noble Bachelor', the 421 pennies and 270 half-pennies in 'The Man with the Twisted Lip' (1891), the blue carbuncle, the counterfeit half-crowns in 'The Engineer's Thumb', the fifty thousand pounds in notes loaned to the illustrious client in exchange for a priceless piece of jewellery in 'The Adventure of the Beryl Coronet' (1892) – all are examples of the most solid forms of capital. Even the opium den in 'The Man with the Twisted Lip' is named 'The Bar of Gold'. Several of these stories belong to a tradition of narratives, stretching back to Chaucer's tale of the Pardoner but including such favourites of Doyle's as Collins's *The Moonstone* and Edgar Allan Poe's 'The Gold Bug' (1843), in which great wealth in material, tactile form motivates characters to perform extraordinary feats.

The stories in *The Memoirs of Sherlock Holmes* (1893), *The Hound of the Baskervilles* (1902) and *The Return of Sherlock Holmes* (1905) reveal a striking and important change. Specie and precious objects become less prominent, and their function is replaced by a form of capital that is insubstantial, abstract and, in some ways, even theoretical. Securities, which include government stocks as well as shares in private companies, are the preferred form of capital in the plots of several of these later stories, and appear with surprising frequency as incidental details. In *The Hound of the Baskervilles*, for instance, we are told that Sir Charles Baskerville made 'large sums of money in South African speculation', after which 'he realised his gains and returned to England', where he invested his profits in 'those schemes of reconstruction and improvement' at Baskerville

Hall 'which have been interrupted by his death' (15). This detail may, in fact, be more than merely incidental, as it provides a pecuniary motive for Stapleton, a disguised Baskerville, to kill the man he knows to be his uncle and to plot the death of his cousin, in addition to all the other benefits of becoming the squire of Baskerville Hall. Sir Charles's investments would have been in what at the time were known as 'Kaffirs' – shares in private companies involved in the enormously lucrative gold and diamond mines of South Africa, such as the Robinson Central Deep mine which Doyle visited in 1900, and in which he bought shares in 1902.[1] South African investments are also mentioned in 'The Dancing Men', when Holmes deduces that Watson has declined to take up an offer from his friend Thurston 'who had an option on some South African property which would expire in a month, and which he desired you to share with him' (74). Here, Watson's investment decision appears to be little more than an excuse for Holmes to show off his inductive reasoning – but such details also form part of the contemporary backdrops of these stories, contributing to their verisimilitude but also pointing to the social and political preoccupations of the late Victorian and Edwardian periods.

'The Adventure of the Stockbroker's Clerk' (1893) and 'The Adventure of Black Peter' (1904) turn this preoccupation with securities into the motive force of the plots of both stories, but in doing so they present a searching examination of how money is made and what is done with it in the modern economy. The clerk of the earlier story, Hall Pycroft, begins his narrative by telling Holmes and Watson that he had been made redundant by a stockbroker's, Coxon and Woodhouse, after the company 'came a nasty cropper' (*Memoirs*, 76) from financing a Venezuelan loan, and therefore had to discharge twenty-seven of its clerks. Coxon and Woodhouse is clearly a small firm seeking to build its business through risky but potentially lucrative investments: Venezuela, location of some of the world's richest goldfields, was also for much of the nineteenth century notoriously politically unstable, and had severed diplomatic relations with Britain in 1887 over a territorial dispute; when Conan Doyle wrote the story, the country had descended into civil war after the overthrow of its dictator Guzmán Blanco in 1889.[2] After a period of unemployment during which Pycroft ran though his entire savings (£70), he says he found a job with the more prestigious firm of Mawson and Williams in Lombard Street, which he describes as 'about the richest house in London', and which offered him £200 a year (76–7). Pycroft's troubles began shortly afterwards, when he was approached by Arthur Pinner, whose business card proclaimed him to be a 'financial agent', with an offer of employment on the basis of rumours about Pycroft's 'financial ability' (77). Pycroft recalls being tested by Pinner on stock prices, a test which Pycroft passed with flying colours, correctly identifying current prices from his knowledge of the Stock Exchange List that he is in the habit of reading 'every morning' (78). As a result, Pinner offered Pycroft the huge salary of £500 to become business manager of the Franco-Midland Hardware Company, Ltd. Although Pinner claimed that the company has 136 branches in France, Belgium and San Remo, Pycroft responded that he had never heard of it. Pinner explained: 'It has been kept very quiet, for the capital was all privately subscribed, and it is too good a thing to let the public into' (78–9). For a smart and knowledgeable clerk to accept this preposterous explanation is a sign that Pinner is a skilful confidence trickster: Pycroft would have known from its name that the Franco-Midland Hardware Company, Ltd. is a public limited company, meaning that it would be listed on the London Stock Exchange and its shares would be available for public purchase. Pycroft, however, accepted the job offer, his acumen no doubt dulled by a £100 advance.

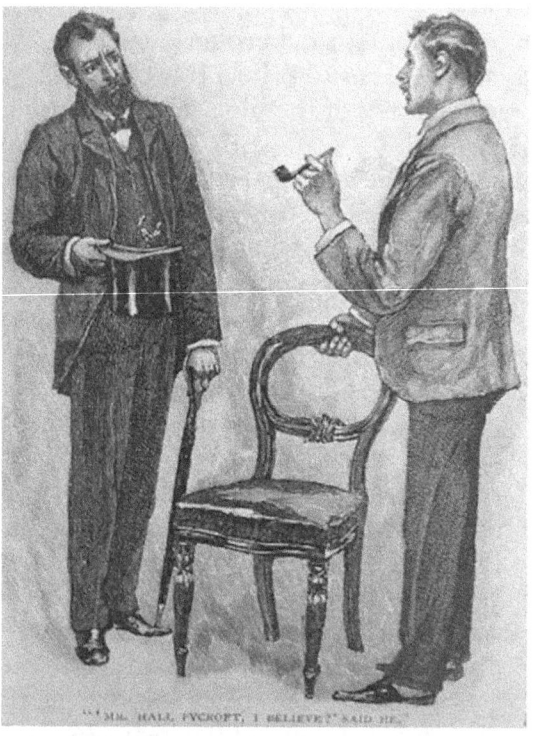

Figure 3 '"Mr. Hall Pycroft, I believe?" said he.' Illustration by Sidney Paget, *Strand Magazine*, March 1893.

The ensuing narrative shows that it is all too good to be true. The company's office in Birmingham appears to lack any of the trappings of a real company; set to work like Jabez Wilson in 'The Red-Headed League' on nugatory tasks, Pycroft soon realises he has been tricked, and consults Holmes. Holmes and Watson, under alias as Mr Harris of Bermondsey and the more appropriately named Mr Price of Birmingham, then accompany Pycroft to the company's office, where they meet Arthur Pinner's brother Harry, who has clearly just received some grave news: he excuses himself, and attempts suicide. After Holmes prevents the suicide, he and a newspaper report reveal what has occurred: the man claiming to be both Arthur and Harry Pinner is really the brother and accomplice of Beddington, 'the famous forger and cracksman' (90). Echoing again 'The Red-Headed League', the plot is an elaborate ruse to get Pycroft out of London so that Beddington could impersonate him and thereby obtain impressions of the locks in Mawson and Williams's Lombard Street office. Beddington attempts a robbery, murdering the night watchman in the process, but is captured by the police. On reading about the plan's failure in the newspaper, Beddington's brother in Birmingham tries to kill himself. The target of the robbery is crucial: Mawson and Williams have become 'the guardians of securities which amount in the aggregate to a sum of considerably over a million sterling' (90). When he is apprehended, Beddington is in possession of nearly 'a hundred thousand pounds' worth of American railway bonds, with a large amount of scrip in other mines and companies' (91).

The specificity of monetary values in this story is striking but, as we have seen, by no means unusual in the Holmes saga. Nor is the financial detail confined to the main plot. Watson begins the narrative with a short history of his new business, a general practice in Paddington. He gives a very precise picture of the economic facts of his acquisition: 'Old Mr Farquhar' has seen his practice decline from £1,200 per year to a mere £300 (73). Watson has presumably bought the practice cheaply, and is confident that, with his energy and determination, he will build it back up to its former glory and income (although the story finds him somewhat underemployed and therefore available to accompany Holmes on the adventure in Birmingham). The story thus thematises employment (and unemployment), business probity, credit (in the sense of what can be trusted as well as in its more specific financial sense), and monetary value, alongside deception and identity. Beddington impersonates Pycroft; Beddington's brother impersonates Arthur and Harry Pinner; Holmes and Watson enter the premises of a fake company under false names. Although a murder occurs (offstage), and there is a more vividly described scene of violence (the attempted suicide, by hanging), this is really a story about detecting the modern economy – its complexity, its global nature, its effects on society, its opportunities and, more than anything, its vulnerability to deception.

To explore this point further, it is worth reflecting on the importance of Pycroft's job and the method by which he is deceived. Both depend on an innovation that had acquired considerable social as well as economic significance by the 1890s: the joint-stock company. In the first decades of the nineteenth century, very few members of the public owned shares in companies: capital was usually in the form of either land or government stock. By the end of the century, largely as a result of the innovation of limited liability – a method of protecting private investors against the risk of losing not just the sum they invested but potentially everything they owned – a million Britons had become shareholders. The first joint-stock companies were created in the mid nineteenth century to finance the expansion of British infrastructure – railways in particular. The second wave of joint-stock companies, in the 1880s and 1890s, capitalised global investments, from railways in South America to the gold mines in South Africa that attracted Sir Charles Baskerville (and Arthur Conan Doyle) but not Dr John Watson.[3] Coxon's Venezuelan loan, and Beddington's swag including American railway bonds and 'scrip' (here presumably a method of paying company dividends) issued by mining companies, are details pointing to this new world of globalised investment in which British citizens were enthusiastic participants. But alongside the enthusiasm there was, evidently, anxiety: opportunities for investment also meant opportunities for criminality, and the new economy's basis in complexity and (in every sense) credit created major hazards for the citizen-investor.

This is exactly the premise of 'Black Peter', in which Holmes and the police detective Stanley Hopkins investigate the violent murder of the retired sea captain Peter Carey, found pinned to a wall in his cabin by a harpoon 'like a beetle on a card' (*Return*, 139). One of the principal clues recovered at the crime-scene is a notebook in which are written 'J.H.N.', '1883', 'C.P.R', several sheets of numbers, and pages of 'signs and figures' with the headings 'Argentine', 'Costa Rica' and 'San Paulo' (140). Hopkins correctly deduces these to be lists of 'Stock Exchange securities' (140). It is clear that both detectives immediately recognise that lists of figures in relation to South and Central American locations would in all likelihood refer to securities; Holmes extrapolates from this assumption to decode 'C.P.R.' as 'Canadian Pacific Railway' (141). The ease with which Hopkins – one of the more acute police detectives in the saga but nonetheless given to grasping the obvious and ignoring alternative explanations, as this story demonstrates – links the Americas to financial instruments demonstrates just how globalised Britain's finance sector had become by this period.

Globalisation provided enormous opportunities for enrichment. However, as Conan Doyle's readers would have been aware, there were also enormous opportunities for criminality. 'J.H.N.' turns out not to be a stockbroker, as Hopkins surmises, but a young man called John Hopley Neligan who is seeking to trace his long-lost father, a West Country banker who absconded with the securities of his firm, Dawson & Neligan, when it 'failed for a million' and 'ruined half the county families of Cornwall' (146). Banking scandals were a feature of nineteenth-century financial history and were memorably replicated in nineteenth-century novels, notably Dickens's *Little Dorrit* (1857), inspired by the scandalous failure of the Tipperary Joint-Stock Bank in 1856, and Trollope's *The Way We Live Now* (1875), whose Augustus Melmotte was based on an amalgam of various mid-century banking swindlers.[4] Neligan Senior is clearly based on more recent cases. In 1890, the oldest merchant bank in Britain, Barings, needed the Bank of England to save it from collapse as a result of its risky investments in Argentina. But the greatest financial scandal of the age came to light in 1892, when the financial empire built by Jabez Balfour around his Liberator Building Society, which also included substantial investments in Argentina, crashed, precipitating further banking collapses that ruined many thousands of ordinary investors. Balfour fled to Buenos Aires, where he was arrested in 1895 and returned to London to face trial: he served ten of the fourteen years of his sentence, finding himself transformed into literature as Bennet Frothingham in Gissing's *The Whirlpool* (1897).[5] Neligan Senior is a rather more sympathetic figure than the appalling Balfour: his son claims that his father planned to realise his securities so that 'all would be well, and every creditor paid in full' (147). But in the context of 1904, the banker absconding with his investments in Argentina after ruining thousands would undoubtedly remind readers of the notorious Balfour.

What matters here is that by making shares and joint-stock companies the motive for two murders, 'Black Peter' dramatises the historic rise of the joint-stock company and share ownership as the motive-power of the British economy and an engine of global growth: the joint-stock company of 'Black Peter' can be seen to replace the gold mines of 'The Boscombe Valley Mystery' and 'The Noble Bachelor'. Similarly, the securities of 'The Stockbroker's Clerk' replace the gold coins of its antecedent story, 'The Red-Headed League'. But given that the enormous social and economic changes were already evident in 1891–2, why do they appear in the Holmes stories from 1893 onwards but not earlier? Andrew Lycett proposes a plausible biographical explanation: *The Adventures of Sherlock Holmes* had made Conan Doyle significantly wealthier, and securities were an obvious vehicle for investing his earnings. The name of a firm of stockbrokers, Pim, Vaughan, begins to appear in Doyle's correspondence from 1892, including details of specific investments, from the Portsmouth Tram Company to mines in Australia.[6] By 1895, Doyle's mining investments had netted him a profit of £2,000, although the following year he complained to his mother that his South African mining shares had taken a hit as a result of the political upheaval caused by the Jameson Raid, and in 1900 he told her he had lost money in Australian mines; by 1903, Doyle was not merely a passive investor but actively promoting companies in which he was investing.[7] But Doyle's own experiences mirrored that of many of his readers: the huge increase in economic participation in the second half of the nineteenth century expanded Britain's middle class and contributed to the profound social changes of the period. Even those who did not participate may have known through the period's expanding financial journalism – reflected in Hall Pycroft's daily bulletin – that the world was changing, while Conan Doyle's readers would, as John Carey has suggested, have included many of the City of London's tens of thousands of clerks, knowledge workers in the new financial economy.[8] They may never have seen a gold mine, or a cellar full of French gold, but they would have known that the global economy had begun to operate on the basis of 'signs and figures' as much as on notes and coins.

Notes

1. *The Return of Sherlock Holmes*, ed. Lancelyn Green, p. 353.
2. Donna Keyse Rudolph and G. A. Rudolph, *Historical Dictionary of Venezuela*, pp. 336–7. These events also contributed to the historical background of Joseph Conrad's *Nostromo* (1904).
3. For background to these developments, see George Robb, *White-Collar Crime*.
4. See Mary Poovey, *Genres of the Credit Economy*, pp. 375–7.
5. See David McKie, *Jabez*.
6. Lycett, *Conan Doyle*, pp. 186, 217, 288.
7. *A Life in Letters*, ed. Jon Lellenberg, Daniel Stashower and Charles Foley, pp. 367, 460.
8. John Carey, *The Intellectuals and the Masses*, p. 64.

Part II: Class

Chapter 4

The Pick of a Bad Lot

A week or so after moving into 221B Baker Street, Watson observes that his fellow lodger Sherlock Holmes receives visits from 'many acquaintances, and those in the most different classes of society'. Among these visitors, Watson is introduced to a 'little sallow, rat-faced, dark-eyed fellow... who came three or four times in a single week' (*Study*, 17). This is a Mr Lestrade, whom Holmes later reveals to be 'a well-known detective' who 'got himself into a fog recently over a forgery case' (20). Lestrade would go on to appear, or at least be mentioned, in a further twelve stories, making him the most frequently trans-textual character in the saga apart from Holmes and Watson themselves, and possibly Holmes's landlady Mrs Hudson.[1]

Holmes's patronising reference to Lestrade being in a fog is characteristic of his attitude to police officers, at least in the early stories. Lestrade may be dim, but his dimness reflects that of Scotland Yard as a whole. When in *A Study in Scarlet* he is invited by Lestrade's colleague Tobias Gregson to attend the crime scene at 3 Lauriston Gardens, Holmes comments: 'Gregson is the smartest of the Scotland Yarders... he and Lestrade are the pick of a bad lot. They are both quick and energetic, but conventional – shockingly so. They have their knives into one another, too. They are as jealous as a pair of professional beauties. There will be some fun over this case if they are both put upon the scent' (24). Scent implies the two detectives are like dogs, but Watson's imagery is more demeaning. Having been 'rat-faced' in Baker Street, at the scene of Enoch J. Drebber's murder Lestrade becomes 'lean and ferret-like' (28). Both he and Gregson are literally clueless ('"There is no clue!" said Gregson... "None at all", chimed in Lestrade'), but Lestrade becomes 'pompous and self-satisfied' when he discovers the word 'RACHE' at the scene. Characteristically, Lestrade turns his triumph into failure as he misinterprets the word – 'it means the writer was going to put

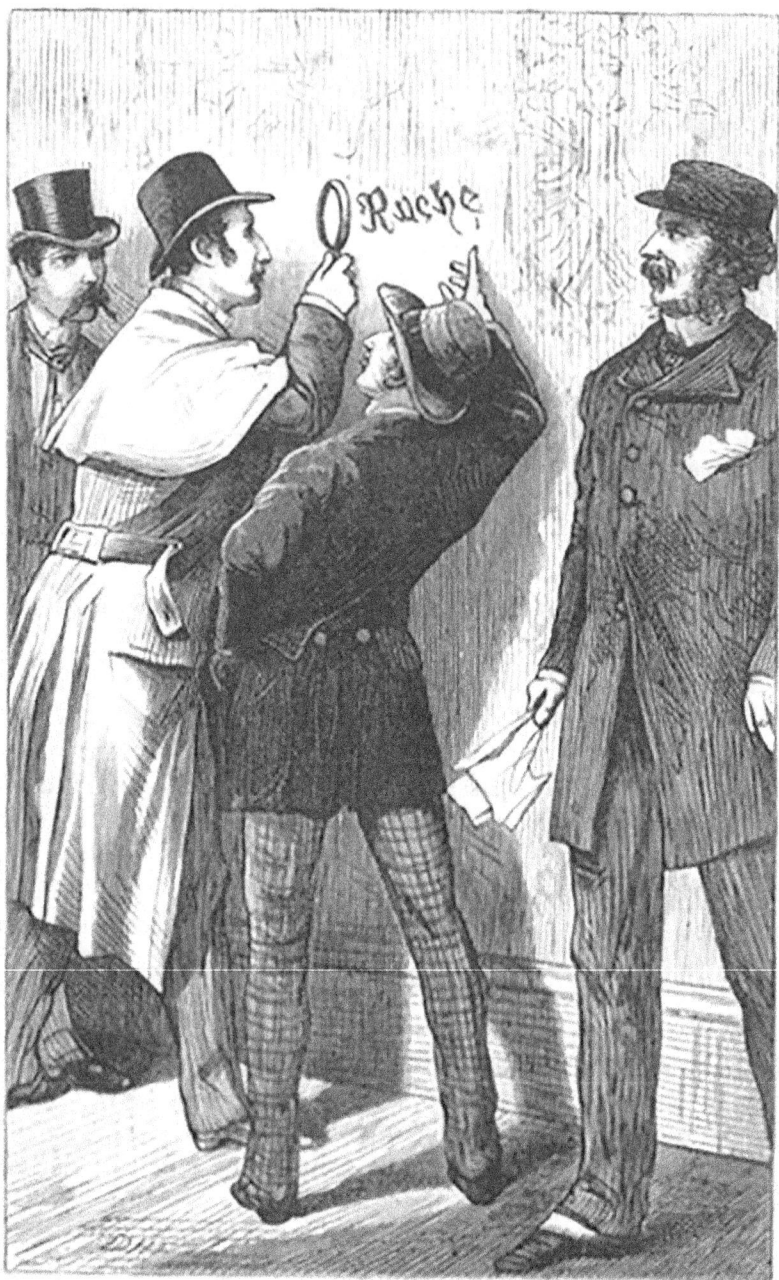

Figure 4 'He examined with his glass the word upon the wall, going over every letter of it with the most minute exactitude.' Illustration by D. H. Friston for *A Study in Scarlet*, in *Beeton's Christmas Annual*, 1887.

the female name Rachel, but was disturbed before he or she had time to finish', prompting 'an explosion of laughter' from Holmes (31). Holmes then examines the scene minutely and systematically, reminding Watson 'of a pure-blooded, well-trained foxhound' (32), prompting 'considerable curiosity and some contempt' from the official detectives. Holmes has the last laugh, as he accurately describes the murderer, the method he used, and the significance of *rache* (German for 'revenge').

These scenes and exchange reveal that social class is an important theme in *A Study in Scarlet*. Holmes, Lestrade and Gregson are all associated metaphorically with animals, but Watson's image of Holmes as a foxhound – that most upper-class of hunting animals – has a class marker attached: he is 'pure-blooded, well-trained'. Lestrade meanwhile is compared to an animal bred for hunting rabbits, a much more working-class sport than hunting with hounds. These images are not incidental. Holmes is introduced to Watson as a student, but he is not enrolled in any programmed course of study: he is a dilettante who converts his leisure time into a self-directed pursuit, the science of deduction. In his article 'The Book of Life', Holmes writes of the basic skill of the detective: 'on meeting a fellow-mortal, learn at a glance to distinguish the history of the man, and the trade or profession to which he belongs' (19). The words 'trade' and 'profession' then recur in the pages that follow. Watson, unaware of the author's identity, objects that the article is 'the theory of some arm-chair lounger who evolves all these neat little paradoxes in the seclusion of his own study' – a description which accurately draws attention to Holmes's membership of what Veblen in 1899 would dub 'the leisure class'.[2] Watson continues: 'I should like to see him clapped down in a third-class carriage on the Underground, and asked to give the trades of all his fellow-travellers' (19). Holmes responds: 'I have a trade of my own . . . I'm a consulting detective, if you can understand what that is. Here in London we have lots of Government detectives and lots of private ones. When these fellows are at fault, they come to me, and I manage to put them on the right scent. They lay all the evidence before me, and I am generally able, by the help of my knowledge of the history of crime, to set them straight' (19–20). Holmes later corrects himself: a consulting detective has a 'profession' (21) rather than a trade. As Douglas Kerr has observed, Holmes in *A Study in Scarlet* resembles the consultant of the medical profession, the specialist who, fully informed by case histories and the professional literature, is able to correct the ill-informed diagnoses of the general practitioners who face the public.[3] A problem arises when the consultant has too little to work on, which is Holmes's situation before receiving Gregson's letter: 'There is no crime to detect, or, at most, some bungling villainy with a motive so transparent that even a Scotland Yard official can see through it' (22).

The difference between Holmes and Lestrade is not, then, merely one of intelligence and training. Holmes, paradoxically, is an amateur who has acquired a profession, but Lestrade (as perhaps his name is meant to indicate) represents trade. Lestrade addresses Holmes as 'sir' (28), and narrates his experience on the trail of Drebber's associate Stangerson in the manner of one who has acquired fluency in English with some effort: 'The question which confronted me was to find out how Stangerson had been employed between 8.30 and the time of the crime, and what had become of him afterwards' (58). His class status is marked most acutely after Jefferson Hope is arrested in Baker Street: he drives the cab which takes Hope, Gregson, Holmes and Watson to the police station. He is capable of applying procedures and drawing obvious conclusions but not of insight or imagination: as Holmes observes in 'The Cardboard Box', 'although he is absolutely devoid of reason, he is as tenacious as a bull-dog when he once understands what he has to do' (*Last Bow*, 42). Holmes brings to bear his knowledge of previous cases – 'There is nothing new under the sun. It has all been done before' (29) – but for Lestrade there is only the case in front of him. Lestrade is not, then, from the professional class, but nor is he from the lowest class, what Victorians called the 'residuum': that position belongs to what Holmes ironically labels 'the Baker Street division of the detective police force'. Watson describes the 'Baker Street Irregulars' (as they are later designated in *The Sign of Four*) as 'half a dozen of the dirtiest and most ragged street Arabs that ever I clapped eyes on'. Holmes drills them like a sergeant major, pays them handsomely, and after they have 'scampered away downstairs like so many rats', comments: 'There's more work to be got out of those little beggars than out of a dozen of the force' (50). These uneducated street-dwellers are below Lestrade in class terms, but his superior in detective skill: they therefore put him firmly in his place.

Class explains why Lestrade is so patronised, demeaned and insulted in *A Study in Scarlet*, but to understand this fully we need to look more broadly at what was happening in Doyle's Britain at the time. The novella appeared at a historical moment when the tectonic plates of the British class system were shifting, but the police were something of an exception to what was happening around them. Howard Perkin has identified the emergence in the late nineteenth century of a new class – the professionals – who differentiated themselves from middle-class industrialists and business people by their training and expertise, on which basis they sought to persuade society to pay their fees and salaries.[4] At the beginning of the nineteenth century there were only seven professions with qualifying associations governing membership, standards and training; by the end of the century the number had grown to forty-eight, including several associated with the medical profession such as chemists, pharmacists and veterinary surgeons.[5] The vast and rapid growth of a white-collar workforce did not, however, include the police or police detectives. When Robert Peel founded the Metropolitan Police in 1829, he decided not to follow the structure of the army and create a class division between officers and men: as a result, police officers were usually recruited from humble backgrounds. When the force acquired a Detective Department in 1842, its officers were drawn from the rank and file, and police detectives in Britain remained largely blue-collar until well into the twentieth century.[6] Not everyone bought into the class prejudice that resulted – Dickens famously wrote admiring essays about police detectives, and created a highly able fictional one in Inspector Bucket in *Bleak House* (1852–3) – but it is evident in the public criticism of the police in newspapers throughout the second half of the century. *Punch* mocked the Metropolitan Police's 'Defective Department' in the 1860s, while the *Times* expressed concern in 1845 at the very creation of a detective force using aliases and plain clothes as being 'mischievous, or even suspicious'. A similar criticism appears, significantly enough, in one of Doyle's major sources for *A Study in Scarlet*, Robert Louis and Fanny Van de Grift Stevenson's *More New Arabian Nights: The Dynamiter* (1885): one character announces that he regards the detective as 'of all dirty, sneaking and ungentlemanly trades; the least and the lowest'.[7] Class prejudice was also clearly evident in the public criticism of Inspector Jack Whicher in the famous case of the Road murder of 1860, which (as Doyle presumably knew) was the major inspiration for Collins's *The Moonstone*. Whicher correctly identified Constance Kent as having committed the murder of her four-year-old brother in the Wiltshire family home, but such was the outcry at a working-class functionary accusing a genteel woman of a violent crime that Kent was released without charge.[8] Collins exploited the class dimension to the full in his novel, as when Lady Verinder vents her patrician fury at what she takes to be Sergeant Cuff's liberties in suspecting her daughter and disturbing the routines of her household.

Watson combines two of the oldest professions – army and medicine – but Holmes is representative of the new professional class, a consultant working in a novel field who is single-handedly developing the ethical code, training programme and case history literature of his specialism. Holmes's disdain for Lestrade is that of the accredited professional for the unqualified worker operating outside the boundaries of training, associations and examinations. But there is more to it than that: his disdain derives also from widespread concern, evident in the response to Whicher's arrest of Constance Kent, that an unprofessionalised cadre cannot be trusted with issues of guilt and innocence. In an age when the wrong decision could send innocent men and women to the gallows, public distrust is perhaps understandable when pharmacists and accountants were expected to abide by high professional standards and police detectives were not. And in the person of Lestrade and his Metropolitan Police colleagues, this distrust was turned into myth.

Lestrade's role in the Holmes saga is to get things wrong. He starts off in *A Study in Scarlet* by earning Holmes's derision for doing just that: '"The fun of it is," he cried, "that that fool Lestrade, who thinks himself so smart, has gone off upon the wrong track altogether"' (51). When he reappears in 'The Boscombe Valley Mystery', investigating the murder of Charles McCarthy in rural Herefordshire, Lestrade is again on the wrong track. He remains in Watson's eyes 'lean, ferret-like', but he is now also 'furtive and sly-looking', while being easily recognisable as a detective in his country clothes (*Adventures*, 84). Before reuniting the reader with him, however, Doyle makes a revealing slip. Holmes claims that Lestrade has been 'retained' by several neighbours of James McCarthy, who is suspected of having murdered his own father, to investigate the case as they believe McCarthy to be innocent (78). As in *A Study in Scarlet*, the 'puzzled' official then refers the case to the specialist Holmes. This is suggestive again of a general practitioner/consultant referral, but also of the relationship between solicitor and barrister: as Richard Lancelyn Green has pointed out, police officers investigated crimes reported to them, and they did not, like legal professionals, act on behalf of clients.[9] But if Lestrade is acting for those in Boscombe Valley who believe James to be innocent, he fails to discharge his professional responsibilities: he assumes his quasi-client to be guilty. 'The case is as plain as a pikestaff', he confidently announces, 'and the more one goes into it the plainer it becomes' (84). Once again, Holmes is dismissive of the official who has referred the case: 'I shall either confirm or destroy his theory by means which he is quite incapable of employing, or even of understanding', and he similarly drives home the gulf in class and training which separates them, using the French word for 'profession' to make the point: 'Therein lies my *métier*' (79). With that, it is clear that whatever Lestrade believes, however probable, cannot be the truth, so we know Holmes is on safe ground when he tells McCarthy's fiancée, Alice Turner, that it is 'very probable' that McCarthy is innocent. Lestrade, not having learned the lesson of the Drebber case, remains 'indifferent and contemptuous' (91) as Holmes pursues his enquiries.

'The Boscombe Valley Mystery' follows a pattern established in *The Sign of Four*, in which Thaddeus Sholto is arrested for the murder of his brother Bartholomew by Athelney Jones: a serious crime is committed, the evidence points clearly in one direction, the police (often but not exclusively Lestrade) assume that the evidence is reliable, Holmes discovers an alternative explanation which turns out to be correct, and the suspected party is saved from prison or execution. In 'The Boscombe Valley Mystery', as in 'The Crooked Man' and 'The Abbey Grange', Holmes also acts as judge and jury, deciding not to intervene in McCarthy's case until the case is in the courts, and allowing the actual murderer, Alice's dying father John Turner, to live out his final months in peace. These stories' distrust of the police, and Holmes's blatant manipulations of the criminal justice system to engineer more naturally just outcomes, imply an anxiety about the capacity and capability of British law and order to get things right. In narrow terms, Holmes can be seen as a plea for greater professionalisation in the detective force; more broadly, he is a reflection of the period's developing society, an exploration of the potential of the emerging professional class to achieve positive social change.

Holmes's relationship with Scotland Yard, and with provincial police forces, improves in the later stories. *The Memoirs of Sherlock Holmes* has a mixed bunch of detectives, from the waspish Inspector Forbes, who accuses Holmes of stealing the credit from Scotland Yard when the reverse is the case, to the 'extremely competent' Inspector Gregory, 'who was rapidly making his name in the English detective service' (11) in 'Silver Blaze'. In *The Return of Sherlock Holmes*, Holmes takes one promising young officer, Stanley Hopkins, under his wing – he has 'high hopes' for Hopkins, who 'in turn professed the admiration and respect of a pupil for the scientific methods of the famous amateur' (136) – but the student remains unable to put the master's methods into practice, and like Lestrade remains wedded to the obvious solution. In 'Black Peter', Holmes tells him: 'You were so absorbed in young Neligan that you could not spare a thought to Patrick Cairns, the true murderer of Peter Carey' (152). Other detectives, though, achieve distinction in their own right, most notably Alec MacDonald in *The Valley of Fear*, a 'young but trusted member of the detective force, who had distinguished himself in several cases which had been entrusted to him'. Described by Watson as 'not having attained the national fame which he has now achieved', his 'tall, bony figure gave promise of exceptional physical strength, while his great cranium and deep-set, lustrous eyes spoke no less clearly of the keen intelligence which twinkled out from behind his bushy eyebrows' (12). Perhaps most significantly, even Lestrade shows himself to be capable of improvement. In *The Hound of the Baskervilles* he has ceased to be sly and ferret-like and become a different kind of animal, who has ascended the social hierarchy: 'a small, wiry bulldog of a man had sprung from a first-class carriage' (145). Since the Boscombe Valley case, he has learned to admire Holmes's methods and his humility is rewarded by a more positive judgement from Holmes, with a revealing choice of words: 'He is the best of the professionals, I think' (142). Holmes thus finally receives Lestrade into the expert fold.

Something clearly caused Doyle to soften, or at least complicate, his presentation of police detectives. His publisher may have been one factor. An American magazine like *Lippincott's*, which carried *A Sign of Four*, could be as critical as it liked about British society – its other publishing coup in 1890 was *A Picture of Dorian Gray* – but, as Jonathan Cranfield has shown, the *Strand* was deliberately aimed at a 'middlebrow' audience which wanted to avoid 'anything salacious or sensational', and preferred its non-fiction to explain 'modern life and institutions in light-hearted, uncritical prose'.[10] Stephen Knight and John Carey have argued that the *Strand*'s readers would have identified with Holmes's clients, but some at least would also have identified with Lestrade and his colleagues, working-class men finding themselves in white collars and doing their best to live up to their employers' expectations.[11] The brutal, socially superior criticism of the police in the first two novellas was increasingly out of place in the *Strand*. A second likely factor was that Scotland Yard detectives had finally found their voices. Stimulated both by press criticism, and by Doyle's brutal caricatures, retired Metropolitan Police detectives wrote a series of memoirs in the 1890s and early 1900s to set the record straight. As Shpayer-Makov observes, these memoirs complain 'that the distorted image of police detectives was the product of the way they were depicted in fiction', and Conan Doyle was singled out by these authors as a repeat offender.[12]

Nevertheless, issues of guilt and innocence in an age of professionalisation continued to dominate Conan Doyle's fiction and, increasingly, his public campaigning. Although he dismissed it as 'carpenter's work'[13] – a somewhat ironic criticism given its principal villain is a builder who, to fake his own death, constructs a false room behind a lath-and-plaster partition in his house – 'The Norwood Builder' is Doyle's supreme examination of contested issues of guilt and innocence, played out between Holmes and Lestrade. Jonas Oldacre appears in person at the very end of the story, flying out of his hidden room 'like a rabbit out of its burrow' (*Return*, 47) after Holmes causes him to think the house is on fire. But throughout the story he has an unwitting accomplice, who is determined to ensure that the Oldacre version of events – that Oldacre has in fact been murdered and the culprit is a young solicitor called John Hector McFarlane – becomes the official truth. Even though he has 'learned by more experiences than he would care to acknowledge' that Holmes's 'razor-sharp brain could cut through that which was impenetrable to him' (34), Lestrade remains just as wedded to the obvious solution as he was in 'The Boscombe Valley Mystery' more than a decade previously. Holmes tries to point out to him the significance of Oldacre's will having been written on a train, but Lestrade does not even bother to consider its implications: 'Is all this not obvious?' (35). The scene that follows is hardly carpenter's work, but a brilliant episode of repartee in which Holmes points out anomalous details and Lestrade doggedly fits them into the narrative that Oldacre has constructed for the authorities to unthinkingly accept. Holmes then travels to Blackheath to interview McFarlane's mother, learning that Oldacre is a particularly repellent sexual bully, but his failure to find substantial exculpatory material causes concern: 'It's all going wrong, Watson – all as wrong as it can go. I kept a bold face before Lestrade, but, upon my soul, I believe that for once the fellow is on the right track and we are on the wrong' (37–8). Lestrade, clearly, is Holmes's adversary here – the detective is not only Oldacre's surrogate, but also a personification of the rough justice which the British system was capable of dispensing: 'I much fear that British juries have not yet attained that pitch of intelligence when they will give the preference to my theories over Lestrade's facts' (38). Watson later tries to reassure Holmes that McFarlane's personable demeanour would ensure his acquittal, but Holmes knows that this is not the case: 'That is a dangerous argument . . . Unless we succeed in establishing an alternative theory, this man is lost' (41). And lost he seems to be the following morning, when Holmes receives Lestrade's 'little cock-a-doodle of victory' in the form of a telegram announcing that McFarlane's guilt has been 'DEFINITELY ESTABLISHED' (42). At Oldacre's home in Norwood, Lestrade, full of an 'insolence' that Watson finds 'maddening' (44), triumphantly displays the clinching piece of evidence – McFarlane's thumb-print in blood upon a wall – which Holmes immediately recognises as final proof of McFarlane's innocence. His victory over Lestrade is celebrated not, as in *A Study in Scarlet* by insulting criticism, but by 'inward merriment' (43) and an elaborate ruse to literally smoke Oldacre out of his hiding place. Holmes's method here has a practical objective, but it also emphatically demonstrates Lestrade's defeat: '"I don't know whether you are playing a game with us, Mr Sherlock Holmes," said he. "If you know anything, you can surely say it without all this tomfoolery"' (46). The demonstration works, and not just because it forces Oldacre's emergence. Lestrade finally grasps the point when he confronts the missing witness: 'You have done your best to get an innocent man hanged. If it wasn't for this gentleman here, I am not sure that you would not have succeeded' (47). Accepting defeat, Lestrade's 'overbearing manner' is suddenly transformed 'to that of a child asking questions of its teacher' (49).

A few weeks after Doyle completed 'The Norwood Builder' in the spring of 1903, another young solicitor found himself accused of a crime he did not commit. But unlike John McFarlane, George Edalji was convicted and went to prison, his supposed crime being a series of horrific animal maimings in Shropshire. After his release from prison in 1906, Edalji sought Conan Doyle's help in his campaign for a pardon. At their first meeting, Doyle immediately recognised that Edalji's astigmatism ruled him out from being the culprit, and he then campaigned vigorously on Edalji's behalf, before taking on the case of Oscar Slater, imprisoned for the brutal murder of an elderly woman in Glasgow in 1908. (Slater was not acquitted until 1927.)[14] Thanks to Julian Barnes's brilliant historical novel *Arthur and George* (2005), the Edalji case is now well known, but life imitates art as well as the other way round: Edalji undoubtedly chose Doyle to be his champion because of stories like 'The Norwood Builder'. Edalji's miscarriage of justice and the similar case of Adolf Beck led directly to the Criminal Appeal Act 1907, which established for the first time in Britain, against strong judicial opposition, a court to hear criminal appeals.[15] But the positive influence of Doyle's prejudiced presentation of Lestrade and his colleagues may be even greater than that. It established in British cultural memory a scepticism about the firmness of criminal convictions, and a wariness about the narratives told by police detectives, that has no doubt been a cause of frustration for practitioners of law and order but which has saved many innocent men and women from prison, execution and disgrace.

Notes

1. Mrs Hudson appears, and is named, in nine stories: *The Sign of Four*, 'The Adventure of the Naval Treaty' (1893), 'The Empty House', 'The Dancing Men', 'Black Peter', 'Wisteria Lodge', 'The Adventure of the Dying Detective' (1913), *The Valley of Fear* (1914), and 'The Adventure of the Three Garridebs' (1925). She is mentioned by name in a further four stories. There are further references to an unnamed landlady, and one anomalous instance, in 'A Scandal in Bohemia', when the landlady is named as Mrs Turner.
2. Thorstein Veblen, *The Theory of the Leisure Class*. See also Dennis Porter, *The Pursuit of Crime*, p. 157.
3. Kerr, *Conan Doyle*, pp. 67–74.
4. Perkin, *The Rise of Professional Society*, pp. 116–17.
5. Ibid., pp. 20; 85–6.
6. Haia Shpayer-Makov, 'Explaining the Rise and Success of Detective Memoirs in Britain', p. 103.
7. Robert Louis and Fanny Van de Grift Stevenson, *The Dynamiter*, p. 9.
8. See Kate Summerscale, *The Suspicions of Mr Whicher*.
9. *Adventures*, ed. Richard Lancelyn Green, p. 328.
10. Jonathan Cranfield, *Twentieth-Century Victorian*, p. 20.
11. See Knight, *Form and Ideology in Crime Fiction*, p. 103, and Carey, *The Intellectuals and the Masses*, p. 64.
12. Shpayer-Makov, 'Explaining the Rise and Success of Detective Memoirs', pp. 199, 122.
13. Qtd in Cranfield, *Twentieth-Century Victorian*, p. 86.
14. For the Edalji case, see Lycett, *Conan Doyle*, pp. 302–6; for Slater, see Lycett pp. 334–5 and 421–4.
15. William Rodolph Cornish et al., *Law and Society in England*, p. 619.

Chapter 5

The Fall of the House of Musgrave

In *Memories and Adventures*, Conan Doyle recounted how his Edinburgh lecturer, Joseph Bell, provided the real-life model for Sherlock Holmes's methods of reasoning: 'It is no wonder that after the study of such a character I used and amplified his methods when in later life I tried to build up a scientific detective who solved cases on his own merits and not through the folly of the criminal.'[1] But Bell was not the only source for Holmes. His literary model was Edgar Allan Poe's 'masterful' Parisian detective, Le Chavalier C. Auguste Dupin, who first appeared in 'The Murders in the Rue Morgue' (1841), and reappeared in 'The Mystery of Marie Rogêt' (1842) and 'The Purloined Letter' (1844). Poe was one of the most powerful literary influences on Doyle's writing. In *Through the Magic Door* (1907), a memoir of his reading, Doyle praised Poe as 'the supreme original short story writer of all time. His brain was like a seed-pod full of seeds which flew carelessly around, and from which have sprung nearly all our modern types of story', including, of course, detective fiction. Each writer in the genre 'may find some little development of his own, but his main art must trace back to those admirable stories of Monsieur Dupin, so wonderful in their masterful force, their reticence, their quick dramatic point'.[2] When introducing Holmes to the world in *A Study in Scarlet*, Doyle acknowledged Poe's influence when Watson compares Holmes to Dupin, only to earn Holmes's retort: 'No doubt you think that you are complimenting me in comparing me to Dupin . . . Now, in my opinion, Dupin was a very inferior fellow . . . he was by no means such a phenomenon as Poe appeared to imagine' (21). This is a textually involved tribute, in that it appears to denigrate Dupin while alluding to Dupin's own repudiation of *his* real-life predecessor, the criminal-turned-investigator Eugène François Vidocq, a founder of the French Sûreté. In 'The Murders in the Rue Morgue', Dupin described Vidocq as 'a good guesser, and a persevering man.

But, without educated thought, he erred continually by the very intensity of his investigations.'³

Such direct acknowledgements aside, the magnetic force of Poe's short stories on Doyle's imagination is evident throughout the Holmes saga. It is discernible in numerous plots: the locked-room mysteries of *The Sign of Four*, 'The Speckled Band' and 'The Empty House' derive from 'The Murders in the Rue Morgue'; the missing documents in 'The Naval Treaty', 'The Adventure of the Second Stain' (1904) and 'The Bruce-Partington Plans' all recall Poe's purloined letter; code-breaking dominates both 'The Gold Bug' and 'The Dancing Men'.⁴ Verbal echoes and images abound, from Holmes's 'What one man can invent another can discover' in 'The Dancing Men' – recalling 'it may well be doubted whether human ingenuity can construct an enigma of the kind which human ingenuity may not, by proper application, resolve' from 'The Gold Bug'⁵ – to the brass tripod in the sinister suburban house in 'The Greek Interpreter', which derives from the mysterious tripod that illuminates Prince Prospero's abbey in Poe's 'The Masque of the Red Death' (1842).⁶ Moreover, some stories can be read as concerted rewritings of Poe's originals, suggesting not so much homage as an attempt to overcome a powerful force. Drawing on Harold Bloom's Freudian theory of 'anxiety of influence', Michael Atkinson has interpreted 'A Scandal in Bohemia' as a sustained (and probably self-conscious) response to 'The Purloined Letter', reversing many of the features of the original so as to turn it inside out: a queen becomes a king, a letter becomes a photograph, Dupin's success becomes Holmes's failure. The climax of both stories is a diversion created by the detective to reveal the location of the sought-after object: Poe hides the letter in plain sight, but Doyle conceals the photograph, so Atkinson concludes that 'Poe's is a story of brazen exposures and surfaces; Conan Doyle's, a tale of clever disguises and hidden depths.'⁷

We can apply a similar method to 'The Musgrave Ritual', a sustained rewriting of Poe's 'The Fall of the House of Usher' which, in its documentary clue to buried treasure, also recalls 'The Gold-Bug'. The ritual of the title is a text, handed down orally from generation to generation of Musgraves, but also recorded in documentary form, originating (as we discover) in the seventeenth century. Holmes realises that the ritual is a key that can unlock the mystery which Reginald Musgrave, his friend from university, has brought to him, concerning the disappearance of Musgrave's butler and maid: 'if I could read the Musgrave Ritual aright, I should hold in my hand the clue which would lead me to the truth concerning both the butler

Brunton, and the maid Howells' (125). 'The Fall of the House of Usher' is also a key which can unlock the hidden chamber of Doyle's later reimagining. Poe's story famously begins with the narrator arriving on horseback at 'the mansion of gloom' to visit his childhood friend, Roderick Usher, obeying 'a very singular summons' conveyed in a letter speaking of 'acute bodily illness – of a mental disorder which oppressed him'.[8] Usher and his dying sister Madeline are the last remnants of a 'very ancient family', previously distinguished in art, charity and music: 'the entire family lay in the direct line of descent, and had always, with very trifling and temporary variation, lain so', entailing 'undeviating transmission, from sire to son, of the patrimony with the name'.[9] In other words, the House of Usher is a house in two senses, estate and family, and the elision of the two is one of the story's principal themes: both family and estate have become degenerated, one through inbreeding, the other by neglect. The house itself, overlooking a sinister tarn, is of 'excessive antiquity', and although apparently intact is subject to 'extensive decay'.[10] The owner is similarly decayed – Roderick Usher is 'terribly altered' – although the narrator makes clear that he has always had an extraordinary appearance:

> A cadaverousness of complexion; an eye large, liquid, and luminous beyond comparison; lips somewhat thin and very pallid, but of a surpassingly beautiful curve; a nose of a delicate Hebrew model, but with a breadth of nostril unusual in similar formations; a finely moulded chin, speaking, in its want of prominence, of a want of moral energy; hair of a more than web-like softness and tenuity; these features, with an inordinate expansion above the regions of the temple, made up altogether a countenance not easily to be forgotten.[11]

Usher's aristocratic physique – his genetic inheritance – is both finely wrought and suggestive of feebleness. His illness, whose symptoms include 'a morbid acuteness of the senses', is also part of his legacy: 'It was, he said, a constitutional and a family evil.'[12] Man and mansion share an uncanny correspondence: Usher has come to be overwhelmed 'by certain superstitious impressions in regard to the dwelling which he tenanted'. He is subject to

> an influence which some peculiarities in the mere form and substance of his family mansion, had, by dint of long sufferance, he said, obtained over his spirit – an effect which the *physique* of the gray walls and turrets, and of the dim tarn into which they all looked down, had, at length, brought about upon the *morale* of his existence.[13]

Roderick's sister Madeline is also afflicted by a wasting disease, no doubt a part of *her* inheritance – glimpsed by the narrator, she apparently dies on the night of his arrival.

Usher spends the ensuing days in solemn contemplation of music and art, and broods over his own 'phantasmagoric conceptions', including a very strange drawing:

> A small picture presented the interior of an immensely long and rectangular vault or tunnel, with low walls, smooth, white, and without interruption or device. Certain accessory points of the design served well to convey the idea that this excavation lay at an exceeding depth below the surface of the earth. No outlet was observed in any portion of its vast extent, and no torch, or other artificial source of light was discernible; yet a flood of intense rays rolled throughout, and bathed the whole in a ghastly and inappropriate splendour.[14]

The vault of Usher's diseased imagination soon finds a physical equivalent in the vault in which he and the narrator entomb Madeline's corpse: 'small, damp, and entirely without means of admission for light; lying, at great depth, immediately beneath that portion of the building in which was my own sleeping apartment. It had been used, apparently, in remote feudal times, for the worst purposes of a donjon-keep.' Its door is of 'massive iron' and 'immense weight', causing 'an unusually sharp grating sound, as it moved upon its hinges'.[15] A few nights later, both the narrator and Usher find themselves sleepless, and the narrator tries to soothe his host by reading to him 'the "Mad Trist" of Sir Launcelot Canning', a story (invented by Poe but redolent of a medieval saga) of a knight who breaks into a hermit's cottage to find a dragon, which he strikes with a mace to earn a brazen shield bearing 'this legend':

> Who entereth here, a conqueror hath bin;
> Who slayeth the dragon, the shield he shall win[16]

At the climax of the story within the story, the two men hear sounds from below that resemble something emerging from Madeline's tomb – and, with Roderick now raving in horror, Madeline appears, bloodied and emaciated, falling dead upon her brother, who himself dies from fear or shock. As the narrator flees, he turns to see the house collapsing into the tarn.

Doyle trims the frenzied excesses of Poe's original, so that the overtly psychological symbolism becomes a more restrained narrative of domestic greed, jealousy and detection. 'The Musgrave Ritual' begins on a winter's night in Baker Street with Holmes tidying his archive, and pulling out a box of souvenirs from one of his earliest cases with the words, 'ah, now! this really is something a little *recherché*' (*Memoirs*, 114). The use of the French word may itself be an echo of Poe's 'The Murders in the Rue Morgue', where it is used by Dupin in a passage explaining his method.[17] Holmes retrieves objects from his past – 'a crumpled piece of paper, an old-fashioned brass key, a peg of wood with a ball of string attached to it, and three rusty old discs of metal' (114–5) – but in designating these as 'relics' (115) which 'have a history' to the extent that 'they *are* history' (115), he alludes to both their antiquity and their present-day significance. For this, like 'The Fall of the House of Usher', is a story about the relationship of the present with the past, and what this means for the future.

Having set the scene of his retrospective narrative by describing his postgraduate domestic arrangements in London's Montague Street, Holmes describes Reginald Musgrave, a fellow-student who would become one of his first clients. On first reading Musgrave seems unexceptional, if well born, demonstrating his upper-class credentials in his looks and bearing: he is 'a man of an exceedingly aristocratic type, thin, high-nosed, and large-eyed, with languid and yet courtly manners'. It is clear that 'aristocratic type' here means physical type, but the word also denotes lineage, and this is what Holmes sets out with characteristic precision: 'He was indeed a scion of one of the very oldest families in the kingdom, though his branch was a cadet one which had separated from the northern Musgraves some time in the sixteenth century, and had established itself in western Sussex, where the manor house of Hurlstone is perhaps the oldest inhabited building in the county' (116). But we can detect in Musgrave Roderick Usher's strange correspondence of bodily and material inheritance when Holmes observes: 'Something of his birthplace seemed to cling to the man, and I never looked at his pale, keen face, or the poise of his head, without associating him with grey archways and mullioned windows and all the venerable wreckage of a feudal keep' (116). 'Venerable' is apt as Hurlstone, 'a labyrinth of an old building' (122), is even more ancient than Usher's mansion: 'Over the low, heavy-linteled door . . . is chiselled the date 1607, but experts are agreed that the beams and stonework are really much older than this' (125), and it has an oak tree, probably dating from the Norman Conquest, which Holmes realises features in the ritual. Both Hurlstone and the House of Usher are characterised by thick, grey walls, narrow windows, Gothic archways and dark passageways. As the corridors of the House of Usher are decorated with 'phantasmagoric armorial trophies',[18] so the 'corridors of Hurlstone have their walls largely decorated with trophies of old weapons' (119). And both buildings are themselves mysteries, clues to which can be discerned in an ancient text.

On one level, Musgrave simply exemplifies Conan Doyle's fascination with genealogy and heraldry which was a feature of his entire writing career and which, in *Memories and Adventures*, he suggests was itself an inheritance from his mother: 'she was great on archaeology, and had, with the help of . . . a relative, worked out her descent for more than five hundred years, and so composed a family tree which lies before me as I write and on which many of the great ones of the earth have roosted'.[19] Doyle begins his autobiography by detailing his family's lineage, one that has some striking similarities to that of the Musgraves:

> The original Doyle, or D'Oil, was a cadet-branch of the Staffordshire Doyles, which has produced Sir Francis Hastings Doyle and many other distinguished men. . . . But the real romance of the family lies in the fact that about the middle of the seventeenth century the Reverend Richard Pack, who was head of Kilkenny College, married Mary Percy, who was heir to the Irish branch of the Percys of Northumberland. By this alliance we all connect up (and I have every generation by name, as marked out by my dear mother) with that illustrious line up to three separate marriages with the Plantagenets. One has, therefore, some strange strains in one's blood.[20]

A similar fascination is evident throughout his loving recreation of fourteenth-century chivalry in *The White Company* (1891), which is replete with exhaustive genealogical accounts and heraldic details, as in Sir Nigel's review of his forces after they have landed at Bordeaux in which he identifies their insignia:

> Close behind us is the moline cross of the gallant William Molyneux, and beside it the bloody chevrons of the Norfolk Woodhouses, with the amulets of the Musgraves of Westmoreland. By Saint Paul! it would be a very strange thing if so noble a company were to gather without some notable deed of arms arising from it.[21]

Barely two years before writing 'The Musgrave Ritual', Conan Doyle included a presumed ancestor of Reginald Musgrave in the heroic force that fought for the Black Prince in the Hundred Years War.

However, Holmes's description of the latter-day Musgrave points to the story's deeper engagement with genealogy and inheritance. Like Roderick Usher, this aristocrat is a broken, enfeebled remnant of an illustrious family, who blithely scorns his family's heraldic devices – 'blazes and charges' – as having, like the ritual, 'no practical use whatsoever' (120). Musgrave has lost contact with his inheritance. Holmes remarks on seeing Musgrave for the first time in four years that (unlike Roderick Usher) he 'had changed little', but both texts go on to describe the enduring features of both men. Musgrave is something of an aesthete: he 'was dressed like a young man of fashion – he was always a bit of a dandy' (117). 'Dandy' has few positive connotations in Conan Doyle's moral lexicon, and this together with his self-designation as 'a bachelor' suggests either asexuality or homosexuality. His physical weakness is indicated at the story's climax, when Holmes locates a hidden cellar containing the treasures entrusted to the Musgraves by King Charles I: he summons a Sussex policeman to help him lift the stone, and does not even ask his university friend to assist. Sidney Paget's illustrations which accompanied the first publication of the story in the *Strand* accentuate Musgrave's dandyish airs: he is shown smoking a cigarette, his legs crossed, his face characterised by high cheekbones and full lips. Moreover, despite his education, Musgrave is as intellectually weak as he is physically feeble: his lack of curiosity over the ritual which is in every sense his inheritance is pointedly noted by Holmes: 'You will excuse me, Musgrave, if I say that your butler appears to me to have been a very clever man, and to have had a clearer insight than ten generations of his masters' (124).

This is the crux of the story. Richard Brunton, the butler, is Musgrave's opposite in almost every respect. Musgrave describes his former employee as 'a man of great energy and character' who became 'invaluable in the household. He was a well-grown, handsome man, with a splendid forehead.' In addition to his impressive physique, his intellectual accomplishments (he was a schoolmaster before becoming a butler) are such that 'he can speak several languages and play nearly every musical instrument'. Musgrave's tribute to his employee even includes the extraordinary admission that a mere servant was one of the most admired features of his ancient estate: 'The butler of Hurlstone is always a thing that is remembered by all who visit us' (118). According to Musgrave, 'this paragon has one fault', although what is perceived by the employer as a weakness is, from another perspective, a source of considerable power and strength: 'He is a bit of a Don Juan, and you can imagine that for a man like him it is not a very

Figure 5 'Reginald Musgrave'. Illustration by Sidney Paget, *Strand Magazine*, May 1893.

difficult part to play in a quiet country district.' Tellingly, his sexual appetites were apparently satisfied by his wife, but after her death 'we have had no end of trouble with him' (118). An engagement to the second housemaid, Rachel Howells, appeared to settle him down again, but he then discarded her in favour of the head gamekeeper's daughter – and it may be significant that Brunton's amorous adventures appear to be confined to fellow servants. As Holmes deduces, it is this physically, sexually and intellectually powerful figure who decodes the Musgrave Ritual, locates the hidden treasure, and with only the help of Rachel succeeds through strength and intelligence in opening the hidden cellar. His only failure in the story is to misjudge the ferocious vengeance of a woman he scorned who, in a reversal of Poe's climactic scene of Madeline escaping from her tomb with a 'low moaning cry', suffers 'a sudden hysterical attack' (119) after entombing her former lover, pines away for three days and disappears.[22]

If Brunton has an equivalent in Poe's story, in which a servant in waiting and a valet are mentioned but remain unobtrusive, it is Ethelred, the knight of 'doughty heart' in the story within the story, who penetrates the hermit's chamber, fulfils the terms of an ancient legend and seizes the treasure. Brunton is also a conqueror, which is the political message contained in Doyle's multi-layered, almost allegorical narrative. And what he represents is the servant class. In telling Holmes his story, Musgrave is strikingly specific about the small army of staff required to keep his estate functioning:

> I have to keep up a considerable staff of servants at Hurlstone, for it is a rambling old place, and takes a good deal of looking after . . . Altogether there are eight maids, the cook, the butler, two footmen, and a boy. The garden and the stables, of course, have a separate staff. (117)

The details are important. Musgrave is, to put it bluntly, outnumbered: his father died two years before his visit to Holmes, and there is no indication of any other Musgrave in the house. He excuses his excessive reliance on the servant class – 'I usually have a house party, so it would not do to be short-handed' (117) – but this unconvincing aside provides another implicit criticism of Musgrave's weakness.

Brunton may be the equivalent of Poe's Ethelred but he and his murderer Rachel also derive from a literary tradition that is closer to home. Victorian novels notoriously often failed to notice the army of servants who kept middle-class as well as aristocratic households going, but servants most certainly came to prominence when those novels concerned themselves with crime. As Anthea Trodd has shown, two stock characters appear repeatedly in the Victorian sensation novel from the 1860s onwards, and have their antecedents in mainstream fiction. One such stock character was the emotional housemaid, of whom Rosanna Spearman in *The Moonstone* is both exemplar and clearly the model for Doyle's Rachel, with some clever variations that show him playing with his source material: as Trodd points out, Collins's Rosanna is employed by a Rachel, and drowns herself in the sea, while preserving the vital clue; Doyle's Rachel is traced to the shore of the mere, but throws the treasure rather than herself into the water.[23] The other stock character is the clever, manipulative valet or butler who discovers the family secret, usually for purposes of blackmail, sometimes labelled 'a Morgan' or 'a Littimer' after the criminal valets in Thackeray's *Pendennis* and Dickens's *David Copperfield*.[24] These figures represented the modern servant, who worked primarily for money, rather than feudal servants motivated by loyalty to the family, and their frequent association with criminality is evidence of anxiety about this aspect of the period's social change. 'The Musgrave Ritual' dramatises the collision of two incompatible conceptions of service when Reginald Musgrave confronts Brunton in the library: '"So!" said I, "this is how you repay the trust which we have reposed in you! You will leave my service tomorrow"' (119). Brunton pleads to be given more time, on the grounds that he cannot bear the disgrace of being sacked, but his real motivation becomes clear when the mystery is revealed: he needed more time to locate the treasure. Musgrave cannot understand Brunton's actions because servants, for him, are part of the estate; Brunton, on the other hand, is an employee who acts to improve his lot in life, and sees Musgrave as an employer, neither more nor less. The location of this confrontation is also significant: Brunton is studying his way to wealth in a library, building on his existing intellectual accomplishments to break free, finally, from the bonds of service.

Doyle wrote 'The Musgrave Ritual' just as Britain's wide-acred aristocrats were losing their ancient privileges of power and wealth, and on the eve of the greatest transfer of territory since the Dissolution of the Monasteries as the great estates were broken up and sold.[25] Brunton represents the forces of social change that will ultimately destroy Hurlstone. In effect he works as a kind of personification of what today we would call social mobility – he is self-educated, determined, vigorous, characterised by 'an insatiable curiosity about things which did not in the least concern him'.[26] And it is his vigour, both professional and sexual, that is the principal threat to the exhausted Musgraves and all that they represent of Britain's diminished aristocratic heritage. As the last of the Musgraves presides over an estate that awaits its dissolution, the countryside around it will, no doubt, be populated by the bastard children of the 'well-grown, handsome' butler and his conquests among the servant class.

Notes

1. Doyle, *Memories and Adventures*, p. 26.
2. Doyle, *Through the Magic Door*, pp. 114–15.
3. Edgar Allan Poe, *Selected Writings*, p. 204. Eugène François Vidocq (1775–1857) was a convicted criminal who became an informer for the French police and, in 1811, helped found a plain-clothes unit which became the Sûreté Nationale. His ghostwritten memoir became a best-seller, and inspired Balzac (whose Vautrin was modelled on Vidocq) and another of Doyle's inspirations, the French detective writer Émile Gaboriau, in addition to Poe. See James Morton, *The First Detective*.

4. Doyle noted in 'Through the Magic Door' that 'all treasure-hunting, cryptogram-solving yarns trace back to his "Gold Bug"' (115). Doyle added that he considered that story and 'The Murders in the Rue Morgue' to be Poe's greatest achievements.
5. Poe, *Selected Writings*, p. 211.
6. For the verbal echoes of 'The Gold Bug' in 'The Dancing Men', see *The Return of Sherlock Holmes* ed. Richard Lancelyn Green p. 352.
7. Atkinson, *The Secret Marriage of Sherlock Holmes*, p. 57.
8. Poe, *Selected Writings*, p. 139.
9. Ibid., pp. 139–40.
10. Ibid., p. 141.
11. Ibid., 142.
12. Ibid., 143.
13. Ibid., 144.
14. Ibid., p. 146.
15. Ibid., p. 150.
16. Ibid., pp. 153–4.
17. Ibid., p. 190.
18. Ibid., p. 141.
19. Doyle, *Memories and Adventures*, p. 9.
20. Ibid., pp. 8–10.
21. Doyle, *The White Company*, p. 188.
22. There may also be an echo of Poe's 'The Cask of Amontillado' (1846), in which the narrator recalls luring his friend Fortunato into a niche in a cellar, where he immures him.
23. Anthea Trodd, *Domestic Crime in the Victorian Novel*, pp. 46–7, 63.
24. Ibid., p. 48.
25. See David Cannadine, *The Decline and Fall of the British Aristocracy*, pp. 88–112.
26. Brunton's curiosity also recalls that of Caleb Williams, the servant of William Godwin's eponymous political novel of 1794 whose discovery of Squire Falkland's secret leads to a drama of pursuit and flight with a tragic denouement. Godwin's novel also features a climactic scene when the master surprises the servant while the latter is penetrating the household's secrets.

Chapter 6

A Scandal in East Yorkshire

Holmes is frequently employed by a client in order to avert, or suppress a scandal. While secrecy is the client's objective, the scandal itself is – usually – revealed to the privileged reader. This is exemplified by the very first Holmes short story, whose scandalous subject is even declared in its title. When the King of Bohemia employs Holmes to save his forthcoming marriage to Clotilde Lothman von Saxe-Meningen, second daughter of the King of Scandinavia, full details of the incriminating evidence – letters and a cabinet photograph[1] – are revealed in a comic catechism between Holmes and the King:

'If this young person should produce her letters for blackmailing or other purposes, how is she to prove their authenticity?'
   'There is the writing.'
   'Pooh, pooh! Forgery.'
   'My private note-paper.'
   'Stolen.'
   'My own seal.'
   'Imitated.'
   'My photograph.'
   'Bought.'
   'We were both in the photograph.'
   'Oh, dear! That is very bad! Your Majesty has indeed committed an indiscretion.' (*Adventures*, 13)

Other clients who employ Holmes to avert scandals include Lady Eva Brackwell, whose 'imprudent letters' to 'an impecunious young squire in the country' (*Return*, 159) threaten her forthcoming marriage to the Earl of Dovercourt in 'Charles Augustus Milverton'; Hilton Soames, tutor at St Luke's College in 'The Adventure of the Three Students' (1904) who is desperate to avoid public knowledge of an attempt at cheating in the examination for the Fortescue Scholarship; and Colonel Sir James Damery, a fixer at the Court of St James who, in 'The Adventure of the Illustrious Client' (1924), employs Holmes to neutralise the threat from Baron Gruner. Gruner is a murderous philanderer whose latest outrage against Edwardian morality is to mesmerise, in Svengali-like fashion, Miss Violet de Merville, daughter of General de Merville 'of Khyber fame' (*Case-Book*, 109), into an engagement. This latter case is the most enigmatic of these society scandal narratives: in contrast with 'A Scandal in Bohemia', in which layers of deception employed by client and detective are seen through and revealed to the reader, 'The Illustrious Client' is permeated by layers of obfuscation, several of which remain opaque at the end. Most Holmes stories reveal the client and his or her motives at the outset (even if, as in 'A Scandal in Bohemia', the client tries to remain incognito), and the client brings a mystery which Holmes's investigations later reveal. 'The Illustrious Client', however, begins with a client whose identity and motivation remain obscure, operating through a surrogate who presents a problem which is far from mysterious: Holmes's subsequent actions and those of his collaborators remove the problem but the client's identity and his motivations remain outside the frame of the story.

Damery, we discover, consults Holmes not on his own behalf but for a principal whom he refuses to name and who, in turn, claims to be acting in the best interests of the de Merville family: the client 'has known the General intimately for many years and taken a paternal interest in this young girl since she wore short frocks. He cannot see this tragedy consummated without some attempt to stop it' (110). However, the client's altruistic stake in this case does not explain the excessive secrecy which extends even to withholding his identity from Holmes. Moreover, Damery's convoluted explanation suggests that the client is not quite so disinterested as he would like to make out, and the very fact that it is he who provides the title of the story, and not the victims, or the perpetrator, or the black book containing details of Gruner's scandalous conquests, urges us to consider his true relation to the case. The obvious explanation – that the client has been the intimate friend of Miss Violet as well as of her father – is unstated.

The client's identity is not revealed to the reader but it is discovered by both Holmes and Watson: the latter spots Damery jumping into a brougham with 'armorial bearings upon the panel' (132). This discovery prompts an astonished and excited Watson to burst into Holmes's room with the news, only to find (unsurprisingly) that Holmes has already deduced the client's identity and decided that discretion remains paramount. The inference we should draw is obvious enough: Sir James Damery is working on behalf of His Majesty King Edward VII, who ascended the throne in 1901; most of the stories in *The Case-Book of Sherlock Holmes* appear to be set in the Edwardian period. In his previous role as Albert Edward, Prince of Wales, 'Bertie' (as he was known to family and friends) appears several times in Holmes's orbit, but always incognito. He is clearly the 'illustrious client' (*Adventures*, 247) of 'The Beryl Coronet', who approaches Alexander Holder, of Holder & Stevenson in Threadneedle Street, with a request to pawn one of the Crown Jewels in return for a short-term loan of fifty thousand pounds: 'a card was brought in to me by one of the clerks. I started when I saw the name, for it was none other than – well, perhaps even to you I had better say no more than that it was a name which is a household word all over the earth – one of the highest, noblest, most exalted names in England' (246).[2] Richard Lancelyn Green even proposes him as an inspiration for the King in 'A Scandal in Bohemia'.[3] And he is also alluded to in 'The Empty House' in the guise of Lord Balmoral.[4]

Before his coronation Bertie was, as Jane Ridley has shown, 'the first modern gossip-column prince' known for his marital indiscretions and his love of gambling: a *Puck* cartoon from 1891, 'L'enfante terrible', shows an irate Queen Victoria castigating her elder son, pointing to a list of indiscretions which include 'inveterate gambling', indebtedness, and 'loose morals'; Bertie himself is shown bearing the Prince of Wales's heraldic badge with the words 'ich deal'.[5] His affairs were common knowledge in society and, to a lesser extent, to the public: he became the first royal since Henry V to appear in court under subpoena in the Mordaunt divorce case in 1870; his long-standing liaisons with Lady Daisy 'Babbling' Brooke and then Alice Keppel were widely known in aristocratic circles; he was rumoured to be the lover of the famous actress Lillie Langtry. After he became king, Henry James christened him 'Edward the Caresser', and it seems entirely plausible that Doyle was discreetly gesturing at the King's amorous reputation in 'The Illustrious Client'.

It is Edward's reputation as a gambler rather than Lothario that animates 'The Empty House', first published in *Collier's Weekly* in the US in September 1903 and in the *Strand* the following month, and written a few months after the King had knighted Conan Doyle in October 1902. (Edward VII had not long before read *The Hound of the Baskervilles* while convalescing from appendicitis in 1902 and pronounced it 'very poor'.[6]) This is the story which brought Holmes back from the dead, following his apparently fatal struggle with Professor Moriarty at a Swiss waterfall in 'The Final Problem'. The story interweaves two plots: the first is the return of Holmes, his account of how he survived his grapple with Moriarty, and what he did next, and the second is a 'locked-room mystery' surrounding the death of the Hon. Ronald Adair, an apparently blameless youth found shot dead in his upstairs sitting room in Park Lane. What connects the two plots is the story's villain, Colonel Sebastian Moran, Moriarty's principal henchman and therefore, before his superior's death, 'the second most dangerous man in London' (*Return*, 23). After trying and failing to finish Holmes off in Switzerland, we learn that Moran returned to London where he became Adair's partner in card games and the two had just won a considerable sum from Godfrey Milner and Lord Balmoral. Both names are suggestive: no commoner would be allowed to take a title from the royal family's estate in Aberdeenshire, while Milner would undoubtedly have reminded a contemporary reader of Lord (Alfred) Milner, previously High Commissioner for South Africa and Governor of Cape Colony, in which role he was one of the main figures behind the Second Anglo-Boer War, who was blamed by the Liberal Party for causing an unnecessary conflict, and who was praised by the war's partisans, Doyle included, for standing up to the Boers. Following the war, and at the time of the story's publication, Milner was the first governor of the Transvaal and Orange Free State – the so-called 'Boer Republics' which were added to Britain's dominion following her victory. Watson reveals (based on facts reported after the inquest) that Adair's 'head had been horribly mutilated by an expanded revolver bullet' (5). This too alludes to the Boer War, in particular the allegation – furiously resisted by Doyle in his propaganda work *The War in South Africa: Its Cause and Conduct* (1902) – that British troops had used soft-nosed, expanding bullets, banned under the Second Hague Conference of 1899, to maximise damage on their human targets.[7]

These allusions to the Boer War may not be as incidental as they might appear. As we learn more about Moran, we discover that – while not as illustrious as his partners at cards – he is nonetheless a highly skilled and much decorated aristocrat with a history of imperial service. Col. Moran has entered the worlds of elite leisure (high-class gambling) and elite crime (Moriarty's gang) from Eton, Oxford and then Her Majesty's Indian Army where he was, Holmes reveals, 'the best heavy game shot that our Eastern Empire has ever produced' (19), famous for stalking tigers in the jungle: Holmes calls him an 'old shikari' (20), an Urdu word for hunter. Like Watson, Moran has served in Afghanistan; unlike Watson, Moran's military exploits in the Second Afghan War were sufficiently distinguished to be mentioned in despatches. Furthermore, Moran has empire in the blood: his father was a former British Minister to Persia. Watson is astonished by this renegade's background as an 'honourable soldier', and indeed Moran can be read as a perverted mirror image of Watson himself, both men having served in the same army in the same places, but the one using his (more limited) talents for good, the other going spectacularly and disastrously wrong. Moran's character thus serves as an implicit commentary on the debate over British military conduct in war into which Doyle had plunged himself with full force in the year prior to writing this story. British officers were capable of atrocities, but as exceptions, not as a rule: Holmes's casual reference to Moran's 'sudden turn' to evil as being the result of some evil genetic inheritance – 'I have a theory that the individual represents in his development the whole procession of his ancestors' – turns Moran's conduct into a biological rather than political phenomenon. And yet, as with other degenerate aristocrats of the Holmes stories, Moran's dissolute career invites us to enquire into the very structure of the British class system. If Moran can use his privileged inheritance to such evil ends, by what right did he enjoy such privilege in the first place?

Such troubling questions are also raised by the circumstances of Adair's death, only to be brushed aside by Holmes. There are some telling details at the crime scene. The door to the sitting room has been locked from the inside, a fact which is judged at the inquest to be both mysterious and potentially significant. On the table next to Adair's corpse are piles of gold and silver coins, some banknotes, and a sheet of paper bearing names of 'club friends' and numbers, apparently of winnings and losses. We are also told that Adair's engagement to his fiancée has just been broken off, but for reasons that are never disclosed. Holmes's solution appears to explain the facts of the case while conveniently allocating all of the blame to the villainous Moran:

> 'I believe that on the day of the murder, Adair had discovered that Moran was cheating. Very likely he had spoken to him privately, and had threatened to expose him unless he voluntarily resigned his membership of the club, and promised not to play cards again . . . The exclusion from his clubs would mean ruin to Moran, who lived by his ill-gotten card games. He therefore murdered Adair, who at the time was endeavouring to work out how much money he should himself return, since he could not profit by his partner's foul play. He locked the door, lest the ladies should surprise him and insist upon knowing what he was doing with these names and coins. Will it pass?' (25)

Figure 6 'Colonel Moran sprang forward, with a snarl of rage.' Illustration by Sidney Paget, *Strand Magazine*, October 1903.

Watson responds affirmatively: 'I have no doubt that you have hit upon the truth.' But as his own question suggests, Holmes's explanation is both entirely speculative and, when considered in the light of the facts, preposterous. It asks us to believe that Adair and Moran could be partners at cards but that only one was cheating; that the second-in-command of Britain's most formidable criminal enterprise is so dependent on income from society gambling that he must kill to preserve his club memberships; and that a man counting his winnings behind a locked door must be doing so in order to provide restitution to those who have been cheated. Nor does Holmes attempt to explain the decision of Adair's fiancée to cut short their engagement, a detail which, in the official version of events, is entirely superfluous.

A clue to what is really going on in the Adair case is suggested by the penalty that Holmes imagines Adair attempted to impose on Moran: the promise not to play cards again. This is the third of three allusions in the Holmes stories to the Tranby Croft Affair, a scandal that gripped the British public as it played out in newspapers and in the High Court in the early 1890s. The first allusion comes in 'The Five Orange Pips' (1891), in which John Openshaw consults Holmes following a recommendation from Major Prendergast: 'I heard ... how you saved him in the Tankerville Club Scandal' (*Adventures*, 104). The second can be found near the end of *The Hound of the Baskervilles*, suggesting that the case was much in Doyle's mind as the new King ascended the throne: Holmes, we learn, 'had exposed the atrocious conduct of Colonel Upwood in connection with the famous card scandal of the Nonpareil Club' (158). The scandal began in September 1890 with a game of baccarat – a variation of pontoon or *vingt-et-un* with a banker, two players and two groups of observers betting on whose hand is closest to nine – at Tranby Croft in East Yorkshire, home of the shipping magnate Arthur Wilson.[8] The game ended with a lieutenant colonel in the Scots Guards, Sir William Gordon-Cumming, being accused of cheating by his hosts and by some fellow former army officers. Gordon-Cumming, a baronet and major Scottish landowner who had fought with great distinction in the Zulu War, and the Egyptian and Sudanese Campaigns (including at the battle of Abu Klea in 1884 as part of the doomed mission to relieve General Gordon at Khartoum), and who was an admired hunter of Indian tigers, sued his accusers for slander and lost. What elevated this from an ordinary tale of greed and loathing among the moneyed and aristocratic elite was the identity of the banker during two evenings of baccarat and who had to take the stand in the witness box at the High Court in 1891: Albert Edward, Prince of Wales.

Baccarat was one of Bertie's favourite games. Both sides in the court case agreed not to refer to the fact that Bertie travelled the country with his own set of baccarat tokens (tokens which are also visible in his hand but hidden from his mother's view in 'L'enfant terrible'). The problem was that playing baccarat for money was actually illegal in Britain at the time, as it was judged by the courts to be a game of chance rather than skill. And the presence in court of the Prince of Wales meant that the press examined every detail of the case. Gordon-Cumming's words and actions on two evenings in 1890 became national news, including the question of whether a sheet of paper on which he recorded the progress of each hand had facilitated his cheating or was evidence to support his innocence. But the main events came after some of the other players observed Gordon-Cumming apparently (and in the rules of the game illegally) raising or lowering his stakes in accordance with the turn of the cards. Gordon-Cumming was confronted, but denied cheating: the matter was passed to the most senior guest present. Bertie's judgment was that the whole thing should be brushed under the carpet, but to preserve everyone's sense of justice, Gordon-Cumming would be required to sign a statement vowing never to play cards again. Bertie hoped that the matter would end there, but months afterwards, rumours began to circulate, and Gordon-Cumming felt he had no option but to sue. After his defeat, he was ostracised by Bertie and the royal courtiers, and required to resign from his four London clubs, so he married an American heiress and retired to a gloomy estate at Gordonstoun in Scotland. The popular verdict, though, appears to have been that he was an innocent man unjustly slandered, and more recent enquiries suggest that the accusation of cheating was revenge from fellow guests fed up at his success in seducing their wives.

In Holmes's solution to the mystery, then, Bertie becomes Adair, adjudicating Moran's offence and assigning the appropriate punishment, exile from the card tables; Gordon-Cumming, the tiger-hunting war hero, is Moran, the bad apple of empire whose moral toxicity is such that he has to be removed from polite society. But there is more than a trace of Gordon-Cumming in Adair too – and not just in that both men were associated with a mysterious sheet of paper interpreted variously as a sign of both guilt and innocence. Adair is also an aristocrat associated with empire, the second son of the Earl of Maynooth, governor of one of the Australian colonies. He is a member of three gaming clubs (the Baldwin, the Cavendish and the Bagatelle). He plays cards 'nearly every day at one club or another', and although Watson reports that 'he was a cautious player', Adair 'has actually won as much as £420 in a sitting some weeks before from Godfrey Milner and Lord Balmoral' (5). It seems obvious from a close reading of these details that there are two versions of the truth here: the official version, sponsored by Holmes and which will no doubt be accepted at Moran's trial ('Will it pass?'), and the subtextual version, in which Adair was clearly Moran's accomplice in card swindles, whose criminal behaviour was discovered by his fiancée and caused her to cancel their engagement.

The official version is one of many examples in the Holmes stories that appears to justify the literary-critical commonplace that detective fiction, especially in the Victorian and Edwardian periods, serves to underwrite bourgeois morality, the disciplinary state and the social status quo: as Stephen Arata puts it, 'the detective story is wholly unsuited to addressing systemic problems in any sustained way. At best, it only translates them into problems of *individual* deviance and transgression.'[9] But if we are to take this alternative reading as the correct version, what are we to make of Holmes's blatant attempt to cover up the true meaning of the facts? One explanation is that he simply wishes to spare Adair's family – his mother, visiting London for an operation on her cataracts, and his sister – the pain of discovering some unpalatable truths about the Hon. Ronald. Another is rather more troubling, and perhaps – for Edwardian society, and loyal citizens like Conan Doyle himself – too unpleasant to bring into the open. The aristocracy – the word means 'rule of the best' – may not be the right or best people to run the empire after all. If inherited wealth and status do not qualify their possessors, even monarchs and princes, to rule, but rather encourage vices, both petty and egregious, then deviance and transgression is far from merely individual: the whole structure of British society is cast in doubt. For anyone unwilling to contemplate radical change, such conclusions, and the facts leading to them, must not see the light of day. Watson begins his account by acknowledging that 'a good deal was suppressed' in reporting of the police investigation, offering the distinctly lame explanation that 'the case for the prosecution was so overwhelmingly strong that it was not necessary to bring forward all the facts' (3). It seems rather more plausible that facts were suppressed at Moran's trial, as they were in Gordon-Cumming's libel action, in order to protect the powerful from the revelation of their vices, and thereby preserve the social order.

Notes

1. Cabinet photographs were of particular size, and were standard souvenirs in Victorian high society: as Lancelyn Green notes, they were '5½ inches by 4 inches, on a mount 6½ inches by 4¼ inches, embossed at the foot and on the verso with the photographer's name'. For an entertaining essay on the story's photograph, which concludes that the photograph must have been rather more revealing than would customarily be the case with a cabinet photograph, see John Sutherland, 'Cabinets and Detectives' in *Who Betrays Elizabeth Bennett*, pp. 232–7.
2. Lancelyn Green proposes the Prince of Wales or his younger brother, Albert Victor, Duke of Clarence, as possible identities. In my view, internal evidence in the story strongly points to the former.
3. Doyle, *The Adventures of Sherlock Holmes*, ed. Richard Lancelyn Green, p. 299.
4. As the Duke of Balmoral, he may also be glimpsed in 'The Noble Bachelor' and 'Silver Blaze'. In the latter story, the Duke of Balmoral is the owner of the horse Iris entered for the Wessex Cup, so the association with gambling may be suggestive of one of Bertie's well-known private passions.

5. Jane Ridley, *Bertie*, p. 208. For the *Puck* cartoon, I am indebted to *The Public Domain Review* who used it to illustrate my essay 'Inside the Empty House'. The following discussion draws on material from that essay.
6. See Lycett, *Conan Doyle*, p. 274.
7. See Doyle, *The Return of Sherlock Holmes* ed. Richard Lancelyn Green, p. 330.
8. This summary is derived from Michael Havers et al., *The Royal Baccarat Scandal*.
9. Stephen Arata, *Fictions of Loss*, p. 143.

Part III: Family

Chapter 7

Singular Occurrence at a Wedding

The action of 'The Noble Bachelor' starts with Watson reading the day's newspapers, and Holmes reading his correspondence. Both, coincidentally, find themselves reading about the same case. Holmes has a letter requesting his services from Lord St Simon, the noble bachelor of the story's title. Watson, meanwhile, reads aloud a story headlined 'Singular Occurrence at a Fashionable Wedding'. We learn that Lord St Simon is a bachelor no more, having just married the American heiress Hatty Doran; however, the bridal party had barely sat down for the wedding breakfast when Hatty, claiming indisposition, left the table, and disappeared, causing Holmes to comment, 'They often vanish before the ceremony, and occasionally during the honeymoon; but I cannot call to mind anything quite so prompt as this' (*Adventures*, 225). Foul play is suspected, leading to the arrest of Flora Miller, one of Lord St Simon's former lovers who tried to force her way into the wedding breakfast, 'alleging that she had some claim upon Lord St Simon' (225).

This rather eventful wedding ceremony is one of several that feature in the early stories. Another happier (but still peculiar) wedding is narrated by Holmes in 'A Scandal in Bohemia': while disguised as a groom, he witnesses, in the legal and the ordinary sense of the term, the hasty marriage of Irene Adler and Godfrey Norton. Other weddings are frustrated, either by violence ('The Speckled Band', 'The Copper Beeches') or deception ('A Case of Identity', in which it is the groom rather than the bride who disappears, this time before the ceremony.) Other marriages are in prospect, such as James McCarthy's to Alice Turner at the end of 'The Boscombe Valley Mystery', and Watson's own, to Mary Morstan, Holmes's client in *The Sign of Four*. Indeed, Watson narrates the matrimonial shenanigans of 'The Noble Bachelor' just weeks before tying the knot himself, which helps to explain why he was so drawn to what otherwise might seem to be a matter of mere society gossip.

This fascination with marriage might seem surprising, given Conan Doyle's negative views about the importance accorded to it by other writers. In an 1890 article, 'Mr Stevenson's Methods in Fiction', he wrote:

> In British fiction, nine books out of ten have held up love and marriage as the be-all and end-all of life. Yet we know, in actual practice, that this is not so. In the career of the average man his marriage is an incident, and a momentous incident; but it is only one of several. He is swayed by many strong emotions; his business, his ambitions, his friendships, his struggles with the recurrent dangers and difficulties which tax a man's wisdom and his courage. Love will often play a subordinate part in his life. How many go through the world without ever loving at all? It jars upon us then to have it continually held up as the predominating, all-important fact in life; and there is a not unnatural tendency among a certain school, of which Stevenson is certainly the leader, to avoid altogether a source of interest which has been so misused and overdone.[1]

This apparent contradiction is partly resolved by the use to which Conan Doyle puts his marriage plots in the Holmes saga. The romantic subplot of *The Sign of Four* certainly fits the pattern which Doyle criticises by delivering a highly conventional form of closure not only to the novella itself but also, it seems, to the Holmes saga: Watson announces his engagement with an apology that it will mean the end of their partnership in crime detection. However, Watson's courtship of Holmes's client is clearly subordinate to the main plot which involves violent revolution, cruel betrayal and murders carried out by an exotic assassin. *The Sign of Four* is also an exception to the general rule in the Holmes saga. In the other cases mentioned, the wedding is far from being the culmination of a traditional courtship: it is either an extraordinary or mysterious event in itself, or is part of a more sceptical examination of the institution of marriage and its social purpose. In particular, it is striking how often marriage in these stories is about power and patriarchy rather than love and romance. Irene Adler, for example, is trying to protect herself from a man of immense privilege who is embarrassed by their earlier liaison and, because he needs to marry dynastically himself, is prepared to pay immense sums in order to remove the threat she poses to his prospects. Lord St Simon is another dissolute aristocrat who, we infer, has gratified his sexual needs with Flora Miller over several years and similarly attempted to silence her with money: 'I have not treated her ungenerously, and she has no just cause of complaint against me, but you know what women are, Mr Holmes' (231). Indeed, money may have been fundamental to their relationship: Rosemary Jann has argued that the newspaper description of Flora as a 'danseuse' suggests prostitution.² The love between Alice Turner and James McCarthy is fortuitous: the motive for John Turner's murder of Charles McCarthy, for which James is nearly convicted, is Charles's plan to force James and Alice's marriage by blackmail.

The Sign of Four's exceptional status is underlined by the fact that Mrs Watson never again appears as a character, and she is barely mentioned except when her absence enables Watson to resume temporarily his adventures with Holmes. Even her apparent death is mentioned by Watson in 'The Empty House' in passing only as 'my own sad bereavement' (*Return*, 13), and it is suggestive that this should be mentioned immediately after Watson discovers that his earlier bereavement – Holmes's death – has been reversed: Watson's homosocial relationship with Holmes is far more significant emotionally than his connubial relationship with Mary. The second Mrs Watson is even more elusive: Watson's remarriage is mentioned only briefly by Holmes in 'The Blanched Soldier', and elsewhere she is entirely absent, without a name, let alone a personality.

More generally, Doyle seeks to defy the conventions of the marriage plot by setting up our expectations and then refusing to meet them. *The Hound of the Baskervilles*, for example, has what appears to be a marriage plot involving Sir Henry and Beryl Stapleton: 'From the first moment that he saw her he appeared to be strongly attracted to her, and I am much mistaken if the feeling was not mutual' (77). However, the prospect of marriage between these two apparently well-matched young people is a constituent part of the novella's criminal plot; Beryl is actually Stapleton's wife, not his sister, and (as Holmes deduces) Stapleton intended to use her as bait to ensnare Sir Henry. But Stapleton realises he has got more than he bargained for when he sees the strength of the attachment between them: 'Stapleton himself seems to be capable of jealousy, and when he saw the baronet playing court to the lady, even though it was part of his own plan, still he could not help interrupting with a passionate outburst which revealed the fiery soul which his self-contained manner so cleverly concealed' (166). The novella ends not with wedding bells but with death, disillusionment and depression: Beryl is widowed, while Sir Henry's nerves are so shattered that Dr Mortimer diagnoses for him a recuperative voyage, with Holmes commenting that Sir Henry's love for Beryl Stapleton 'was deep and sincere, and to him the saddest part of all this black business was that he should have been deceived by her' (166). This is a story in which, as Diana Barsham has observed, children are conspicuous by their absence, and wives are either desperate victims – we will come to the case of Laura Lyons later – or (like Mary Watson) absent.[3] The one exception is Mrs Barrymore, but even she leads Watson to suspect, with her uncontrollable nocturnal sobbing, that her husband is 'a domestic tyrant' (81). The real domestic tyrant turns out, of course, to be Stapleton, who binds his wife in sheets when she disobeys him. This suggests that the failed marriage plot in *The Hound of the Baskervilles* is part of a wider theme: marriage is an imperfect mechanism reflecting power relationships and social pressures – including, as Joseph Kestner has pointed out, 'aberrant male authority and criminality'[4] – rather than idealised physical and spiritual love.

A Study in Scarlet is a more sustained and direct examination of this theme. It is significant that Doyle's discussion of his contemporaries' over-emphasis of the marriage plot comes in a discussion of Stevenson, one of his favourite authors but who, in Doyle's view, reacted so strongly to the Victorian novel's fetishisation of love and marriage that he went to an opposite extreme and largely removed women from his fiction. The result was the 'modern masculine novel, dealing almost exclusively with the rougher, more stirring side of life, with the objective rather than the subjective'.[5] Doyle's argument – that Victorian literary realism and the masculine romance are at opposite ends of a spectrum and that neither, by itself, does justice to the reality of life or the possibilities of fiction – is itself an appropriation from Stevenson, who set out similar views on the art of fiction in a famous essay of 1884, 'A Humble Remonstrance'.[6]

A Study in Scarlet represents Doyle's first, sustained attempt to challenge the conventions practised by his contemporaries, and he did so by very deliberately rewriting 'Story of the Destroying Angel', one of the interlinked short stories in *The Dynamiter*. In 'Mr Stevenson's Methods in Fiction', Doyle described *The Dynamiter* as one of Stevenson's more uneven works, but he drew particular attention to the 'sudden flashes of extraordinary lucidity and vigour' of 'The Destroying Angel': 'the Mormon story in The Dynamiter might fade away as a connected tale, but how are we to forget the lonely fire in the valley, the white figure which dances and screams among the snow, or the horrid ravine in which the caravan is starved'.[7] 'The Destroying Angel' is the increasingly fantastical narrative of Asenath, whose parents stumble into the path of Mormon caravans and become unwilling converts; their attempt to escape is thwarted, leading to Asenath's father being killed by Dr Grierson, one of the Mormons' 'Destroying Angels', which are clearly the source of Doyle's 'Danite Band, or the Avenging Angels' (87). *The Dynamiter*'s engagement with what it presents as the brutal, tyrannical and exploitative society of the Mormons under the leadership of Brigham Young becomes little more than a backdrop as Grierson is shown to be a mad scientist seeking the elixir of life, but it is clearly the backdrop rather than the main action which interests Doyle. In *A Study in Scarlet* he created a rather more realistic tale, told apparently by Jefferson Hope in a long retrospect (although it is presented as a third-person narration) of state-sanctioned murder, forced marriage and transatlantic revenge. Doyle follows the Stevensons in making the Mormon state the epitome of political tyranny: the state's symbol in 'The Destroying Angel' is an open eye, carved on mountainsides and emblematic of the ability of the Destroying Angels to see and to know all, including in England to where the action shifts; in Jefferson Hope's narrative, the Mormon Church 'appeared to be omniscient and omnipotent' (87). In *The Dynamiter*, the state's practice of polygamy and forced marriage is incidental; in *A Study in Scarlet* it is the central theme.

For Doyle's Mormons, marriage is both the means and the end of patriarchal power, enabling the state's growth and its control, as well as being the principal element of the Church's ideology:

> At first this vague and terrible power was exercised only upon the recalcitrants who, having embraced the Mormon faith, wished afterwards to pervert or to abandon it. Soon, however, it took a wider range. The supply of adult women was running short, and polygamy without a female population on which to draw was a barren doctrine indeed. Strange rumours began to be bandied about – rumours of murdered immigrants and rifled camps in regions where Indians had never been seen. Fresh women appeared in the harems of the Elders – women who pined and wept, and bore upon their faces the traces of an unextinguishable horror. (87)

John Ferrier, father of Hope's fiancée Lucy, is upbraided by Brigham Young for not practising polygamy, before ordering that his daughter be betrothed not to 'a Gentile' (Hope) but to the son of one of two Mormon Elders, Drebber and Stangerson (89).[8] The two sons, Enoch and Joseph, then bicker over which is entitled to be Lucy's bride, and John's refusal to grant the privilege to either leads to a futile escape attempt, led by Hope, but which culminates in Ferrier's murder and Lucy's capture. There is no mistaking the distaste we are meant to feel at Lucy's subsequent fate:

> There was some words between young Drebber and young Stangerson as to which was to have her. They'd both been in the party that followed them, and Stangerson had shot her father, which seemed to give him the best claim; but when they argued it out in council, Drebber's party was the stronger, so the Prophet gave her over to him. (106)

As Douglas Kerr has pointed out, the 'sexual subjugation of a woman seems to have been the worst thing Conan Doyle could think of',[9] and it is significant that this subjugation is institutionalised: Doyle's Mormon men are not simply oppressing their womenfolk, but have built an edifice of legality and formalised decision-making around their sexual tyranny, in which marriage has a central function.

This theme of sexual subjugation through marriage is not confined to the long retrospect of Hope's backstory. It is integral to the plot: Hope's self-appointed mission to avenge Lucy's fate – inscribed, literally, at the crime scene – is the motive for his murders of Drebber and Stangerson, crimes for which (as with other cases of similar vengeance in the saga) he receives remarkably little condemnation. And marriage supplies the first major, material clue in the Holmes saga: a woman's wedding ring, discovered beneath Drebber's body. Unlike the dull-witted Gregson and Lestrade, Holmes recognises it as a symbol on two different levels. It symbolises marriage, but it has also been deliberately placed under Drebber's body by Hope to symbolise the purpose of the murder.

The saga's most peculiar wedding, and in some ways its most illuminating, comes at the climax of 'The Adventure of the Solitary Cyclist' (1904). This story seems to have given the normally fluent Conan Doyle unusual trouble: his first draft was effectively rejected by the *Strand*'s editor, Herbert Greenhough Smith, leading to a very defensive admission by Doyle of its faults – 'It has points but as a whole is not up to the mark' – and a subsequent reappraisal ('I have gone over the Cyclist again. It strikes me as a dramatic & interesting & original story . . . I have gone over it carefully & can do no more to strengthen it.')[10] And 'The Solitary Cyclist' is dramatic and interesting in several ways. Its opening prelude by Watson suggests that it 'culminated in unexpected tragedy' (*Return*, 52), but no such tragedy appears to be narrated – the story concludes with the would-be victim of the story, Violet Smith, marrying Cyril Morton, a senior partner in a well-known firm of Westminster electricians. But even stranger is that the villain's plan, to force Violet Smith to marry, would fail legally on every count.

Violet Smith is introduced to the reader as particularly good-looking. Indeed, both Holmes and Watson are notably insistent on this point: Holmes is preoccupied with an important case but finds it 'impossible to refuse to listen to the story of the young and beautiful woman, tall, graceful and queenly . . . Holmes begged the beautiful intruder to take a seat' (53). Before making his enquiries, Watson tells us that 'his keen eyes darted over her' and he 'took the lady's ungloved hand and examined it with as close an attention and as little sentiment as a scientist would show to a specimen' (53). After scrutinising her with such unconcealed interest, Holmes comments to Watson: 'It is part of the settled order of Nature that such a girl should have followers' (58). Her problem is that she has a follower in a quite literal sense: while cycling, she has been followed repeatedly at a distance by a suspiciously bearded man. This is later revealed to be her employer, Bob Carruthers, who confesses that he did not warn her of the danger posed by his friend Jack Woodley as this would have immediately deprived him of the company of a beautiful and much younger woman: 'Even if she couldn't love me it was a great deal to me just to see her dainty form about the house, and to hear the sound of her voice' (69). Miss Smith, it is clear, is the object of voyeuristic attention by friends as well as foes.

But her principal foe, Woodley, is determined to do more than merely look at her. As she tells Holmes and Watson, he 'made odious love to me . . . and finally, when I would have nothing to do with him, he seized me in his arms one day after dinner – he was hideously strong – and he swore that he would not let me go until I had kissed him' (55). Only Carruthers's violent intervention saves her from Woodley's sexual advances. The next time she meets Woodley is when she is abducted by him and taken to a glade in Charlington Wood. Holmes, Watson and Carruthers, in pursuit, hear her 'shrill scream' before seeing the aftermath of the sham wedding:

> under the shadow of a mighty oak, there stood a singular group of three people. One was a woman, our client, drooping and faint, a handkerchief round her mouth. Opposite her stood a brutal, heavy-faced, red-moustached young man, his gaitered legs parted wide, one arm akimbo, the other waving a riding-crop, his whole attitude suggestive of a triumphant bravado. Between them an elderly, grey-bearded man, wearing a short surplice over a light tweed suit, had

Figure 7 'As we approached, the lady staggered against the trunk of the tree.' Illustration by Sidney Paget, *Strand Magazine*, January 1904.

evidently just completed the wedding service, for he pocketed his Prayer-Book as we appeared, and slapped the sinister bridegroom upon the back in jovial congratulation. (67)

There is no mistaking the sexual violence implicit in this scene. Woodley's pose is undoubtedly sexual; Miss Smith is over-matched by two men with a single purpose. Joseph Kestner interprets his riding-crop as a phallic symbol, but there is no need to attach a symbolic value to an instrument designed to inflict pain: Woodley's intention, by abducting, gagging and beating Miss Smith, is clearly rape.[11] The ostensible motive of the villains was to acquire her inheritance through marriage following the death of their acquaintance Ralph Smith in South Africa: Woodley and Carruthers played cards to determine who would win the privilege of marrying her. And yet this explanation crumbles under examination. First, the forced marriage is one that has no legal force – as Holmes points out, the officiating clergyman has been defrocked, and the marriage licence has been obtained by deception. As a method for extorting an inheritance, an illegal marriage would be utterly futile. Secondly, even if they were legally married, Woodley would have no automatic claim to his wife's money. The Married Women's Property Acts of 1870 and 1882 were among the nineteenth century's most important reforms, establishing a married woman's right to independent ownership of property including her earnings, returns on investments, and physical property.[12] In theory at least, Violet Smith would be able to enjoy her fortune, if nothing else, even if she were forced to become Woodley's spouse. Significantly, after Carruthers told Woodley that their deal was off, the latter 'went off cursing... swearing that he would have her yet' (71). Woodley's primary objective is clearly the woman, not the money.

Kestner observes that the 1870 and 1882 Acts are readable in the many plots in the Holmes saga involving heiresses and marriage, suggesting that they inscribe male anxieties at female empowerment.[13] While he correctly emphasises 'issues of male power' in 'A Case of Identity', 'The Speckled Band' and 'The Copper Beeches', he does not explain why the women in the Holmes saga do not appear to be able to enjoy their statutory rights. 'The Solitary Cyclist' does not (as Kestner suggests) imply that South Africans would have been ignorant of the legislation, but rather that legal rights for women have only limited traction in a man's world.[14] Despite legislative advances entitling women to the rights of ownership, they were still subject to the overwhelming social, political and, above all, sexual power of men in Victorian and Edwardian Britain. The King of Bohemia and Lord St Simon do what they want with women, and buy their compliance, while Jack Woodley relies upon and appears to enjoy the use of brute force in satisfying his sexual needs. He can only be stopped by superior masculine force, from Carruthers (first knocking him down, then shooting him) and Holmes, whose 'straight left' (63) in a country pub sends Woodley home in a cart, and whose 'strong, masterful personality... dominated the tragic scene' (68). Throughout the Holmes saga, women are victims of male exploitation, both sexual and economic. And in 'The Solitary Cyclist', Doyle attempted to demonstrate this by coming as close as he dared to describing a scene of rape. This, then, explains the 'unexpected tragedy' (52) and 'tragic scene' (68) which otherwise stand out as anomalous phrases in a story with an ostensibly happy ending.

Notes

1. Conan Doyle, 'Mr Stevenson's Methods in Fiction', first printed in the January 1890 issue of the *National Review*, and reprinted in the February 1890 issue of *The Living Age*, pp. 417–24, from which these quotations are taken. Sections of the essay, with only very minor editorial changes, were subsequently included in *Through the Magic Door*, pp. 265–6.
2. Rosemary Jann, *Detecting Social Order*, p. 114.
3. Diana Barsham, *The Meaning of Masculinity*, p. 136.
4. Kestner, *Edwardian Detective*, p. 43.
5. 'Mr Stevenson's Methods in Fiction', p. 421.
6. Reprinted in *Memories and Portraits* (1887).
7. 'Mr Stevenson's Methods in Fiction', pp. 418–19
8. Doyle's choice of name is a clear echo of the 'The Destroying Angel', in which Asenath gives her mother the name of Lucy, apparently as an alias. Stevenson and Stevenson, *The Dynamiter*, p. 22.
9. Kerr, *Conan Doyle*, p. 145.
10. Doyle, *A Life in Letters*, pp. 514, 516. See also McDonald, *British Literary Culture*, p. 143,
11. Kestner, *Sherlock's Men*, pp. 144–5.
12. See Joseph A. Kestner, *Mythology and Misogyny*, p. 35.
13. Kestner, *Sherlock's Men*, pp. 88–94.
14. Ibid., p. 145.

Chapter 8

The Rock of Gibraltar

Marital unhappiness is a persistent theme of the Holmes stories, from the first (*A Study in Scarlet*) to several of the last ('The Adventure of the Retired Colourman' and 'The Adventure of the Veiled Lodger', both published in 1927). *A Study in Scarlet* begins as a detective story but its backstory is, as we have seen, a melodrama of forced marriage and domestic tyranny. 'A Case of Identity' concerns a courtship that is an elaborate deception, and the story opens with a digression on the 'Dundas separation case'. This is reported in a newspaper as a 'husband's cruelty to his wife', prompting Watson to claim that he knows the details without even reading the article: 'There is, of course, the other woman, the drink, the push, the blow, the bruise, the sympathetic sister or landlady. The crudest of writers could invent nothing more crude.' However, Holmes has investigated the case and reveals that it is actually more unusual: 'The husband was a teetotaller, there was no other woman, and the conduct complained of was that he had drifted into the habit of winding up every meal by taking out his false teeth and hurling them at his wife' (*Adventures*, 31). In 'The Blue Carbuncle' Holmes deduces from a hat that Henry Baker's wife has ceased to love him. Mary Cushing in 'The Cardboard Box' marries a sailor, Jim Browner, who blames everyone but himself and his alcoholism for the catastrophic collapse of the couple's relationship and the ensuing acts of infidelity, murder and mutilation.

Unhappy marriages are particularly frequent in the Holmes stories written in the first decade of the twentieth century, when, according to Jane Eldridge Miller, novels were 'filled with unhappy marriages' and 'the institution of marriage [was] relentlessly scrutinized'.[1] One of the major red herrings in *The Hound of the Baskervilles* is the story of Laura Lyons, who has been deserted by her blackguard of a husband; we later discover that he has been seeking through the courts to force her to live with him again, and that she has sought money from Sir

Charles Baskerville, and obtained it from Stapleton, in order to institute divorce proceedings. Mrs McFarlane in 'The Norwood Builder' is happily married but had a lucky escape many years previously when she broke off her engagement to the appalling Jonas Oldacre after hearing 'a shocking story of how he had turned a cat loose in an aviary, and I was so horrified at his brutal curiosity that I would have nothing more to do with him'; she shows Holmes a photograph of herself, sent to her by Oldacre on the day of her wedding, 'shamefully defaced and mutilated with a knife' (*Return*, 38). Oldacre would clearly have made a pathologically violent husband, an implication supported by textual evidence: in a cancelled passage in the manuscript, Lestrade dismisses McFarlane's evidence that he was admitted to Oldacre's house by a middle-aged woman with the words, 'Jonas Oldacre is well known as a woman hater, he has no servant except an old Charwoman.'[2] Peter Carey in 'Black Peter' is perhaps the saga's most brutal husband: 'The man was an intermittent drunkard, and when he had the fit on him he was a perfect fiend. He had been known to drive his wife and his daughter out of doors in the middle of the night, and flog them through the park until the whole village outside the gates was aroused by their screams' (*Return*, 137); Watson describes Mrs Carey as 'a haggard, grey-haired woman ... whose gaunt and deep-lined face, with the furtive look of terror in the depths of her red-rimmed eyes, told of the years of hardship and ill-usage which she had endured' (143). 'The Adventure of the Golden Pince-Nez' (1904) features an estranged anarchist couple, Professor Coram and his wife Anna, the latter responsible for the manslaughter of the professor's secretary Willoughby Smith while she was hunting for documents that would exonerate her imprisoned lover, another anarchist. In 'The Adventure of the Devil's Foot' (1910), the explorer Leon Sterndale is unable to marry the love of his life, Brenda Tregennis, as he is already married to a woman who has deserted him; Brenda's death prompts Sterndale to take revenge against her killer, Mortimer Tregennis. The plutocrat Neil Gibson in 'Thor Bridge' is trapped in a loveless marriage with his fiery Brazilian wife Maria, and so cannot marry Grace Dunbar, the woman he loves. In 'The Retired Colourman', the deranged Josiah Amberley gasses his wife and her lover in a strong room and hides their bodies in a disused well. Mrs Ronder, a former circus artiste in 'The Veiled Lodger', plots with her lover to kill her cruel and violent husband, and to make the death appear accidental with the help of the circus lion.

The source of unhappiness in several of these cases is a cruel and violent husband: in the poetic justice which Holmes sometimes administers at the end of a story, marital cruelty is powerful mitigation, even for the crime of murder. This is particularly evident in 'The Abbey Grange', one of several stories in which Holmes investigates the death of an alcoholic, brutal man who is both victim and perpetrator. In this instance, Conan Doyle advances a kind of legal case study of what he considered to be a particularly destructive social evil, and to which he would later devote a significant quantity of his political and social capital. It begins as a story of high society: Holmes remarks, on receiving a request from Scotland Yard's Stanley Hopkins to attend the scene of Sir Eustace Brackenstall's murder, 'we are moving in high life, Watson – crackling paper, "EB" monogram, coat-of-arms, picturesque address' (*Return*, 267). The victim is 'one of the richest men in Kent' (268), and his house is another of the impressive country piles that appear so frequently in the Holmes stories, complete with 'lines of ancient elms', a Palladian frontage, and an entire wing for no fewer than nine servants. The motive for what appears to be a burglary gone wrong is theft, the loot being the Brackenstall family silver. The surviving victim of the burglary is Lady Brackenstall, described rather breathlessly by Watson as

> no ordinary person. Seldom have I seen so graceful a figure, so womanly a presence, and so beautiful a face. She was a blonde, golden-haired, blue-eyed, and would, no doubt, have had the perfect complexion which goes with such colouring had not her recent experience left her drawn and haggard. (268)

Despite having been beaten and tied up by the burglars, Watson records that 'her quick, observant gaze as we entered the room, and the alert expression of her beautiful features, showed that neither her wits nor her courage had been shaken by her terrible experience' (268–9). It seems that we are in the presence of a natural aristocrat.

However, this is a story in which nothing is as it first appears. Lady Brackenstall, urged by her loyal maid Theresa Wright, has concocted the entire story. The killer is Jack Croker, who became besotted with Lady Brackenstall when she was known more simply as Mary Fraser. Mary had arrived in England from Adelaide eighteen months previously on board the *Rock of Gibraltar*, the ship on which Croker was presumably first mate (he was promoted to the rank of captain before his next voyage). But Croker is not a murderer in the legal sense: in his confession to Holmes at the end of the story, he reveals he acted in self-defence when he visited the Abbey Grange for one final meeting with the love of his life; an enraged Sir Eustace attacked him with a cudgel, and he fought back with an iron poker.

Nor is Mary Fraser really an aristocrat, but a young woman from the colonies who finds English high society to be constraining and debilitating: 'I was brought up in the freer, less conventional atmosphere of South Australia, and this English life, with its proprieties and its primness, is not congenial to me' (269). There are strong indications, in fact, that she was something of a young woman on the make, coming to England with only her maid for company in order to find a rich husband – which explains her initial lack of romantic interest in Croker, who describes himself as 'a penniless sailor' (287). Within six months of her arrival, Mary had married Sir Eustace who, Theresa reveals, 'won her with his title and his money and his false London ways' (269). A woman who marries for property and wealth rather than love is unlikely to be an object of pity, but she has learned the hard way that, as elsewhere in the Holmes stories, estate is rarely correlated with virtue, and wealth does not bring happiness. Sir Eustace was, she discovered, 'a confirmed drunkard' (269) who, as Theresa tells Holmes,

> was for ever ill-treating her, and she too proud to complain. She will not even tell me all that he has done to her. She never told me of those marks on her arm that you saw this morning, but I know very well that they come from a stab with a hat-pin. (281)

Whatever her motives in marrying, Mary does not deserve this fate: 'To be with such a man for an hour is unpleasant. Can you imagine what it means for a sensitive and high-spirited woman to be tied to him for day and night?' (269). Even in death, Sir Eustace radiates violence and malice: Watson describes his 'white teeth grinning through his short, black beard', and his 'dark, handsome, aquiline features were convulsed in a spasm of vindictive hatred, which had set his face in a terribly fiendish expression' (273). That 'fiendish' is an accurate reading of Sir Eustace's character is confirmed by Theresa's verdict of him as a 'sly devil – God forgive me that I should speak of him so, now that he is dead, but a devil he was if ever one walked the earth' (281).

A victim not of premeditated murder but of his own vile and violent instincts, Sir Eustace clearly deserves his violent but accidental death, which is why Croker is exonerated by Holmes's impromptu (and entirely extrajudicial) court; Holmes is similarly magnanimous with Leon Sterndale in 'The Devil's Foot', who also kills for love having been prevented from remarrying 'due to the deplorable laws of England' (*Last Bow*, 91). Croker is commenting on more than the physical effect of his strike with the poker when he says, 'I went through him as if he had been a rotten pumpkin' (288). But while the

Figure 8 'It was the body of a tall, well-made man, about forty years of age.' Illustration by Sidney Paget, *Strand Magazine*, September 1904.

forty-something Brackenstall is, in moral terms, a lost cause, it is an important message of the story that people – and young people especially – make mistakes, and that they should not be punished for them for life. In particular, hasty and ill-conceived marriages should not oblige both parties to live, as Sir Eustace and Lady Brackenstall have done, in a state of marital tyranny and despair. In a notable moment, Lady Brackenstall is unable to conceal her fury when she exclaims: 'It is a sacrilege, a crime, a villainy to hold that such a marriage is binding. I say that these monstrous laws of yours will bring a curse upon the land – Heaven will not let such wickedness endure' (269).

Here, Lady Brackenstall is referring to England's divorce laws under the Matrimonial Causes Act 1857, which notoriously restricted the availability of divorce to the more prosperous by requiring expensive and time-consuming litigation without the availability of legal aid. The Act also made adultery the only ground for divorce, and insisted on a much higher standard of proof for wives: men had to prove adultery only, but women had also to prove another matrimonial crime such as cruelty or violence. These restrictions meant that remarkably few couples divorced in England: the divorce rate increased steadily in the late nineteenth century from four per year in 1857 to around 600 just before the First World War, but, as Lawrence Stone has demonstrated, this was still 'statistically minute' by comparison with other countries.[3] The Act therefore ensured that most unhappy couples stayed together, especially when the husband was either poor or intent on keeping his wife. Sir Eustace, and Mr Lyons in *The Hound of the Baskervilles*, both belong to the latter category: as Laura Lyons complains, 'My life has been one incessant persecution from a husband whom I abhor. The law is upon his side, and every day I am faced by the possibility that he may force me to live with him' (114).[4]

The solution to this deplorable state of affairs for Doyle and other arbiters of public opinion, such as the novelist and playwright John Galsworthy, was divorce law reform. Doyle was so committed that he published a pamphlet on the issue in 1909 and became president in the same year of the Divorce Law Reform Union; no other cause bar Spiritualism excited his passions so much in the last twenty years of his life. Doyle's life provides an obvious explanation for his commitment. His marriage to Louise Hawkins (known as 'Touie') was, from the moment that she was diagnosed as suffering from tuberculosis in 1893, likely to have been sexless, and we know that he met the second Lady Doyle, Jean Leckie, in 1897 – a full decade before Touie's death enabled him to remarry.[5] (Doyle's willingness to appear in public with Jean while still married to Touie prompted scandalised objections from the latter's family, notably from her brother, the writer E. W. Hornung.) More resonant for the Holmes stories was his parents' marriage. Charles Altamont Doyle married Mary Foley in 1855 but, by the early 1860s, he had become alcoholic and mentally unstable, at times reduced, according to Mary, to dragging 'himself around the floor . . . unable to remember his own name'.[6] Following violent episodes, he was detained in the Montrose Royal Mental Hospital in 1885, where he claimed to be in communication with God, and was moved in 1892 to another asylum in Dumfries, where he died the following year.[7] Alcohol is a principal ingredient in the lives of many of Doyle's unhappy couples, symbolised in 'The Abbey Grange' by one of Sir Eustace's characteristic acts – throwing a decanter at his wife's maid.

Lady Brackenstall's characterisation of the problem might sound extreme – her metaphor of a curse upon the land alludes perhaps to the biblical plagues of Egypt, or the cursed desolation of Sophocles' *Oedipus Rex* – but there is an intellectual argument behind it which accords entirely with Conan Doyle's publicly expressed views on the subject. In a series of letters to the *Daily Mail* in 1912, Doyle argued that England's divorce laws were 'the most conservative and, from the reformer's point of view, reactionary in Europe – far more so even than the divorce laws of Scotland'. The problem was not just marital unhappiness, grievous though this was for couples comprising 'a sane person and a hopeless idiot, an innocent person and a criminal suffering penal servitude, or a normal man or woman and a dipsomaniac partner'. The laws also encouraged separation and prevention of remarriage: 'the existence of this great number of enforced celibates must have a subversive effect upon public morals, and incidentally a depressing influence upon that dwindling birth-rate which everyone deplores as a national disaster'.[8] Lady Brackenstall's curse, then, is sterility: the divorce laws are inhibiting the English from obeying the biblical injunction to go forth and multiply.

'The Abbey Grange' follows this logic and extends Doyle's interest in legislative reform into a fable inscribing what at the time was described as the racial health of the English. Had Sir Eustace not been killed, the divorce laws would have prevented his wife from finding a more suitable mate in Jack Croker, and thereby depriving the nation of their offspring. The text leaves us in no doubt as to the severity of this loss. Lady Brackenstall's significant attractions have already been described, but Croker is an equally impressive physical specimen. At the crime scene, Holmes deduces that the killer is

> [s]trong as a lion – witness the blow which bent that poker. Six foot three in height, active as a squirrel, dexterous with his fingers; finally, remarkably quick-witted, for this whole ingenious story is of his concoction. Yes, Watson, we have come upon the handiwork of a very remarkable individual. (280)

Summoned to Baker Street, Croker impresses Watson as a physical paragon:

> our door was opened to admit as fine a specimen of manhood as ever passed through it. He was a very tall young man, golden-moustached, blue-eyed, with a skin which had been burned by tropical suns, and a springy step which showed that the huge frame was as active as it was strong. (285–6)

His ships, *Rock of Gibraltar* and *Bass Rock*, are aptly named: Croker is solid and dependable, but also a symbol of British strength and power.[9] At the shipping office, Holmes discovers that Croker's character is strong in every sense: 'His record was magnificent. There was not an officer in the fleet to touch him. As to his character, he was reliable on duty, but a wild, desperate fellow off the deck of his ship, hot-headed, excitable, but loyal, honest, and kind-hearted' (283). Holmes does not take the documentary evidence for granted: he appears to give Croker the opportunity to save himself while condemning Lady Brackenstall, but Croker loyally refuses. 'I was only testing you, and you ring true every time' (290) is Holmes's response: Croker's character is vindicated and his destiny assured.

Seen in this light, Holmes's valedictory comment to Croker takes on a new significance: 'Come back to this lady in a year, and may her future and yours justify us in the judgement which we have pronounced this night' (290). Holmes is thinking of their future, but marital happiness is not the only result that he anticipates. One of Doyle's most insistent arguments in favour of divorce law reform was that, by preventing remarriage, the existing system caused population decline. Holmes does not exercise extrajudicial mercy for its own sake, but for the benefit of posterity – Jack and Mary Croker will unite and populate the land with blue-eyed, golden-haired children, their contribution to the racial health of the nation.

Notes

1. Jane Eldridge Miller, *Rebel Women*, p. 45.
2. Doyle, *The Return of Sherlock Holmes*, ed. Richard Lancelyn Green, p. 341.
3. Lawrence Stone, *Road to Divorce*, p. 387; for the statistics see F. M. L. Thompson, *Cambridge Social History of Britain, 1750–1950*, p. 31.
4. Laura Lyons is, however, wrong to assert that her husband has the legal power to command cohabitation: in 1884 Parliament legislated to end the powers of the Matrimonial Causes Court to force a wife to cohabit with her husband, while in 1891 a judge reversed a principle from case law (the 1840 Cochrane case) that a husband could prevent his wife from eloping. See Stone, *Road to Divorce*, pp. 389–90.
5. Lycett, *Conan Doyle*, pp. 232–3.
6. Ibid., p. 19.
7. Ibid., pp. 104, 194.
8. Conan Doyle, *Letters to the Press*, pp. 160–1.
9. In choosing these names, Doyle was also accurately reflecting the practice of shipping companies to follow themes in naming their vessels: see *The Return of Sherlock Holmes*, ed. Richard Lanceleyn Green, p. 402.

Chapter 9

The Discreetly Shadowed Corners

In a famous passage at the beginning of 'A Case of Identity', Holmes imagines surveying the inner workings of the households of London from the air:

> If we could fly out of that window hand in hand, hover over this great city, gently remove the roofs, and peep in at the queer things which are going on, the strange coincidences, the planning, the cross-purposes, the wonderful chains of events, working through generations, and leading to the most *outré* results, it would make all fiction with its conventionalities and foreseen conclusions most stale and unprofitable. (*Adventures*, 30)

Besides the clear reference to Shakespeare's *Hamlet*, this passage alludes to a French reinterpretation of an ancient myth which, as Anthea Trodd and others have shown, fascinated Victorian writers: Alain-René Lesage's *Le Diable boiteux* (1707) takes the figure of Asmodeus from Hebrew myth and turns him into a satirical figure who leads 'a favoured human companion on a roof-top excursion of Madrid, and lifts the roofs of the houses to expose the secret crimes habitually being enacted beneath'.[1] Dickens, Thackeray and George Eliot all invoked Asmodeus in their writing, with the most celebrated instance coming in *Dombey and Son* (1848):

> Oh for a good spirit who would take the house-tops off, with a more potent and benignant hand than the lame demon in the tale, and show a Christian people what dark shapes issue from amidst their homes, to swell the retinue of the Destroying Angel as he moves forth among them! For only one night's view of the pale phantoms rising from the scenes of our too-long neglect; and from the thick and sullen air where Vice and Fever propagate together, raining the tremendous social retributions which are ever pouring down, and ever coming thicker![2]

Dickens's concern is to expose the want and suffering of which Dombey is blithely ignorant, while Conan Doyle suggests that what lies beneath our rooftops is a more diverse set of mysteries and complications. But in both cases, Asmodeus's power is a metaphor for the revelation of domestic secrets and this, for Doyle as for his Victorian predecessors, was a major theme. The plots of the Holmes stories, like those of the Victorian novels with which Doyle was deeply familiar, turn again and again on a suppressed family history. The Holmes saga is insistently concerned with the discovery of what goes on under the domestic roof: Trodd estimates that more than half of the stories 'centre on the household and on conflicting interests between members of the household'.[3] The mythical demon finds its late nineteenth-century avatar in Holmes himself: as Lynn Cain points out in her study of Dickens, the Latin root of detective – *detegere* – literally means 'to unroof'.[4] Rather than lifting roofs, though, Holmes tends to cross thresholds, usually (but not always) with an invitation to do so, and he has a knack of finding out more than his clients bargain for.

'A Case of Identity' is a case in point: for all that Holmes dismisses Mary Sutherland's problem as 'rather a trite one' (39), one does not have to be a Freudian to consider the revelation that she is being courted by a man she calls her father as suggestive of an incest fantasy.[5] As we have seen, suggestions of incest are also apparent in 'The Speckled Band': taken together, the wicked stepfathers of *The Adventures* suggest perverted patriarchy as well as pecuniary greed. Parent-child relationships are stranger still in 'The Copper Beeches', a case which provides ample justification for Holmes's observation that the thinly populated countryside is far more conducive to crime – isolation breeds 'deeds of hellish cruelty' and 'hidden wickedness which may go on, year in, year out, in such places, and none the wiser' (*Adventures*, 280) – than dense cities. The story's grotesque effect lies partly in this unsettling isolated backdrop, and partly in its marrying of the horrors of a fairy tale to a very modern plot of financial exploitation. The Bluebeard figure of the story, Jephro Rucastle, is in the business of recruiting surrogate daughters rather than finding wives to replace those he has murdered. But he goes about his criminal business in a peculiarly fetishistic manner. After employing Violet Hunter, he insists that she wears an electric-blue dress to his exact specification, cuts her hair to a required length and sits in a particular position while adopting a particular pose. We eventually discover that this is all part of Rucastle's elaborate plot to ensure that Alice, his real daughter imprisoned in an uninhabited wing, does not become financially independent, but this explanation, given by Mrs Toller at the end of the story, does little to efface the disturbing details of Violet's narrative, such as the discovery of what initially appears to be her own hair in a locked drawer, or her confrontation with Rucastle after she tries to enter the forbidden chamber: 'you cannot think how caressing and soothing his manner was', before he threatens to throw her to his savage mastiff. And this is not the only perverted family relationship in the story. Violet is employed as governess to six-year-old Edward, the apple of his father's eye: '"Oh, if you could see him killing cockroaches with a slipper! Smack! Smack! Smack!, three gone before you could wink!" He leaned back in his chair and laughed his eyes into his head again' (275). The Dickensian turn of phrase cannot quite conceal the disturbing flavour of the father's admiration. Violet initially believes Jephro to be joking, but she soon finds that she is babysitting a sadist: 'Giving pain to any creature weaker than himself seems to be his one idea of amusement, and he shows quite remarkable talent in planning the capture of mice, little birds, and insects' (283). Edward evidently is a chip off the Rucastle block, and the Copper Beeches a rural house of horror.

The Rucastles are just one of many bad families in the Holmes saga. As Diana Barsham has pointed out, '[d]ysfunctional fathers and husbands' who maintain 'a problematic relationship both with their children and the spoken word' are a feature of ten stories among the dozen in *The Adventures*.[6] The husbands and fathers lie, and build (or try to build) their families on the basis of a lie – the misappropriation of a legacy, a dual identity, or the erasure of previous liaisons. The Rucastles are not, however, Doyle's most dysfunctional family. That honour belongs instead to the family of the Duke of Holdernesse in 'The Priory School'. First impressions are that the duke – a former cabinet minister – has led an impeccable *public* life: Holmes remarks, on reading in an encyclopaedia of the duke's credentials and record in politics, that he is 'one of the greatest subjects of the Crown!' (101).[7] His son, Lord Saltire – whose disappearance is investigated by Holmes – is something of a paragon: Dr Huxtable, the headmaster of the Priory School who brings Holmes into the case, describes him as a 'charming youth' (102). However, that all was not well even before the young lord's disappearance is indicated by Dr Huxtable's revelation of the 'open secret that the Duke's married life had not been a peaceful one, and the matter had ended in a separation by mutual consent' – a development that had strongly affected the young lord, whose 'sympathies are known to have been strongly with his mother' (102–3), providing a possible explanation for his disappearance. Despite the duke's marital unhappiness being an 'open secret', he is nonetheless so anxious 'to avoid all public scandal' that he seems to have ordered that any investigation into Lord Saltire's disappearance be conducted so discreetly as to be ineffective: 'He was afraid of his family unhappiness being dragged before the world. He has a deep horror of anything of that kind' (104). The story thus sets up an opposition between the duke's public and private lives: Huxtable reports that he is 'completely immersed in large public questions' which makes him 'rather inaccessible to all ordinary emotions' (106). He is, simultaneously, a most public and a most private man, and this contradiction is explained by what motivates his desire for privacy: the story turns on the fact that the duke is really protecting his illegitimate son, James Wilder, whom he has brought into his household in the guise of his secretary. Even former cabinet ministers – Doyle's manuscript has him as a former Foreign Secretary – have household secrets, and the Duke of Holdernesse's secret is Wilder himself.

Holmes's solution to the mystery of Lord Saltire's disappearance suggests that the duke's public virtues conceal even darker private vices. Wilder, intending to force his natural father to break the entail which makes Lord Saltire the duke's sole heir, has arranged for the young lord to be kidnapped by a coarse villain called Reuben Hayes, landlord of a 'forbidding and squalid' public house on the moor, the Fighting Cock Inn (119). But Holmes discovers that Hayes, after luring the boy out of the school, was pursued on a bicycle by the young lord's German master, Heidegger; in a confrontation on the moor, Hayes struck and killed Heidegger before concealing Lord Saltire in the inn. The duke discovered the truth but instead of rescuing his son and heir, became an accessory after the fact by conspiring with Wilder to cover up the kidnapping and murder, and facilitate Hayes's escape. Holmes condemns the duke's conduct, but (in return for a cheque for the huge sum of six thousand pounds) agrees to the duke's scheme to allow Hayes to take the blame for the kidnapping and murder, and keep secret the scandal of Wilder's birth and his criminal behaviour. The obvious question here is why the duke should risk so much to protect Wilder. The duke's explanation is simply that he was overpowered by his affection for his illegitimate son, which, in spite of everything, remained undiminished. The duke's version of events, however, strains credibility. As he admits, Wilder has subjected Lord Saltire to 'a persistent hatred' (129), but instead of removing his illegitimate son, the duke chose to remove Lord Saltire, to a nearby boarding school. After learning

Figure 9 'Beside him stood a very young man.' Illustration by Sidney Paget, *Strand Magazine*, February 1904.

of his kidnapped son's whereabouts, the duke discovers that boy has been traumatised by witnessing a brutal murder, but he nonetheless consents to Wilder's plan to keep the young lord locked up in the squalid moorland inn for three days. The duke then conspires with Wilder to cover up murder and kidnapping. A doting father may do much to protect an errant child, but to permit and even facilitate the sustained victimisation of one son by another suggests deeper and murkier currents.

There are several clues in the text to suggest that incest and paedophilia may be among the secret vices at Holdernesse Hall. The duke's own explanation of his doting affection for James Wilder has a distinctly sexual flavour:

> You may well ask me why, under these circumstances, I still kept James under my roof. I answer that it was because I could see his mother's face in his, and that for her dear sake there was no end to my long-suffering. All her pretty ways, too – there was not one of them which he could not suggest and bring back to my memory. I *could* not send him away. (129)

Wilder, then, despite his evident capacity for cruelty, is also by implication coquettish, feminine and physically appealing to his own father. It is also clear that the duke's second marriage is in trouble at least partly because of the dynamics of his relationship with his illegitimate son: as Holmes points out, 'any unhappiness in your married life was caused by his presence' (132). As we read on, we may suspect that Wilder's relationship with Reuben Hayes may also have been sexual: Hayes 'was a rascal from the beginning; but in some extraordinary way James became intimate with him. He had always a taste for low company' (129). The duke's delicate reference to the 'extraordinary' nature of their intimacy may also account for Hayes's turbulent employment history: Hayes had been the duke's head coachman, but reveals to Holmes that the duke 'sacked me without a character on the word of a lying corn-chandler' (120). We can only speculate at what the corn-chandler could have witnessed, but it was clearly no minor offence for Hayes to be dismissed on the spot. The suggestions of a sexual element to Wilder and Hayes's relationship and Wilder's history of cruelty to his half-brother force us to reappraise their plot to kidnap and imprison Lord Saltire. Although the duke claims that he was looked after by the kindly Mrs Hayes, Holmes dismisses this feeble excuse: 'What are the promises of people such as these? . . . To humour your guilty elder son you have exposed your innocent younger son to imminent and unnecessary danger' (131). Given these suggestions, it is difficult to put out of our minds the possibility that Wilder's victimisation of his half-brother also had a sexual element.

What emerges from this sinister and unsettling story is perhaps Conan Doyle's most trenchant attack on aristocratic mores. In many ways a socially conservative writer, Doyle was nonetheless apt to criticise those born to high office who failed to live up to the standards of their caste. That good breeding still has a positive effect is evident not just in the innocence and conduct of Lord Saltire, but also in the duke's ability to master his emotions under Watson's watchful gaze: 'Never shall I forget the Duke's appearance as he sprang up and clawed with his hands like one who is sinking into an abyss. Then, with an extraordinary effort of aristocratic self-command, he sat down and sank his face in his hands' (127). However, in this story the containment of baser instincts is successful only on a superficial level: Holdernesse Hall has the appearance of a stately home, with its 'famous yew avenue' and 'magnificent Elizabethan doorway' (124), but the facade of respectability conceals not only criminality and vice, but also the abuse of power. This becomes evident in the story's most dramatic scene – of which Doyle was particularly proud – when Holmes confronts the duke with his knowledge:[8]

> 'And whom do you accuse?'
> Sherlock Holmes's answer was an astounding one. He stepped swiftly forward and touched the Duke upon the shoulder.
> 'I accuse *you*,' said he. (126)

In the passage that follows, the duke demonstrates the arrogance of power and wealth and class. Offering Holmes twice the advertised reward for locating Lord Saltire and identifying the perpetrator, the duke assumes that his social inferior will accept the bribe and acquiesce to the aristocratic demand. Not only that, but the duke proceeds to ascribe guilt and blame, identifying the lower-class Hayes as the villain who bears the guilt, and his upper-class co-conspirator Wilder – ringleader of the plot – as little more than a bystander. That Wilder has confessed to the duke and expressed remorse is, in this world of privilege, sufficient to atone for murder, kidnapping and deception.

In the end, Holmes goes along with the duke's demands, but only up to a point. In an unprecedented display of reward-seeking, he makes a particular show of taking the duke's money – '"I am a poor man" said he', as he patted his notebook containing the duke's cheque 'affectionately' (133) – causing Watson to comment on its uniqueness in the following story, 'Black Peter' (*Return*, 134). There is clearly a social point to his insistence on receiving the duke's cheque: it is a token of the duke's acknowledgement of Holmes's success. But while Holmes agrees that the duke and Wilder can take their chances to escape not only the British justice system but also the shame and dishonour that would accompany a revelation of the plot, Holmes nonetheless punishes the duke by upbraiding him strongly on his despicable conduct: 'The proud lord of Holdernesse was not accustomed to be so rated in his own ducal hall. The blood flushed into his high forehead, but his conscience held him dumb' (131). Holmes does not go as far as to disturb the social edifice which the duke represents, but he effectively issues a warning that the ruling class should heed, for its own sake. 'The Priory School' thus continues Doyle's analysis of aristocratic decline that he began in 'The Speckled Band' and continued in 'The Musgrave Ritual'. The duke possesses the greatest political power, high status and great landed wealth. Partly as a result of external factors, but also because of their own inability to keep pace with the times, the landowning nobility were in the process of losing their immense privileges. They were being replaced in Parliament, in government and in the country itself by new plutocratic forces, a process that would be almost complete by Doyle's death in 1930. The Duke of Holdernesse represents the past; the future belongs to men like Neil Gibson, the American 'Gold King' in 'Thor Bridge', who has purchased, presumably from some indigent aristocrat, Thor Place and its Hampshire estate with its lakes and pheasant preserves.

Doyle was not alone in suggesting that the aristocracy's declining wealth, political power and social status were the symptoms of a moral degeneration. The MP Arthur Ponsonby, himself a landed aristocrat (he was 1st Baron Ponsonby of Shulbrede and son of Queen Victoria's private secretary), wrote in 1912 that 'the suspicion is growing that our aristocratic model is deteriorating, that our patricians are inadequately performing the duties which fall to them, that they are by no means alive to their responsibilities'. He added:

> There is an increasing impatience against the existence of a class that merely vegetates, lives off the fat of the land, and squanders, according to their whim and fancy, the wealth that others have toiled to create . . . Physically, morally and intellectually, they are a species in a steady decline.[9]

Holmes's uncharacteristic insistence on being handsomely rewarded is not only his punishment of the duke's inadequate performance of his family duties. It is a symbolic act, the transfer of wealth from the landowning nobility to a new, self-made, professional elite.

Reading 'The Priory School' as a fable of aristocratic privilege – which must be earned as well as inherited – also helps to explain one of the story's more curious details. Hayes covers his tracks – literally – by shoeing his horses with cloven shoes to mimic the feet of cattle. Wilder evidently obtained the shoes from the duke's private museum, which Holmes examines at the story's conclusion: the 'thin film of recent mud' (133) on them indicates that they were deployed in the kidnapping plot. But the horseshoes, which were probably inspired by an article about counterfeit horseshoes in the May 1903 edition of the *Strand*, are more than a mere plot device.[10] As the duke explains: 'They are supposed to have belonged to some of the marauding Barons of Holdernesse in the Middle Ages' (133). This detail thus reminds us that the duke owes his position not to his personal character or political talents, but to an inheritance originating in violence, deceit and force. His older son's dissolute cruelty, and his own suspect morality, are suggestions that the dubious legacy of the marauding medieval barons lies not just in the land and buildings, but also under their roofs.

Notes

1. Trodd, *Domestic Crime in the Victorian Novel*, p. 4.
2. Charles Dickens, *Dombey and Son*, p. 738.
3. Trodd, *Domestic Crime in the Victorian Novel*, p. 158.
4. Lynn Cain, *Dickens, Family, Authorship*, p. 62.
5. For an elaboration on this point, see Atkinson, *Secret Marriage*, p. 112.
6. Barsham, *Conan Doyle and the Meaning of Masculinity*, p. 128.
7. Lancelyn Green suggests he is a composite portrait of Lord Salisbury, three times British prime minister who died in 1903, on whom Paget appears to have based his illustration for the *Strand*, and Spencer Compton, eighth Duke of Devonshire and Marquis of Hartington, former leader of the Liberal and Liberal Unionist parties and former Secretary of State for India. Doyle, *The Return of Sherlock Holmes*, ed, Richard Lancelyn Green, pp. 360–1. The duke's extramarital affairs were common knowledge in Victorian Britain and earned him the nickname 'Harty-Tarty'.
8. Doyle included 'The Priory School' in a list of the twelve best Holmes stories for a competition in the *Strand* in March 1927. He explained that the story 'is worth a place if only for the dramatic moment when Holmes points his finger at the Duke'. Doyle, *The Uncollected Sherlock Holmes*, p. 324.
9. Arthur Ponsonby, *The Decline of Aristocracy*, pp. 23; 141.
10. McDonald, *British Literary Culture*, p. 159.

Part IV: Sex

Chapter 10

The Worst Man in London

Charles Augustus Milverton, blackmailer of society women in the 1904 story that bears his name, is assumed by critics to be based on a real person – but which real person is open to doubt. The favourite is Charles Augustus Howell, a larger-than-life associate of the Pre-Raphaelite Brotherhood (whose members knew him as 'Owl'), friend to James McNeill Whistler and Algernon Charles Swinburne, and one-time secretary to John Ruskin. However, it is by no means established that Howell was, in Lancelyn Green's words, a 'scoundrel and blackmailer'.[1] He certainly seems to have fallen out with a lot of people, but the more outlandish stories about his life and death – Oscar Wilde may be the source for the claim that Howell was found dying outside a Chelsea public house 'with his throat cut and a ten shilling piece between his clenched teeth' – may be urban myths rather than actual facts: his death certificate, for instance, records that he died of pneumonia.[2] Howell's reputation as a blackmailer seems to have originated with Swinburne, who blamed Howell for pawning some of his more colourful letters; these fell into the hands of an antiquarian bookseller who then offered to reunite them with their author for a fee.[3] Even so, Swinburne's post-mortem verdict on his former friend – that he lies 'in that particular circle of Malebolge where the coating of eternal excrement makes it impossible to see whether the damned dog's head is or is not tonsured'[4] – seems a little excessive.

Another candidate identified by Lancelyn Green is Dr Charles Augustus Bynoe, a London general practitioner convicted in 1892 for forgery with intent to defraud. There are good reasons for thinking that Doyle was aware of the Bynoe case, not least as W. T. Stead, a friend and fellow Spiritualist who became Doyle's political opponent over the Boer War, had campaigned for Bynoe to be exonerated, and published a detailed investigation of the case in 1895 under the title *Wanted: A Sherlock Holmes! A Chance for Amateur Detectives.*[5] The

Bynoe case, at least as Stead tells it, is indeed Holmesian in its combination of elaborate deception, subtle clues which are misread by police detectives determined to convict the obvious suspect, and prosecution of an innocent victim who has been deliberately ensnared by the villains. But the very features that make this case so Holmesian also serve to make Bynoe an unlikely model for Milverton: although both narratives turn on letters and other documents (forged in Bynoe's case, bought in Milverton's), it is hard to believe that Doyle would have based his villain on the victim of an apparent miscarriage of justice. If Stead's book inspired anything in Doyle's writings, we should look more to his writings on the cases of George Edalji and Oscar Slater. In particular, Doyle's outrage in the Edalji case at the resistance of the Home Office to even consider the possibility of a miscarriage of justice echoes Stead's furious invective directed at the same department.

As neither of the usual suspects seem a close match, are there others? Perhaps Doyle was thinking of Charles Augustus Bennet, the 6th Earl of Tankerville, whose ancestor features in Doyle's *Micah Clarke* (1889), and whose title pops up in 'the Tankerville Club Scandal' in 'The Five Orange Pips'. Alternatively, he may have had in mind the British diplomat Charles Augustus Murray (d. 1895). But speculating in this way does not get us very far in identifying a source for Milverton: there are very few actual people who match him in terms of conduct, even if his two given names were, in the nineteenth and early twentieth centuries, actually not that uncommon among the British upper classes. Real equivalents are hard to identify because sexual blackmail was, until quite recently, a very uncommon type of crime, and when it did occur its victims were rarely the aristocratic women victimised by Milverton: most, in fact, were men.[6] The notorious Labouchere amendment to the 1885 Criminal Law Amendment Act led to increasing fears of sexual blackmail, particularly on the part of homosexual men. Even though the Act as a whole was framed to protect 'Women and girls', the amendment's focus was exclusively on male homosexuals: 'Any male person who, in public or private, commits, or is a party to the commission of, or procures, or attempts to procure the commission by any male person of, any act of gross indecency with another male person, shall be guilty of a misdemeanour.'[7] Milverton is certainly a rogue, but not one any late nineteenth-century woman was likely to meet in reality.

Sources for Milverton are to be found in fiction, not in fact. Blackmailing of women, especially in high society, is a literary trope that stretches back at least to the dastardly lawyer Tulkinghorn in Dickens's *Bleak House* (1853), but in Britain it reached its peak

Figure 10 '*You couldn't come any other time–eh?*' Illustration by Sidney Paget, *Strand Magazine*, April 1904.

in the voguish sensation fiction of the 1860s with works such as Mary Braddon's *Aurora Floyd* (1863) and Wilkie Collins's *No Name* (1863) in which women who have married illegally find themselves blackmailed by men. Conan Doyle knew his sensation novels but he probably also drew on two of his favourite detective stories, Poe's 'The Purloined Letter' and Emile Gaboriau's *Le Dossier No. 113*, published in English as *File No. 113* in 1887 and then as *The Blackmailers* in 1907. Poe's story (which, as we have seen, is also a source for 'A Scandal in Bohemia') begins with the Prefect of Police requesting Dupin's assistance in locating a compromising letter stolen from a female royal by Minister D—, described by the Prefect as one 'who dares all things, those unbecoming as well as those becoming a man'.[8] Gaboriau's novel, meanwhile, features the detective Lecoq investigating in various disguises the theft of an enormous sum from a Paris bank. From this he unravels a decades-long history of aristocratic family feuds, dispossessed inheritance and sexual jealousy, in which the motive for the crime and much associated deception is a blackmail plot: the novel's villain is blackmailing a wealthy banker's wife by threatening to reveal the existence of her love child.

'The Adventure of Charles Augustus Milverton' also responds to a source text closer to home, in every sense. *The Amateur Cracksman* (1899) was the first collection of stories featuring the gentleman thief A. J. Raffles and his confidant Bunny, written with great flair by E. W. ('Willie') Hornung, who had married Conan Doyle's sister Connie in 1893. Hornung dedicated the book 'TO // A.C.D. // THIS FORM OF FLATTERY'.[9] 'Charles Augustus Milverton' shows Doyle returning the compliment by reworking Hornung's 'Wilful Murder', in which Raffles decides to murder Angus Baird, a moneylender and fence who has begun to suspect that Raffles is 'not quite the common cracksman I would have him think me', and has begun a pursuit with the clear aim of extortion. Raffles and Bunny break into Baird's house in Willesden, only to find that another of Baird's victims has beaten them to it: Baird is lying dead, beaten to death with his own poker. Raffles and Bunny locate the killer, Jack Rutter, hiding in Baird's house, who admits he has 'killed a robber, a usurer, a jackal, a blackmailer, the cleverest and cruellest villain unhung'.[10] Doyle's story similarly includes a set-piece scene in which Holmes and Watson break into Milverton's house to remove incriminating documents, but whereas Raffles is acting on his own account, Holmes is in the service of a client, Lady Eva Brackwell, 'the most beautiful *débutante* of last season' (*Return*, 159). Doyle's story follows Hornung's particularly closely in an exchange in which Holmes tries to prevent Watson from joining him in his mission to burgle Milverton's house (164), and in the details of the burglary itself (166): Holmes's skill in housebreaking and cracking the safe reveals him to be as skilled an amateur cracksman as his fictional rival.[11] Whereas Hornung's Baird is already dead, Holmes and Watson find Milverton very much alive; concealed in his study, they then witness his murder by another of his victims.

Doyle's rewriting of Hornung's story is, though, more than an intra-familial tribute to one of his most talented imitators. Doyle actually disagreed with Hornung's decision to reverse the morality of the conventional detective story and make the criminal into the hero. In *Memories and Adventures*, Doyle wrote:

> I think I may claim that his famous character Raffles was a kind of inversion of Sherlock Holmes, Bunny playing Watson. He admits as much in his kindly dedication. I think there are few finer examples of short-story writing in our language than these, though I confess I think they are rather dangerous in their suggestion. I told him so before he put pen to paper, and the result has, I fear, borne me out. You must not make the criminal a hero.[12]

Why, then, did Doyle do exactly this in 'Charles Augustus Milverton'? The answer is that Doyle's story is more rebuttal than tribute. By taking up the challenge that Hornung posed to the entire genre of detective fiction, Doyle creates a kind of morality story in which the criminal behaviour of the heroes is weighed in the balance of a higher good. This idea is certainly not absent from Hornung's story, as Rutter's defence of his actions demonstrates, but Doyle takes this further by setting out a wide range of criminal activities and explicitly inviting the reader to judge their legal and moral justifications. Holmes (with Watson's assistance) attempts to take Milverton's notebook by force (162), and some days later announces his plan to commit burglary: 'Let us look at the matter clearly and fairly. I suppose that you will admit that the action is morally justifiable, though technically criminal. To burgle his house is no more than to forcibly take his pocket-book – an action in which you were prepared to aid me.' Watson's response is even more illuminating: 'it is morally justifiable so long as our object is to take no articles save those which are used for an illegal purpose' (164). In other words, Holmes and Watson convince themselves that the ends justify the illegal means: in an area where legal protections are inadequate, the upstanding citizen is permitted to take the law into his own hands to protect the vulnerable.

In this way, the hero of the detective story remains on the right side of morality even if theoretically liable to legal sanction. As for the law, its limitations set the context in which the champions of morality must act. Watson protests that Milverton 'must be within the grasp of the law', but Holmes demurs: 'Technically, no doubt, but practically not. What would it profit a woman, for example, to get him a few months' imprisonment if her own ruin must immediately follow?' (158). By the same logic, Holmes prevents Watson from intervening to save Milverton's life:

> as the woman poured bullet after bullet into Milverton's shrinking body, I was about to spring out, when I felt Holmes's cold, strong grasp upon my wrist. I understood the whole argument of that firm, restraining grip – that it was no affair of ours; that justice had overtaken a villain; that we had our own duties and our own objects which were not to be lost sight of. (172)

Here, then, is Watson, whose professional instinct is to prevent harm, whatever the circumstances, being restrained by Holmes who acts as the arbiter of natural justice; recollecting the events, Watson concludes that he would have been morally wrong to have followed his instincts and saved Milverton's life. (He also conveniently observes that he would probably not have succeeded in any case.) Holmes then follows his moral verdict to its logical conclusion by refusing to assist Scotland Yard investigate the case, again pleading an ethical argument: 'I think there are certain crimes which the law cannot touch, and which therefore, to some extent, justify private revenge. No, it's no use arguing. I have made up my mind. My sympathies are with the criminals rather than with the victim' (174). Watson's narrative rather slyly reminds us that the 'criminals', in Inspector Lestrade's understanding of the case, are actually Holmes and Watson, but Holmes's reasoning is not merely self-serving: Milverton deserved to die; his crimes were worse than murder.

This brings us to one of the story's more important mysteries. The story was originally 'The Worst Man in London', but the existence of a successful play with the same title, performed the previous year in London, necessitated the change. The earlier title persists in Holmes judgement that Milverton is the 'worst man in London' (157). But why, among the violent and brutal criminals who populate the Holmes saga, does Milverton earn such a damning moral verdict? Holmes goes on to labour the point:

> Do you feel a creeping, shrinking sensation, Watson, when you stand before the serpents in the Zoo and see the slithery, gliding, venomous creatures, with their deadly eyes and wicked, flattened faces? Well, that's how Milverton impresses me. I've had to do with fifty murderers in my career, but the worst of them never gave me the repulsion which I have for this fellow. (158)

Milverton's oleaginous manner – Watson comments that 'there was something of Mr Pickwick's benevolence in his appearance' (159) – only goes so far in explaining Holmes's response. Throughout the story, we are reminded that there is something intrinsically and morally wrong about sexual blackmail that makes even murder a lesser crime. Holmes's own explanation is revealing: 'I would ask you how could one compare the ruffian who in hot blood bludgeons his mate with this man, who methodically and at his leisure tortures the soul and wrings the nerves in order to add to his already swollen money-bags?' (158). This was, indeed, a contemporary view of the crime of blackmail: one judge declared in 1895 that blackmail was 'one of the worst offences known to the law', and its highly premeditated nature, alongside the studied indifference to the harm it causes, appears to have been a source of particular horror to the

Victorian and Edwardian public.[13] But what is most striking about the history of the British state's response to the crime was the extent to which it was constructed upon imagination rather than fact – and a highly gendered imagination at that. The 1843 Libel Act, which specified blackmail as an offence (albeit as a misdemeanour rather than a felony), responded to what the subject's historian calls 'the pleasing fantasy of honourable men ... coming to the defence of besieged womanhood'.[14] The Slander of Women Act 1891 was a further protection for victims real and imagined, lowering the burden of proof so that a woman accused of unchastity or adultery did not have to prove harm.[15] Seen in this light, the values determining the literary treatments of the subject, culminating in 'Charles Augustus Milverton', become clear: the crime of blackmail, directed against women by men, was an assault on some of the most cherished gender norms and assumptions of the age. Milverton, even more than Dickens's Tulkinghorn, Braddon's James Conyers, and Poe's Minister D—, preys on women because they are women; the victims have no recourse to the law because they must at all costs protect their reputations for chastity. Doyle's rewriting of 'Wilful Murder' takes Hornung's exploration of criminal justice and higher morality and combines with it a story of female vulnerability to male aggression which Doyle found in his other literary sources, and which reflects a wider, cultural preoccupation with gendered violence.

However, Doyle's story is more than a simple morality tale. Two issues in particular stand out as suggesting a more troubling subtext. The first is Holmes's own complicity in sexual exploitation. In order to gain information on the inner workings of the Milverton household, Holmes disguises himself as a plumber called Escott and courts Milverton's housemaid to the point that he proposes to her. Justifying his actions to an incredulous Watson, he calls it 'a most necessary step', but does not conceal the extent of his deception: 'I have walked out with her each evening, and I have talked with her. Good heavens, those talks! However, I have got all I wanted. I know Milverton's house as I know the palm of my hand' (163). In any Holmes story, this admission of exploiting and then discarding a vulnerable woman – 'I have got all I wanted' – would be problematic. But in a story which explicitly justifies crime up to and including murder as a means of righting women's wrongs, Holmes's behaviour forces us to reappraise the neat hierarchy of measures of justice that Holmes and Watson propose. Holmes's use of the word 'necessary' makes it clear that we should see his actions in that hierarchy. But how can they be justified? It is only when we consider the issue of class can we accept that, in his terms, Holmes has done the right thing. Seducing the maid is morally acceptable if it is done to protect the reputations of upper-class women.

This brings us to the second issue: the morality of the victims. From the outset, Holmes frames the case in terms of a simple moral dichotomy between the imprudence of the victims and the criminal's scheming exploitation. Significantly, Holmes does not classify the victims as 'innocent' (that is, chaste): 'If ever he blackmailed an innocent person, then, indeed, we should have him; but he is as cunning as the Devil' (159). Holmes evidently is in no doubt that Milverton's victims, such as his client Lady Brackwell, have committed acts that they are ashamed of, but in her case he goes out of his way to minimise the significance of the evidence: 'This fiend has several imprudent letters – imprudent, Watson, nothing worse – which were written to an impecunious young squire in the country' (159). (The squire's lack of funds suggests an explanation as to how the letters ended up in Milverton's hands.) But when Holmes confronts Milverton, it swiftly becomes clear that the letters are more than 'imprudent', as can be judged by Holmes emotional responses to Milverton's revelations that the letters are in fact 'sprightly – very sprightly': first 'baffled', then 'grey with anger and mortification' (160), Holmes – never having seen the letters in question – has clearly been misled by Lady Brackwell.

Whatever Lady Brackwell has or has not done, her victimisation by Milverton is unjust as well as unlawful. But the narrative shows the aristocracy and squirearchy in a far from flattering light: concealing their indiscretions, marrying for money, selling secrets and resorting to murder rather than allow their reputations to be tarnished. Holmes and Watson are complicit in this system, and not simply in refusing to investigate Milverton's murder, as the final scene of the story demonstrates. Holmes summons Watson to view a photograph in a shop window in Oxford Street 'filled with photographs of the celebrities and beauties of the day':

> following his gaze I saw the picture of a regal and stately lady in Court dress, with a high diamond tiara upon her noble head. I looked at that delicately curved nose, at the marked eyebrows, at the straight mouth, and the strong little chin beneath it. Then I caught my breath as I read the time-honoured title of the great nobleman and statesman whose wife she had been. (175)

This is Milverton's murderer. The pluperfect tense reminds us that, at the scene of the crime, she revealed that her husband had died of a broken heart (171). Her description as 'regal', 'stately' and 'noble', and his designation as a 'great nobleman and statesman', emphasise that this was a marriage that combined political power and inherited wealth as well as beauty and gallantry. When Holmes puts 'his finger to his lips', he demonstrates that he is determined to do more than keep secret the sexual peccadilloes of the ruling class. He is helping to keep them in power.

Notes

1. *The Return of Sherlock Holmes*, ed. Richard Lancelyn Green, pp. 371–2.
2. C. L. Cline, *The Owl and the Rossettis*, p. 26.
3. Ibid., p. 15.
4. Nicholas Freeman, *1895*, p. 208.
5. W. T. Stead, *Wanted: A Sherlock Holmes!*
6. Angus McLaren, *Sexual Blackmail*, p. 35.
7. Criminal Law Amendment Act 1885 (c. 69, section 11).
8. Poe, *Selected Writings*, p. 332.
9. E. W. Hornung, *Raffles: The Amateur Cracksman*, ed. Richard Lancelyn Green (London: Penguin, 2003) p. 2. The stories were first published in 1898 as *In the Chains of Crime* in *Cassell's Magazine* (June to November) and *Adventures of A. J. Raffles* (September to October) in *Collier's Weekly*.
10. Ibid., p. 83.
11. Lancelyn Green, who has edited both texts, sets out the parallels in the Oxford World's Classics edition of *The Return of Sherlock Holmes*, pp. 372, 374–5. The killing with the poker may have also influenced the method in 'The Abbey Grange', published five months after 'Charles Augustus Milverton'.
12. Doyle, *Memories and Adventures*, p. 259.
13. McLaren, *Sexual Blackmail*, p. 20.
14. Ibid., p. 35.
15. Slander of Women Act 1891, c.51, section 1.

Chapter 11

The Whole Queer Business of Wisteria Lodge

'Wisteria Lodge', published in the *Strand* in 1908 and collected in *His Last Bow* (1917), is in two parts. The first, entitled 'The Singular Experience of Mr John Scott Eccles', covers the client's narrative of a most unusual dinner at Wisteria Lodge, a house near Oxshott in Surrey; the dinner is given by a Mr Garcia, who is found murdered the following morning. The second part, 'The Tiger of San Pedro', tells the story of the investigation of Garcia's murder. 'Wisteria Lodge' turns out to be a story of revolution and tyranny: Don Murillo, the former kleptocratic dictator of a South American country, has escaped with his loot and his life, adopted a new identity in Surrey, but is being pursued by a syndicate of his surviving victims led by Garcia.

The word used by both Holmes and his client for this case is 'grotesque', and Holmes's reflections on the meaning of this word bookend the tale (*Last Bow*, 5, 36). 'Grotesque' is one of many adjectives signifying the unusual or abnormal – Watson defines the word as '[s]trange – remarkable' (5) – that recur throughout the story. The subtitle tells us that the case is 'singular' (5). Scott Eccles describes his experience as 'incredible and grotesque' (5), 'most singular and unpleasant', and 'most improper – most outrageous' (6). His subsequent narrative is, Watson records, 'extraordinary' (8) and 'bizarre' (11), while Holmes describes it as 'perfectly unique' (11), 'remarkable' (15) and 'extraordinary' (16). In the second part, Holmes's deductions lead him to Don Murillo, posing as Mr Henderson of High Gable, who 'was by all accounts a curious man, to whom curious adventures might befall' (26). Describing Henderson's 'strange household' (27), Holmes identifies them as a 'singular set of people' and 'the man himself the most singular of them all' (26); labouring the point, he exclaims: 'Curious people, Watson! I don't pretend to understand it all yet, but very curious anyway' (27). Reflecting on the business more than six months later, Holmes describes it rather differently as a 'chaotic case': 'It covers two continents, concerns two groups of mysterious persons, and is further complicated by the highly respectable presence of our friend Scott Eccles, whose inclusion shows me that the deceased Garcia had a scheming mind and a well-developed sense of self-preservation' (35).

Why should this text be so emphatic on being out of the ordinary – even by the standards of Holmes's casebook? The story's exotic details supply part of the answer. Some of the more sinister elements in the story are provided by one of Don Murillo's pursuers, a giant mixed-race cook who practises voodoo, and the effect of this story relies, in part, on the juxtaposition of Latin American exoticism with Home Counties familiarity. The neighbours of Wisteria Lodge and High Gable (Henderson's house) include a lord, a JP and someone luxuriating in the name of Sir George Ffoliott; to find living among them a South American dictator and a house containing a mummified child (or perhaps an ape) and other trappings of voodoo worshippers is, indeed, grotesque. But there is something else that is remarkable and out of the ordinary, at least so far as the kind of material one is used to finding within the pages of the *Strand* magazine. And that is the largely unexplored mystery of Mr John Scott Eccles.

There are, in fact, two questions connected to Scott Eccles, only one of which Holmes and the police choose to investigate. The first is why Garcia should invite Scott Eccles to Wisteria Lodge. As they discuss Scott Eccles's narrative, Holmes asks Watson: 'What could Eccles supply? I see no charm in the man. He is not particularly intelligent – not a man likely to be congenial to a quick-witted Latin' (15). The investigations of Holmes and the Surrey Constabulary supply an answer, albeit a rather unsatisfactory one, in the suggestion that Garcia needed an alibi for his vengeance against Don Murillo. (It is unsatisfactory in that it requires us to believe that Garcia and his co-conspirators, including a gigantic voodoo worshipper, would remain in suburban Surrey while the police investigated the murder of a man whom they would be sure eventually to identify as the 'Tiger of San Pedro'.) The second, unexamined question is why Scott Eccles should accept the invitation.

Scott Eccles prefaces his story by emphasising his marital status: 'I am a bachelor . . . and, being of a sociable turn, I cultivate a large number of friends' (8). He tells Holmes that, some weeks beforehand, he met Garcia at a dinner party. Garcia 'spoke perfect English, was pleasing in his manners, and as good-looking a man as ever I saw in my life' (9). They strike up a friendship at the dinner table:

> He seemed to take a fancy to me from the first, and within two days of our meeting he came to see me at Lee. One thing led to another, and it ended in his inviting me out to spend a few days at his house, Wisteria Lodge. (9)

One thing led to another: Scott Eccles kept the appointment, but on arrival at 'an old, tumbledown building in a crazy state of disrepair' (9), he confesses he 'had doubts as to my wisdom in visiting a man I knew so slightly' (9). Despite having been promised 'an excellent dinner' (9), the house was 'depressing' (9), Garcia was distracted, and the food 'was neither well served nor well cooked' (10). A thoroughly disappointed Scott Eccles then went to bed at eleven, only to be woken by Garcia on a pretext at nearly one o'clock – though Holmes surmises that it was probably earlier, as Garcia clearly wanted to give the impression that he remained at Wisteria Lodge throughout the night.

Even though Scott Eccles acknowledges that his actions were potentially unwise, nothing in this account seems to arouse suspicion from the three detectives to whom he tells his story (Holmes, Gregson of Scotland Yard and Baynes of the Surrey Constabulary). But to today's reader, and probably to an Edwardian one, familiar with the moral panic that followed Oscar Wilde's libel action and criminal prosecution in 1895, it is surely obvious that Scott Eccles's admiration for the 'pleasing' and 'good-looking' Garcia is sexual – an impression that is further confirmed by the repeated use in the story of another adjective to denote the remarkable or unusual. Prior to the arrival of the two police officers at Baker Street, Scott Eccles announces that he will tell Holmes about 'the whole queer business' (7). He recalls that Garcia 'remarked what a queer household it was to find in the heart of Surrey, and that I agreed with him, though it has proved a good deal queerer than I thought' (9). 'Queer' is subsequently used by a constable to describe the voodoo relic in the kitchen at Wisteria Lodge and the complexion of Garcia's 'mulatto' assistant (19), and there it is clearly a synonym for 'strange'. But in the context of Scott Eccles's narrative it is suggestive of homosexuality. Although 'queer', like 'gay', can be said to have changed its meaning over the twentieth century, the first recorded use in the *OED* to mean homosexual actually dates from 1894.[1] Scott Eccles's

Figure 11 'This is awful! You don't mean – you don't mean that I am suspected?' Illustration by Arthur Twidle, *Strand Magazine*, September 1908.

decision to spend the night at Wisteria Lodge with a man he hardly knows becomes entirely explicable if we imagine that he interpreted Garcia's invitation as an assignation, an impression that Garcia presumably intended to create – 'He seemed to take a fancy to me from the first' (9) – in order to lure the potential witness.

What purpose does this apparently undeveloped subplot serve? Whether or not we recognise its sexual implications, Scott Eccles's narrative seems oddly unconnected to the grotesque events that follow, and his connection to the story's main plot is, ultimately, a tenuous one. An explanation comes into view, however, when we look more closely at the presentation of Scott Eccles's character. In their descriptions of Scott Eccles, and their assessment of his social position, Holmes and Watson go out of their way to emphasise his respectability: a 'measured step' on the stairs precedes the arrival of 'a stout, tall, grey-whiskered and solemnly respectable person'; 'His life history was written in his heavy features and pompous manner.

From his spats to his gold-rimmed spectacles he was a Conservative, a Churchman, a good citizen, orthodox and conventional to the last degree' (6). After they have heard his narrative, Holmes asks:

> Has he any one outstanding quality? I say that he has. He is the very type of conventional British respectability, and the very man as a witness to impress another Briton. You saw yourself how neither of the inspectors dreamed of questioning his statement, extraordinary as it was. (16)

Focusing on the apparent conventionality of Eccles's character turns 'Wisteria Lodge' into an exploration of double lives: Don Murillo poses as a respectable Surrey householder; Garcia poses as an urbane man about town; Scott Eccles is a Conservative and a Churchman but, in late Victorian England, he would have been unable to be open about his homosexuality. This was, after all, what Lord Alfred Douglas described in 'Two Loves' (1894) as 'the Love that dare not speak its name', a phrase that became one of the most celebrated issues of Oscar Wilde's cross-examination at the Old Bailey in April 1895.[2]

Homosexuality was far from secret in the period but it could only speak its name in certain kinds of specialist literature – pornography, like the anonymous novel *Teleny, or, The Reverse of the Medal* (1893), reportage of events such as Wilde's trials, or medical literature. In fiction designed for wide circulation, it could only be mentioned in coded terms. 'Wisteria Lodge' is not the only example from the period of such encoded sexuality. Joseph Conrad's short story 'Il Conde', published in the same year, tells of a highly respectable man – 'I have no doubt that his whole existence had been correct, well ordered and conventional' – who is robbed and humiliated at an assignation with a younger man, with a similarly obvious implication that the victim's motive for agreeing to the assignation is sexual.[3] In both cases, homosexuality had to remain sub-textual because it could not, in view of the prevailing conventions of the age, be openly discussed in popular publications. Both stories were published in magazines oriented towards a 'family' readership; *Cassell's Magazine* (formerly *Cassell's Illustrated Family Paper*), which carried 'Il Conde', was developed by its editor Max Pemberton (himself a popular writer of genre fiction) to compete directly with the *Strand* in the 1890s. And in both cases, the authors' inability to be open about the topic becomes an asset to the story because it supplies hidden mysteries of motivation, and because it engages the theme of deceptive appearances.

What, though, do we make of the detectives' lack of curiosity about Scott Eccles's intentions? It is significant that Eccles approaches Holmes specifically because he does not want to trouble the police, but his desire to keep the matter unofficial is frustrated when Inspectors Gregson and Baynes arrive at Baker Street to trouble him. In 1892, the year in which (according to most editions) the story is set, a homosexual man would have had a lot to fear from the police, thanks to the Criminal Law Amendment Act 1885.[4] This was the legislation under which Oscar Wilde was prosecuted and imprisoned for two years with hard labour in 1895: the Act's so-called Labouchere Amendment, named after the Radical Liberal MP Henry Labouchere – an acquaintance of Conan Doyle's – who tabled it, created the offence of gross indecency. This offence was both less serious and considerably more wide-ranging and easier to prove than the more serious offence of buggery which had been on the statute books since the reign of Henry VIII.[5] (Both offences were repealed in 1967.) Gregson and Baynes's apparent lack of curiosity could be read as discretion: Scott Eccles's sexual orientation was none of their business, even if homosexual activity was, notoriously, proscribed at the time.

The story's thematic insistence on the grotesque might suggest that Eccles's homosexuality is presented as an abnormality, like voodoo or the physical form of Garcia's accomplice, whose appearance terrifies a police constable minding Wisteria Lodge. Such a reading, requiring us to interpret the story's morality as homophobic, is an uncomfortable one today, but by no means unwarranted by late Victorian and Edwardian views of homosexuality. Evidence for this can be found in the period's most highly developed investigation of homosexuality, *Sexual Inversion* by Henry Havelock Ellis and John Addington Symonds, published in German in 1896 and in an English translation in 1897. Although its first English edition was banned as an obscene publication, it was widely reviewed in the medical press, including *The Lancet* and *The British Medical Journal* (*BMJ*), journals which Conan Doyle read and which occasionally published his correspondence; a second American edition in 1901 was also noticed by the *BMJ*.[6] Although the book contains a concerted appeal for the decriminalisation of homosexuality, it nonetheless treats it as a congenital, medical condition, and frequently applies the word 'abnormal' to distinguish same-sex attraction and sexuality from the 'normal': as Stephen Arata has commented, 'Despite the laudable intentions of both men, *Sexual Inversion* effectively pathologises its subjects, in part turning them into "case studies".'[7] Furthermore, Oscar Wilde himself subscribed to this medicalised view of homosexuality in his appeal against conviction to the Home Secretary in 1896.[8] It would be no surprise, then, if Dr A. C. Doyle were to subscribe to the most advanced scientific thinking of his contemporaries, and view homosexuality not as a set of preferences, or a social identity, but as a congenital medical condition.

Scott Eccles's character, however, suggests a different and more generous view of same-sex relationships. The *fin de siècle* was, according to cultural historians like Karl Miller, Jeffrey Weeks and Elaine Showalter, a period of uncertainty and flux in gender and sexuality. In Miller's words, 'Men became women. Women became men. Gender and country were put in doubt.'[9] The period's theorists of sexuality speculated that same-sex desire was a result of a blurred genetic line between male and female. One theorist of the armchair variety was Doyle's friend Bram Stoker, who opined: 'Each individual must have a preponderance, be it ever so little, of the cells of its own sex, and the attraction of each individual to the other sex depends upon its place on the scale between the highest and lowest grade of sex.' While the most masculine men mate with feminine women, those 'close to the borderline' are 'easily satisfied to mate with anyone'.[10] This view of homosexuality as akin to hermaphrodism was widespread in the period, even among champions of what today we would call gay rights: the poet and social critic Edward Carpenter, for instance, author of *Homogenic Love and Its Place in a Free Society* (1894), proposed the existence of an 'intermediate sex' which crossed the threshold of male and female. But Scott Eccles could not be more dissimilar to the caricature of the *fin de siècle* homosexual, identified in the public mind with Wilde himself. Indeed, it is worth comparing Eccles to the decadent aesthete Thaddeus Sholto in *The Sign of Four*, generally assumed to be based on Wilde, whom Doyle met at the 1889 dinner during which the American publisher J. M. Stoddart commissioned both *The Sign of Four* and Wilde's *The Picture of Dorian Gray* for *Lippincott's Magazine*.[11] Sholto, with his perpetual twitching, 'obtrusive baldness' (despite being only thirty years old), 'pendulous lip', and 'too visible line of yellow and irregular teeth' (*Sign*, 22) is as grotesque as Eccles is ordinary; where Sholto has a 'thin, high voice' and a taste for oriental luxury, Scott Eccles prefers spats and 'gold-rimmed spectacles' and is characterised by his 'heavy features and pompous manner' (6). Indeed, 'Wisteria Lodge' is insistent that Scott Eccles is masculine in every sense, a point made at the story's opening in a strikingly loaded exchange between Watson and Holmes. The latter reads out Scott Eccles's telegram, prompting

Watson to ask, 'Man or woman?' Holmes replies: 'Oh, man of course. No woman would ever send a reply-paid telegram. She would have come' (5). Leaving aside Holmes's sweeping gender assumptions, this seems a particularly gratuitous reference to the gender of Holmes's prospective client: the name which Watson has already heard is hardly ambiguous, but Watson's question adumbrates the story's concern with sexual and gender identity. Whereas the investigations of sexologists like Havelock Ellis framed homosexuality as 'inversion', and theorised that it resulted from the incomplete 'process' of male or female 'germs' developing 'the upper hand', 'Wisteria Lodge' suggests that homosexuality is just a different kind of normal.[12]

We can push this interpretation further still by reading the story through the lens of queer theory, which seeks to challenge the very notion of what is normal as presented in literature. Viewed in this way, 'Wisteria Lodge' becomes less a compendium of Gothic effects, yoking political murder to voodoo to transgressive sexuality, and more an exploration of the myriad possibilities of domestic and social organisation. Don Murillo lives, under his assumed name, with his daughters, a governess and 'Mr Lucas' – 'the two men, close and confidential friends, are the centre of the household' (26). Garcia lives with 'a faithful servant . . . who looked after all his needs' and the 'mulatto' cook (9). The latter's ritualistic magic involves a fetish which Watson cannot identify – it is 'a mummified negro baby' or 'a very twisted and ancient monkey' (20) – as well as a dismembered white cock and a pail of blood. But whereas Baynes, the story's very English police detective, interprets this as evidence that 'there must have been some very strange people with some very strange ways', Holmes's final conclusion is strikingly at odds with this view. With the benefit of an anthropological study, Eckermann's *Voodooism and the Negroid Religions*, he concludes that the cook was actually 'very orthodox in his ritual' (36). It may be 'grotesque', as he immediately concedes, but the implication is that what appears in one context to be outlandish may, in another, be highly conventional.

Conan Doyle returned to the topic of homosexuality in 'The Blanched Solider' (1926), one of two stories in *The Case-Book of Sherlock Holmes* which is entirely narrated by Holmes. Indeed, Holmes establishes the theme of same-sex relationships by revealing at the outset that he found himself without his amanuensis as Watson 'had at that time' – January 1903 – 'deserted me for a wife' (*Case-Book*, 151). That Holmes and Watson's ménage would give rise to gossip has become a mainstay of the more playful adaptations of the saga, notably Billy Wilder and I. A. L. Diamond's *The Private Life of Sherlock Holmes* (1970) and the first series of the BBC's hugely successful *Sherlock* (2010–). In Conan Doyle's hands, Holmes and Watson's relationship – 'the depth of loyalty and love' (104) characterises Holmes's anguished reaction when Watson is shot in 'The Three Garridebs' – exemplifies the asexual and high-minded homosocial relationship that was something of a Victorian ideal. In this story, though, Holmes's regret at Watson's absence seems to suggest something a little less platonic. Moreover, Holmes seems unusually appreciative of his client, the stockbroker and former Imperial Yeoman James M. Dodd, who is 'a big, fresh, sunburned, upstanding Briton' (151), 'a gentleman of virile appearance' (152), and 'the sort of person whom it would be better to have as a friend than an enemy' (154).

But Holmes's admiration for the impressive Dodd is as nothing to Dodd's admiration for another absent male, Godfrey Emsworth, with whom Dodd served in the Boer War. 'There was not a finer lad in the regiment', Dodd tells Holmes. 'We formed a friendship – the sort of friendship which can only be made when one lives the same life and shares the same joys and sorrows. He was my mate – and that means a good deal in the Army' (153). A battle wound sees Godfrey Emsworth repatriated to England but his silence in the face of repeated letters causes Dodd such sorrow that he embarks on a campaign to reunite himself with his former comrade-in-arms, much to the irritation of Colonel Emsworth, Godfrey's father, whose rebuffs prompt Dodd to exclaim, 'You must put it down, sir, to my real love for your son' (156). This admission follows a question that is at the heart of the story: 'I was fond of your son Godfrey, sir . . . Is it not natural that I should wonder at his sudden silence and should wish to know what has become of him?' (155).

Dodd's appeal to what is natural alerts us to a major theme of 'The Blanched Soldier'. As in 'Wisteria Lodge', the story's covert exploration of same-sex desire is central to its effect and crucial to its examination of the meaning of normality and the effects of the social codes demanded by convention. Colonel Emsworth, a stiff and traditionalist patriarch, retorts: 'Every family has its own inner knowledge and its own motives, which cannot always be made clear to outsiders . . . Such inquiries serve no useful purpose, sir, and place us in a delicate and difficult position' (156), thereby suggesting that Godfrey's absence is connected to some family shame. At this point, Godfrey's sexual orientation seems the most likely explanation for the family secret, and Dodd's own speculations seem to confirm this:

> That stern old man had sent his son away and hidden him from the world lest some scandal should come to light. Godfrey was a reckless fellow. He was easily influenced by those around him. No doubt he had fallen into bad hands and been misled to his ruin. (157)

When Dodd finally glimpses Godfrey, watching him through the window, he detects 'something slinking, something furtive, something guilty' in his motions, in sharp contrast to 'the frank, manly lad' he had known in South Africa (158). Dodd's interpretation, then, is that a healthy relationship had become corrupted into something shameful.

Throughout this story, Holmes invites us to draw our own conclusions. Dodd's narrative 'presented, as the astute reader will already have perceived, few difficulties in its solution, for a very limited choice of alternatives must get to the root of the matter' (161–2). The whole point of the story, though, is that the solution is far from what most astute readers will have assumed at this point. Godfrey's shame is not sexual but medical: he is believed to have contracted leprosy in South Africa. In fact, Godfrey's condition is diagnosed as pseudo-leprosy, a potentially psychosomatic condition brought on by fear of having contracted the disease. But the astute readers so flattered by Holmes's aside may not be quite so satisfied by the story's solution. Godfrey believes he has contracted leprosy in a bed; he wakes to find himself surrounded by men. 'Not one of them was a normal human being. Every one was twisted or swollen or disfigured in some strange way' (167). Godfrey's response on waking in the leper hospital, and seeing what he perceives to be abnormal humanity, is first horror, then fear, and finally shame.

'The Blanched Solider', then, is a story about the physiological effects that emotions can exert on a sensitive mind. The sexual subtext of Godfrey's relationship with Dodd appears to give way to a medical explanation, but the suspicion remains that the two are in fact linked. Reassured by a medical diagnosis, and forced to reveal the facts of his experiences, Godfrey will, we assume, be able to confront his fears, and may revert to being the 'frank, manly lad' who had so attracted Dodd in the veldt. But we can also read Godfrey's fear of disease as a fear of what is natural in him – and that, as in 'Wisteria Lodge', the normal and abnormal, the grotesque and natural, are dependent on one's point of view.

Notes

1. *OED*'s source, significantly enough, is a letter from the Marquess of Queensberry to his father-in-law concerning the death of his eldest son: 'I write to tell you that it is a *judgement* on the whole *lot of you*. Montgomerys, The Snob Queers like Roseberry [*sic*] & certainly Christian hypocrite Gladstone.' As Richard Ellmann suggests, Queensberry suspected that his son, fearing blackmail over his relationship with the Liberal Prime Minister, Lord Rosebery, had committed suicide. Richard Ellmann, *Oscar Wilde*, p. 402.
2. See Ellmann, *Oscar Wilde*, p. 435.
3. Joseph Conrad, *A Set of Six*, p. 290.
4. The Oxford edition, edited by Owen Dudley Edwards, 'corrects' the date of the story's events from 1892 to 1895, on the Sherlockian logic that in 1892 Holmes was out of the country following the death of Professor Moriarty. This unwarranted editorial intervention could mislead readers into thinking that Conan Doyle had written 1895, which would suggest that he selected the year as a specific allusion to the Wilde case.
5. When Labouchere was pursued in the civil courts for libel, Doyle contributed £40 to his defence. Lycett, *Conan Doyle*, p. 195.
6. For the early publication history of *Sexual Inversion*, see Ivan Crozier, Introduction to Ellis and Symonds, *Sexual Inversion*, pp. 57–67.
7. Arata, *Fictions of Loss*, p. 81.
8. Ellis and Symonds, *Sexual Inversion*, p. 201n.
9. Karl Miller, *Doubles*, p. 97. Qtd in Elaine Showalter, *Sexual Anarchy*, p. 3.
10. Qtd in Showalter, *Sexual Anarchy*, p. 8.
11. See McDonald, *British Literary Culture*, pp. 135–6.
12. Ellis and Symonds, *Sexual Inversion*, pp. 202–3.

Part V: Race

Chapter 12

Nice, Amiable People!

The Sign of Four was Conan Doyle's second attempt at rewriting Wilkie Collins's landmark detective novel *The Moonstone*. His first, published between *A Study in Scarlet* and *The Sign of Four*, was *The Mystery of Cloomber* (1888), a short novel that Doyle later came to regard as mere apprentice work. It is certainly derivative: its setting in a coastal village in south-west Scotland is strongly redolent of Stevenson, with an atmosphere recalling that of some of Doyle's favourites, such as 'The Pavilion on the Links' (1880). Technically, though, it follows Collins in its use of multiple narrators presenting their testimony, some of which takes the form of legalised witness statements and other official documents. But the influence of Collins is even more apparent in *The Mystery of Cloomber*'s characters, plot and orientalist tropes. Like *The Moonstone*, it features a fugitive soldier haunted by a dark secret from his days of Indian service, a trio of mysterious Indians determined to fulfil a sacred trust, and a climactic scene at a sinister and remote watery location. All of these elements appear again in one form or another in *The Sign of Four*, albeit with the Indian trio becoming warlike and pragmatic Sikhs rather than mystical Hindus or Buddhists, and acquiring an Englishman to become a multiracial quartet. Furthermore, *The Sign of Four* adds further elements drawn from *The Moonstone*, including a wronged heiress, a cursed treasure and a killer gaining access to the victim via a trapdoor in the roof.

In terms of literary history, the most significant common factor in the three novels is their imperialist contexts, specifically Britain's wars in India. The primal scene of *The Moonstone* takes place during the Siege of Seringapatam at the end of the Fourth Anglo-Mysore War (1798–9): the siege provides an opportunity for the wicked Colonel John Herncastle to commit murder and then make off with an enormous diamond which, unbeknownst to him, has great mystical significance. The genesis of the curse in *The Mystery of Cloomber* is a great imperial defeat: Britain's disastrous experiences in Afghanistan, now dubbed the First Anglo-Afghan War (1839–42), during which Doyle's brutal General Heatherstone kills a Buddhist priest trying to stop the vengeful slaughter of a troop of defeated Afridis. *The Sign of Four* draws on what was probably the only imperial-military catastrophe of the Victorian age that eclipsed the Afghan disaster of 1841–2 – the events which Britain named as the Indian Mutiny, and which are recorded by modern Indian historians as the First War of Independence, or more neutrally as the Indian Rebellion of 1857.

It is hard to overstate the impact of 1857 on the British national psyche. As the novelist Hilda Gregg ('Sydney C. Grier') remarked in an essay for *Blackwood's Magazine* in 1897: 'Of all the great events of this century, as they are reflected in fiction, the Indian Mutiny has taken the firmest hold on the popular imagination. By comparison, the impression made on imaginative literature by the Crimean War is a very faint one.'[1] Patrick Brantlinger estimates at least fifty novels about the Mutiny appeared before 1900, although Gautam Chakravarty counts only twenty-nine (of which nineteen, including *The Sign of Four*, appeared in the 1890s).[2] Despite its present action being confined to London and its suburbs, *The Sign of Four* is distinctively also a book about India – or, more specifically, the influence of India on British society – from almost the first page. Referring to his experiences in the Second Anglo-Afghan War (1878–80), Watson complains that his 'constitution has not got over the Afghan campaign yet' (*Sign*, 5), and as he listens to Holmes's lecture on the deductive method he nurses his leg wound: 'I had had a Jezail bullet through it some time before, and though it did not prevent me from walking, it ached wearily at every change in the weather' (5). Watson's wound is emblematic of the novella's theme: the violent confrontations of West and East do not remain confined to India and its peripheries, but make themselves insistently present in the imperial centre. Everywhere we look in *The Sign of Four*'s London we can find traces of India – the ashes of the Trichinopoly cigar which Holmes claims to be able to distinguish from any other, 'the curiosities from the Andaman Islands' (13) in Captain Morstan's luggage left unclaimed at the Langham Hotel after his disappearance, the 'Hindoo servant, clad in a yellow turban, white loose-fitting clothes, and a yellow sash' (21) who attends the extraordinary bohemian figure of Thaddeus Sholto. Watson observes 'something strangely incongruous in this Oriental figure framed in the commonplace doorway of a third-rate suburban dwelling-house' (21) in the vicinity of Brixton's Coldharbour Lane, and similar incongruities persist throughout: Thaddeus's suburban collection of oriental art and furniture, including 'a huge hookah'; his brother Bartholomew's home in Upper Norwood taking its name from the Indian coastal town of Pondicherry (which was captured and recaptured throughout the Anglo-French wars of the mid eighteenth century); the 'peculiar instrument – a brown, close-grained stick, with a stone head like a hammer, rudely lashed on with coarse twine' (38) which is discovered next to Bartholomew's corpse; Holmes's discoveries of a poisoned thorn in Bartholomew's body and, on the roof of Pondicherry Lodge, of

> a small pocket or pouch woven out of coloured grasses and with a few tawdry beads strung round it . . . In shape and size it was not unlike a cigarette-case. Inside were half a dozen spines of dark wood, sharp at one end and rounded at the other. (53)

The Sign of Four is a canonical exemplar of what Brantlinger influentially called 'Imperial Gothic' – the use of the themes, tropes and techniques of Gothic fiction to explore Britain's relationship with its overseas acquisitions. As is common in this sub-genre, the menace comes in the form of a psychologically and politically repressed force that arrives from both the past and the East. It brings with it a reminder that actions (especially criminal ones) have consequences, that political obligations persist and that alien cultures may not be quite as easy to master as initially assumed. When *The Sign of Four* turns specifically to the events of 1857, as it does when Jonathan Small is captured and tells his story, it seems at first to align itself with the customary portrayal of the Mutiny in nineteenth-century British fiction. Small, who in 1857 was an employee on Mr Abel White's indigo plantation, tells Holmes during his confession that the Mutiny was a sudden, irrational, or even diabolical irruption on a peaceful and well-ordered land: 'One month India lay still and peaceful, to all appearance, as Surrey or Kent; the next there were two hundred thousand black devils let loose, and the country was a perfect hell' (97–8). His first realisation that 'the crash' had come was discovering Mrs Dawson, the wife of Abel White's bookkeeper and plantation manager, 'all cut into ribbons, and half eaten by jackals and native dogs' (98). This strikes the characteristic note of Mutiny fiction which, as Brantlinger and others have shown, dwelt almost obsessively on the violence done to women's bodies, pre- and post-mortem. The Mutiny novel returned again and again to one incident in particular, the Bibighar Massacre during the Siege of Cawnpore, when over two hundred European women and children were hacked to death and their dismembered remains thrown into a well, to be followed later by the few remaining survivors who suffocated among the body parts. Small's narrative refers to this incident obliquely:

> if you look at the map you will see that we were right in the heart of it. Lucknow is rather better than a hundred miles to the east, and Cawnpore about as far to the south. From every point on the compass there was nothing but torture and murder and outrage. (99)

When in Agra two Sikh soldiers hold a knife to his throat, Small immediately assumes that 'these fellows were in league with the rebels', meaning that 'the place must fall, and the women and children be treated as they were in Cawnpore' (101). He also mentions, again only in passing, the figure consistently blamed by Victorian writers for the Bibighar Massacre. This is the Maratha aristocrat Nana Sahib, who assured the British authorities of his loyalty before leading the rebels' attack on Cawnpore, and who became for the Victorians 'the Demon of Cawnpore', a treacherous and brutal monster.[3] In *The Sign of Four*, Nana Sahib's disappearance 'over the frontier' (108) is a sign that the Mutiny is over, but Small's reference to him without any gloss shows that he (and of course Doyle) knew that, decades after the event, he was still a household name, such was his dominant position in how the Mutiny was memorialised.

Also typical of the Mutiny novel is Small's characterisation of the rebels. Watching them set fire to Abel White's house, Small recalls: 'From where I stood I could see hundreds of the black fiends, with their red coats still on their backs, dancing and howling round the burning house' (98). Later, Small recalls hearing from the comparative safety of Agra Fort the 'beating of drums, the rattle of tomtoms, and the yells and howls of the rebels, drunk with opium and with bang' (100). In Small's telling, the Sepoys are demonic arsonists and drug-crazed murderers, not political actors – which is exactly how they would have been seen by British readers. British fiction, following the eyewitness accounts and numerous histories that appeared in the decades after 1857, did not dwell for long on the complex politics of the Mutiny, as Brantlinger notes: 'The problem of general causes is reduced to that of the motives of the mutineers, which are in turn reduced to Nana Sahib's allegedly deceitful, lustful, bloodthirsty impulses.'[4] Or, as Winwood Reade puts it in *The Martyrdom of Man* (1872), the work which Holmes urges Watson to read in *A Sign of Four*, 'The Indian Mutiny was only a mutiny, not a rebellion.'[5]

However, Small's narrative is not quite the simplistic recycling of British official propaganda that it may appear to twenty-first-century readers armed with the sceptical instruments of post-colonialism. *The Sign of Four* is deeply concerned with the subject of loyalty, from its title, referring to the oath of allegiance between Small and his three Sikh accomplices, Mahomet Singh, Abdullah Khan and Dost Mohammed, to the final words of Small's confession. This is not incidental: loyalty to British rule was a central issue in British responses to the Mutiny. Indeed, the framing of the conflict as 'only a mutiny, not a rebellion' derives from the assumption that it was primarily an act of disloyalty to an employer, an ultra-violent breach of contract, rather than an expression of resistance or attempt to rectify political grievances. And this is why Nana Sahib's actions – promising safe passage to the British contingent before cruelly betraying them to the rebels – were held to be so emblematic of the conflict.

At first glance, Small's confession appears to underwrite the British version of events:

> It was a fight of the millions against the hundreds; and the cruellest part of it was that these men that we fought against, foot, horse, and gunners, were our own picked troops, whom we had taught and trained, handling our own weapons and blowing our own bugle calls. (99)

But this is not the only betrayal in the story, and as far as the plot is concerned, it is considerably less important than the betrayal of Small by his fellow Englishman, Major Sholto. More importantly, not only does Sholto renege on his promise, betraying Small as well as his fellow officer Captain Morstan, but he also sees no reason to regard Indians as deserving of his trust or loyalty. When Small objects that the treasure must be split five ways, Sholto retorts, 'What have three black fellows to do with our agreement?' (113). Sholto's morality stands in stark contrast not only to Small's ('"Black or blue," said I, "they are with me, and we all go together"') but also to that of three 'Punjaubees'. Even though Dost Mohammed is absent when Small is first brought into the plot, Abdullah Khan points out that he 'must have his share', before observing to Small:

> I know that an oath is binding upon a Feringhee, and that we may trust you. Had you been a lying Hindoo though you had sworn by all the gods in their false temples, your blood would have been upon the knife and your body in the water. But the Sikh knows the Englishman, and the Englishman knows the Sikh. (102)

Figure 12 'I shall reward you, young Sahib, and your governor also, if he will give me the shelter I seek.' Illustration by Herbert Denman in *Lippincott's Magazine*, February 1890.

The Four remain true to a verbal contract that is assured by honour and integrity, whereas the most senior representative of British power in the novella does not even bother to pay lip service to fidelity. Like General Heatherstone in *The Mystery of Cloomber*, the debt-ridden and unscrupulous Major Sholto gives the lie to the myth of the loyal Englishman officer in India. Similarly, in 'The Crooked Man', the other Holmes story to deal with the matter of the Mutiny, the principal villain is again a British soldier guilty of imperial betrayal: the treacherous Sergeant (later Colonel) James Barclay betrays Wood to the Sepoys in order to keep the beautiful Nancy Devoy to himself.

There is also an intriguing hint that, prior to the Mutiny, India might not be the well-ordered extension of the Home Counties that Small appears to suggest. By allocating the name Abel White to the indigo planter, Conan Doyle can hardly have expected his contemporaries to miss his most direct and obvious allusion to *The Moonstone*. In Collins's novel, the diamond's thief turns out to be the hypocritical charmer Godfrey Abelwhite, who seduces heiresses and rich widows under the guise of his philanthropic endeavours, and who steals the moonstone in order to settle his crippling debts. Abelwhite's direct equivalent in *The Sign of Four* is, of course, the disgraceful Major Sholto, who similarly attempts to satisfy his creditors by walking off with treasure obtained from its rightful owners by someone else. By transferring Abelwhite's name to another character, Doyle is clearly trying to tell us something. For Lillian Nayder, 'Conan Doyle reinforces racist stereotypes of Indian lawlessness and treachery, defending the Empire against its critics and implicitly justifying British rule' by transforming 'Collins's English villain into a martyr of sorts, and identifying natives rather than Englishmen as the enemies of the women.'[6] But a very different reading is equally possible – that Abel White is not so kindly as his erstwhile employee Jonathan Small assumes. After all, Collins's Abelwhite seems to be the model Victorian gentleman and philanthropist, a false impression confirmed by the implications of his name. Doyle's Abel White is an agent in a regime that administered India as if it were Surrey or Kent, expropriating its natural resources under a guise of benign governance. Moreover, far from simplistically justifying British rule, *The Sign of Four* implicates a wide range of loyal characters in what is increasingly shown to be a kleptocratic system. It is notable that despite their Muslim-sounding names – a failure, one presumes, of Conan Doyle's background knowledge – the three 'Punjaubees' who steal the Agra treasure are Sikhs, a religious group that remained famously loyal to the Raj during the Mutiny. Abdullah Khan's offer to bring Small into their conspiracy is expressed in the clearest terms: 'We only ask you to do that which your countrymen come to this land for. We ask you to be rich' (102). Neither Khan and his accomplices nor Small see any contradiction between stealing a northern rajah's fortune and remaining loyal to the Raj. Khan goes on to justify the planned theft by alleging that the rajah is himself disloyal, but is hedging his bets by dividing his fortune between his estate and the Agra fort. Even if this is true, the logic that a wealthy prince's political decision justifies a major heist is, to put it mildly, self-serving.

The Sign of Four's surprisingly even-handed examination of the ethics of loyalty is continued in the character of Tonga. To the novella's post-colonial critics, Tonga is a classic instance of the 'subaltern', a character who is seen and not heard, confined at the base of the novel's social hierarchy and presented to the reader exclusively by a westerner. Tonga is voiced by Small, the novella's most prominent internal narrator after Watson himself: despite his own low position in the social hierarchy, Small is privileged by the power of speech and by the charismatic control he appears to exert over 'the

Islander'. And there is certainly plenty of evidence to support the argument that Tonga is confined, along with the red-coated fiends who lay waste to Abel White's plantation, to the novella's lowest circle of hell. Watson's glimpses of Tonga on board the *Aurora* during the climactic chase down the Thames paint a picture beyond any orientalist stereotype. Tonga is at first inhuman – 'Beside him lay a dark mass, which looked like a Newfoundland dog' (86). This then resolves itself into 'a little black man – the smallest I have ever seen – with a great, misshapen head and a shock of tangled, dishevelled hair', and the sight of 'this savage, distorted creature' causes both Holmes and Watson to draw their revolvers (86). The inhuman thus becomes subhuman, before reverting metaphorically to the animal kingdom: 'Never have I seen features so deeply marked with all bestiality and cruelty. His small eyes glowed and burned with a sombre light, and his thick lips were writhed back from his teeth, which grinned and chattered at us with half animal fury' (86–7). And then this 'unhallowed dwarf with his hideous face, and his strong yellow teeth gnashing at us in the light of our lantern' raises his blowpipe to his lips. Holmes and Watson fire simultaneously, and Tonga disappears into the Thames, leaving one final impression of implacable hatred: 'I caught one glimpse of his venomous, menacing eyes amid the white swirl of the waters' (87).

Watson throws the full range of dehumanising animal metaphors at Tonga – dog, ape, venomous reptile – and when Tonga is acknowledged to be human it is in a defective (misshapen, dwarfish, black and yellow) form. When we move from Watson's metaphorical description to the facts of Small's narrative, we find further evidence that Tonga's behaviour is brutal and violent, even if Small is a more sympathetic narrator. In particular, we discover that Tonga murdered Bartholomew Sholto unnecessarily, earning a ferocious rebuke from Small, who 'cursed him for a little bloodthirsty imp' (117). The strongest evidence of the novella's indulgence of racist stereotyping, however, comes not in the accounts of Tonga's appearance and action but in the haven of Holmes and Watson's lodgings in Baker Street. There Holmes discovers what he needs to know about the Andaman Islands and their aboriginal inhabitants from 'the first volume of a gazetteer which is now being published', endorsed by Holmes as 'the very latest authority':

> What have we here? 'Andaman Islands, situated 340 miles to the north of Sumatra, in the Bay of Bengal.' Hum! hum! What's all this? Moist climate, coral reefs, sharks, Port Blair, convict barracks,

Rutland Island, cottonwoods – Ah, here we are! 'The aborigines of the Andaman Islands may perhaps claim the distinction of being the smallest race upon this earth, though some anthropologists prefer the Bushmen of Africa, the Digger Indians of America, and the Terra del Fuegians. The average height is rather below four feet, although many full-grown adults may be found who are very much smaller than this. They are a fierce, morose, and intractable people, though capable of forming most devoted friendships when their confidence has once been gained.' Mark that, Watson. Now, then listen to this. 'They are naturally hideous, having large, misshapen heads, small fierce eyes, and distorted features. Their feet and hands, however, are remarkably small. So intractable and fierce are they, that all the efforts of the British officials have failed to win them over in any degree. They have always been a terror to shipwrecked crews, braining the survivors with their stone-headed clubs, or shooting them with their poisoned arrows. These massacres are invariably concluded by a cannibal feast.' Nice, amiable people, Watson! If this fellow had been left to his own unaided devices, this affair might have taken an even more ghastly turn. (68)

Clearly, this is the source of the ethnological knowledge that Watson reproduces in his narrative of the chase on the Thames: the gazetteer describes a racial type to which Tonga the individual clearly belongs. The gazetteer, strikingly presented as an independent, extrinsic source of authority, probably derives from a real text, the *Imperial Gazetteer of India*, compiled by William W. Hunter and published in 1881. This described the Andaman Islands as 'cannibal islands', and its inhabitants as 'a very low type', although in other respects the fictional *Gazetteer* departs significantly from the real version.[7] Nor is this Holmes's only source of anthropological knowledge. Winwood Reade's *The Martyrdom of Man* – a sprawling history of human civilisation which, although forgotten today, was astonishingly influential in Conan Doyle's time, running to twenty-three editions by 1915 – is permeated by observations about the practices of different ethnic groups but frequently assigns to them a position in a global hierarchy, with Western colonial powers at the summit. By aligning his narrative with such source material, *The Sign of Four* underwrites the use of ethnological investigation and documentation not merely to generate and disseminate knowledge, but to exert political control. As John McBratney has shown, the *Imperial Gazetteer of India* was part of a concerted operation in the decades following the Mutiny to map, classify and categorise the subcontinent's vast and complex population, all with a view to ensuring that the events of 1857 would never be repeated. The *Gazetteer* followed the first census in India (1871) and, in the same year, the passing of the first Criminal Tribes Act, ostensibly aimed at the Thuggee cult, but enabling the Indian government to designate particular ethnic groups to be subject to close control. (Initially confined to parts of northern India, the Act was progressively amended to expand its scope in 1876, 1911 and 1924.)[8] We also see Holmes applying his distinctive deductive method to imperialist, anthropological ends, when he classifies Tonga's footprints:

> Some of the inhabitants of the Indian Peninsula are small men, but none could have left such marks as that. The Hindoo proper has long and thin feet. The sandal-wearing Mohammedan has the great toe well separated from the others, because the thong is commonly passed between. (68)

While we might condemn Holmes's 'knowledge' as absurd essentialising, attributing specific and consistent characteristics to vast populations united only by religious identity, it provides another example of the application of positivist, scientific techniques to imperialist knowledge systems. As McBratney has shown, the connection between ethnicity and criminality in the imperial mindset was a significant one: *The Sign of Four* follows British policy in reframing political challenge as ethnically determined criminality. Tonga thus joins the drug-fuelled, red-coated rebels as a way of making sense of the Mutiny without having to consider the implications of British imperial policy and conduct.

But is this 'very latest authority' in any way scientifically accurate? This is a question that bothered one of the novella's earliest critics, the anthropologically minded author, editor and Spiritualist Andrew Lang, whose positive reader's report on *Micah Clarke* in 1888 led to that novel's publication and a subsequent literary alliance with Doyle.[9] Lang's long and otherwise admiring survey of Conan Doyle's *oeuvre* in the *Quarterly Review* in 1904 singles out *The Sign of Four*'s anthropological knowledge for a rare passage of censure: 'the Andamanese are cruelly libelled, and have neither the malignant qualities, nor the heads like mops, nor the weapons, nor the customs, with which they are credited by Sherlock'. Doyle 'has detected the wrong savage, and injured the character of an amiable people. The *bo:jig-ngijji* is really a religious, kindly creature, has a Deluge and a Creation myth, and shaves his head, not possessing scissors.' Lang goes on to attack Holmes's supposed source of authority: the gazetteer 'is full of nonsense', as the average height of the Andamanese is four feet ten inches and a half, they do not use blowpipes or poisoned arrows, and 'show no traces of cannibalism'.[10] Lang suggests that Doyle would have done better to have looked to the tribes of the Amazon for blowpipes and poison – if he was interested in anthropological accuracy, at any rate.

A South American aborigine would not, however, have served Doyle's purpose, and not only because it would have required some additional and possibly incredible plotting to have moved Small's incarceration from the Bay of Bengal to the Amazon basin. Small's imprisonment on 'Blair Island' (109), meaning Port Blair in the Andamans, is both historically accurate and maintains the novella's focus on the Mutiny and its aftermath. As Shafquat Towheed has shown, a penal colony at Port Blair was established in the aftermath of the Mutiny as a destination for political prisoners, becoming 'India's largest facility for transported convicts'.[11] The choice of the Andaman Islands was both practical (for their remoteness) and political: one of the penal colony's founders, F. J. Mouat, saw

> something poetical in the retributive justice that thus rendered the crimes of an ancient race the means of reclaiming a fair and fertile tract of land from the neglect, the barbarity, and the atrocities of a more primitive, but scarcely less cruel and vindictive race.[12]

Tonga's entry into the story is yet another consequence of the Mutiny, and in reflecting on this we might consider him to be one of the novella's victims, as much as a perpetrator: Towheed brilliantly imagines *The Sign of Four* from Tonga's perspective, giving voice to the subaltern so as to show the British as thoughtlessly destructive intruders.

Tonga is also connected thematically to the novella's exploration of loyalty. In contrast to the Sepoys, Tonga is 'devoted' (115) to Small. In one way this only dehumanises him further: his devotion causes him, dog-like, to wish to please his master, as when he murders Bartholomew Sholto in the mistaken belief that his master wished it. For post-colonial theorists like Frantz Fanon or Homi Bhabha, this is an entirely predictable manoeuvre: Bhabha observes that stereotypes are 'curiously mixed and split', combining seemingly irreconcilable opposites. Thus the 'black is both savage (cannibal) and yet the most obedient and dignified of servants'.[13] However, in terms of the novella's ethical analysis, Tonga shows a consistency in human values that is not observed by the British officers. Indeed, Small's choice of words to describe his companion – 'He was staunch and true, was little Tonga. No man ever had a more faithful mate'

(115) – are keywords in the Victorian moral lexicon. Although their relationship could be seen as exploitative – Small earns his money in London by exhibiting Tonga as a cannibal freak (117) – it is also a notably warm and human one. The maimed convict Small, more a victim of circumstances than a scheming villain, finds a sick aboriginal in the jungle, takes 'him in hand' (114), and nurses him back to health.[14] Small learns Tonga's language, thereby (as Towheed notes) demonstrating a curiosity and sympathy absent from the researches of the aloof and misinformed Holmes. The gazetteer and Small's narrative are at cross purposes, but it is Small who has the last word on the 'staunch and true' Islander.

The Mutiny novel 'reworks antecedent and metropolitan literary idioms to represent indigenous resistance, and in doing so serves for a time as the potent medium of popular imperialism and jingoism'.[15] However, *The Sign of Four*'s contribution is less to underwrite the comforting illusions of Victorian historiography as to offer a horror story of the aftermath of the Indian Mutiny at home as well as abroad: in the last pages of the novella we discover that Bartholomew Sholto was betrayed by his Indian servant Lal Rao, an instance of the treacherous violence of the Mutiny as it was imagined in the Victorian mind, but even more alarming and close at hand. While this might seem to inscribe the dominant view of the conflict as an expression of disloyalty, it also suggests that the Mutiny is unfinished business, and so may implicate more fundamental issues than the contractual obligations of the East India Company's native soldiers. As with 'The Crooked Man', the suburban Home Counties cannot escape the consequences of white men's misdeeds in the East, however much dubious orientalist knowledge Holmes deploys to reassure us.

Notes

1. Cited in Brantlinger, *Rule of Darkness*, p. 199.
2. Brantlinger, *Rule of Darkness*, p. 199; Gautam Chakravarty, *The Indian Mutiny and the British Imagination*, pp. 215–36.
3. Brantlinger, *Rule of Darkness*, p. 201.
4. Ibid., p. 201.
5. Winwood Reade, *The Martyrdom of Man*, p. 504.
6. Lillian Nayder, 'Victorian Detective Fiction', p. 186.
7. John McBratney, 'Racial and Criminal Types', pp. 154–6.
8. Ibid., pp. 151–4.
9. Lycett, *Conan Doyle*, p. 140.

10. Shafquat Towheed (ed.), 'Appendix E: Contemporary Reviews', in Arthur Conan Doyle, *The Sign of Four* (Peterborough, Canada; Buffalo, NY; London; Moorebank, NSW: Broadview, 2010), p. 214.
11. Towheed, 'Introduction' to *The Sign of Four*, p. 32.
12. Ibid., p. 32.
13. Homi K. Bhabha, *The Location of Culture*, p. 82.
14. McBratney, 'Racial and Criminal Types', p. 155.
15. Chakravarty, p. 16.

Chapter 13

A Nobler Man Never Walked the Earth

One of the most problematic characters in any Holmes story is Steve Dixie, the black gangster who bursts into Holmes's room at the beginning of 'The Three Gables'. He is a man of contradictions, simultaneously ridiculed and full of menace. His size and apparent physical aggression – 'his sullen dark eyes' have 'a smouldering gleam of malice in them' (*Case-Book*, 133) – are in counterpoint to his comic appearance: Watson remarks on his 'very loud grey check suit with a flowing salmon-coloured tie' (133). Instructed by his superior to warn Holmes that his life is at threat 'if he go down Harrow way' (134), he enters like 'a mad bull' and twice threatens Holmes with physical violence: 'It won't be so damn fine if I have to trim you up a bit' (133); 'you'll get put through it for sure if you give me any lip' (134). However, Dixie is 'easily cowed' by Holmes's 'icy coolness' (134–5) and Holmes's suggestion that he knows about Dixie's involvement in 'the killing of young Perkins outside the Holborn Bar' (134). After Dixie's departure, Holmes laughs off the encounter: 'he is really rather a harmless fellow, a great muscular, foolish, blustering baby' (135). Dixie's contradictions are, indeed, his essence. He cannot be presented as thoroughly menacing as that would concede power and agency to a figure who is Holmes's inferior mentally, physically and socially. But nor can he be a firmly comic character, as that would make him harmless or likeable. Dixie has to be both comic and threatening in order for him to be so thoroughly demeaned.

Reading 'The Three Gables' today, it is impossible not to be repelled by Doyle's offensive characterisation. This is the only Holmes story to feature the word 'nigger' (143), used by a police inspector but with apparent approval from Holmes. Despite having a geographical scope that stretches from Harrow in West London to Birmingham's Bull

Ring, Dixie speaks in an end-of-the-pier Deep South patois, addressing Holmes as 'Masser' (133) and employing formulations like 'this boy done get into trouble' and 'So help me the Lord!' (134).[1] But the naked racism of the portrait is most apparent in Holmes and Watson's reactions to Dixie's physicality: Watson remarks on his 'broad face and flattened nose' and 'hideous mouth' (135), while Holmes mocks the size of his fist – '"Where you born so?", he asked. "Or did it come by degrees?"' – and asks him not to sit down 'for I don't like the smell of you' (134). Later, seeing Stevie outside the Three Gables, Mary Maberley's home, Holmes quips that he is looking for 'my scent-bottle' (141).

This scene is as out of place as it is unpleasant. No other visitor to Baker Street is treated in this way – even Dr Grimesby Roylott and Professor Moriarty are treated with more respect. And Holmes even begins to respond to Dixie in kind, his rejoinders – '"Keep on talking," said Holmes. "It's fine"' – more in keeping with the tenor of the hard-boiled American detective fiction that would reshape the genre at the end of the decade than that of the Holmes saga. It is tempting to speculate that, in this late story, Doyle was so running out of creative puff that he found himself importing the matter of the American dime novel or the Victorian music hall in order to maintain momentum: one critic has labelled Stevie 'a minstrel figure, a caricature of an American black' familiar to the late Victorian or Edwardian theatregoer.[2] Indeed, at least one Sherlockian has gone so far as to reject the story from the canon altogether, relying on purely internal evidence, including Holmes's racist jeers.[3] W. W. Robson speculates more convincingly that Doyle originally conceived and perhaps even drafted 'The Three Gables' as a non-Holmes story, before shoehorning Holmes and Watson into the narrative in response to a looming deadline.[4]

Conan Doyle is certainly not alone among his contemporaries in offending more recent readers with what appear to be antediluvian attitudes towards race and ethnicity: the casual racism with which Kipling, in Orwell's words, 'describes a British soldier beating a "nigger" with a cleaning rod in order to get money out of him', and Chinua Achebe's charge that Joseph Conrad was a 'thoroughgoing racist' spring to mind.[5] Comparing Conan Doyle with those contemporaries helps us see that, for all that the Holmes saga usually confines its real-time settings to London and the Home Counties, it also narrates a long series of cross-cultural encounters, often in the form of the threat to the imperial centre of repressed or suppressed forces from the Asian empire, or embedded narratives of encounters in Asia or the Americas. But Stevie in 'The Three Gables' is a very different case from Tonga in *The Sign of Four* or the lepers in 'The

Blanched Soldier'. His backstory is undisclosed, and as for geography, the Bull Ring in Birmingham, The Three Gables in Harrow, and Holmes's rooms in Baker Street are the only domains with which he is associated. Despite his Americanese patois, Stevie is a study in purely domestic racial prejudice, not an exploration of the cultural strains and opportunities that result from imperial obligations and Britain's position as a global power.

Was racism of this kind a new development in Doyle's writing, an index either of an author's increasingly parochial and intolerant outlook, or of hardening social attitudes in the 1920s? Certainly, if we look beyond the Holmes saga for a moment, we can see Doyle as a thoroughgoing racist at the very outset of his writing career. In 1882, Doyle published a two-part article in the *British Journal of Photography* entitled 'On the Slave Coast with a Camera'. This was one of the fruits of his adventures as ship's surgeon on board the *Mayumba,* a passenger ship plying the Liverpool-West Africa route for the African Steamship Company.[6] Doyle went down with an unnamed fever in West Africa and hated the ports, writing to a friend from the Niger Delta that 'Never was there such a hole of a place, it is good for nothing but swearing at'; in a foreshadowing of Holmes's disgust at Stevie's smell, Doyle added that the only way to distinguish one 'dirty little port' from another was to compare 'the smell of the inhabitants, though they all smell as if they had become prematurely putrid and should be buried without unnecessary delay'.[7] These unpleasant responses seem to have influenced 'On the Slave Coast with a Camera'. Amidst all the technical details of wide-angle lenses, an improvised tripod and the difficulties of using developing chemicals in a tropical climate, Doyle admits to a colonialist ambition 'to "astonish the natives" by representations of their own hideous faces', combining in a single sub-clause a triumphalist certainty in the superiority of Western technology and a sense of disgust at the otherness of African people.[8] As with 'The Three Gables', disgust vies with amused contempt in Doyle's reactions to Africans. At Accra he cannot summon the words to capture adequately the comic appearance of Ghanaian fishermen:

> The effect of the row of woolly heads glaring at me from the other side of the boat was so ludicrous that I attempted to make good use of the opportunity and expended a plate upon the group. I am sorry to say, however, that the results exhibited little better than a chaotic mass of white foam, distorted faces, and waving paddles, hardly distinguishable from each other.[9]

Disgust re-enters the essay further on, when Doyle recounts photographing a 'native prince' in Duke Town in the British colony of Old Calabar in modern-day Nigeria:

> His highness did me the honour of informing me that it was wonderfully unlike him. The delight of his retinue, however, at seeing the ugliness of their lord so faithfully represented more than assuaged my wounded photographic feelings. It was an excellent likeness; but the monarch probably missed the smell of premature putridity which was so characteristic of the original, and yet could not be transferred to paper.[10]

While the subject of the photograph disputes its accuracy, its author concedes that while the visual record is reliable, it fails to do adequate justice to the awfulness of the subject: as Jinny Huh has pointed out, 'Doyle implies that some elements of savagery are so vile and grotesque that even technology and the most skilled of photographers cannot capture it.'[11] In other words, when it comes to black Africa, the truth is even worse than the assumption. And Doyle makes this point even more insistently in what may be his most unsavoury verdict of all:

> A great deal has been said about the regeneration of our black brothers and the latent virtues of the swarthy races. My own experience is that you abhor them on first meeting them, and gradually learn to dislike them a very great deal more as you become better acquainted with them.[12]

Doyle's purpose in the articles is, clearly, to bring home to readers of the *British Journal of Photography* that any feelings of contempt they may feel at seeing photographic evidence of Africa are not only justified by his first-hand experience, but actually underestimate the reality.

Doyle's unvarnished racism – more damning than anything in Achebe's case against Conrad in 'An Image of Africa' – stands in contrast, however, with the considerable biographical and textual evidence that Doyle was also capable of much more progressive attitudes. George Edalji's father was a Parsi from Bombay, and Doyle was convinced that racial prejudice played a role in the state's persecution of him. In 1909, Doyle took up the cause of the atrocities that were being committed on an astonishing scale in the Congo, which had been colonised not by a country but on behalf of a single individual – Leopold II, King of the Belgians. This and the enslavement of Putamayo Indians by the Peruvian Amazon Company lie behind Doyle's buccaneering adventurer and human rights activist Lord John Roxton in *The Lost World* and subsequent Professor Challenger stories. But the most eloquent evidence of Doyle's relatively enlightened views on race can be found in 'The Adventure of the Yellow Face' (1893). Like 'The Three Gables', this has long been viewed as an unsatisfactory story.[13] One complaint from critics has been that Holmes's most remarkable feat of detection in the story comes not in solving the client's problem but in reading the client's physiognomy and history from the evidence of his pipe.[14] The client in question, Grant Munro, has come to Holmes with what appears to be a very humdrum problem – although he does not say as much, he clearly suspects his wife Effie of having an affair: 'It's a very delicate thing . . . One does not like to speak of domestic things to strangers. It seems dreadful to discuss the conduct of one's wife with two men whom I have never seen before' (*Memoirs*, 56). Although he is certain she loves him, she has requested substantial sums of money for reasons which she will not divulge, and has begun to make clandestine visits to a cottage near to Munro's villa in Norbury. A standard matrimonial case would not, of course, have interested Holmes or been worthwhile for Watson to record, but what marks out Munro's narrative is that he has glimpsed in the Norbury cottage a face watching him from an upstairs window: 'I don't know what it was about that face, Mr Holmes, but it seemed to send a chill right down my back . . . there was something unnatural and inhuman about the face . . . the colour was what impressed me most. It was of a livid dead yellow, and with something set and rigid about it, which was shockingly unnatural' (59–60). Munro describes an incident when he forced his way into the cottage and discovered a comfortable bedroom with a full-length photograph of his wife, appearing to confirm in his mind that this was the scene of her illicit relationship. After Munro leaves Baker Street, Holmes constructs a scenario to explain the facts of the narrative, drawing a somewhat different conclusion from his client: 'There's blackmail in it, or I am much mistaken.' The blackmailer, Holmes supposes, is a previous husband who 'developed some hateful qualities, or, shall we say, that he contacted some loathsome disease, and became a leper or an imbecile' (67). But Holmes's scenario, which even Watson realises is 'all surmise', is profoundly wrong. This is indeed a case about skin colour, but the social implications could not be more different from what Holmes and Munro assume. The 'creature' (67, 69) is Effie's daughter, Lucy, by her deceased first husband, John Hebron: Holmes unmasks her to reveal, behind the yellow face, 'a little coal-black negress with all her white teeth flashing in amusement at our amazed faces' (70). Hebron was a black lawyer from Atlanta,

Figure 13 'There was a little coal-black negress.' Illustration by Sidney Paget, *Strand Magazine*, February 1893.

'and a nobler man' Effie says, 'never walked the earth' (71). Effie left Lucy under the care of a servant in America, but after she remarried arranged for her to take up residence in the cottage, fearful that her second husband would object to the presence of a black stepdaughter. In a touching moment of reconciliation, Grant Munro responds to his wife's elaborate deception by announcing: 'I am not a very good man, Effie, but I think that I am a better one than you have given me credit for being' (72).

One of the most remarkable features of the story is the degree to which Holmes is proven wrong. Indeed, Watson warns us in the opening paragraph that this is a story of failure, or what Huh calls 'racial undetection':

> it is only natural that I should dwell rather upon his successes than upon his failures ... where he failed it happened too often that no one else succeeded, and that the tale was left for ever without a conclusion. Now and again, however, it chanced that even when he erred the truth was still discovered. (53)

The final paragraph confirms the cases's status as a failure, this time in Holmes's words: 'if it should ever strike you that I am getting a little over-confident in my powers, or giving less pains to a case than it deserves, kindly whisper "Norbury" in my ear' (72). 'The Yellow Face', then, is a story about failure as well as a story of failure: by surmising in advance of some of the facts, a practice which is actually integral to his method but which he condemns in others (notably police detectives), Holmes is shown to prejudge the case. And as Cuningham and Huh have shown in different ways, Holmes's fallibility is not incidental but thematic: Holmes, Watson, Grant Munro and Effie all prejudge the facts or the responses of each other and are forced to reappraise their assumptions. The result is almost a complete reversal of the racist argument proposed by Doyle in 'On the Slave Coast with a Camera', a point underlined by Lucy's response to her unmasking. The black girl laughs at the bewildered reactions of the white onlookers: the ethnographic gaze is reversed, and the onlookers are chastened.

The context of the story is just as important as its dramatic reversal in its climactic scene. Effie tells her story of interracial marriage in Atlanta (presumably Georgia – although some Sherlockians have ingeniously suggested that Atlanta, New York is a more plausible location for a black lawyer marrying a white woman). Effie says, 'I cut myself off from my race in order to wed him', and the racial politics of the United States are clearly important here. Grant Munro reveals to Holmes that there is no photograph of Effie's first husband because 'there was a great fire at Atlanta very shortly after his death, and all her papers were destroyed' (66) – presumably a reference to the destruction of Atlanta by the Union army under General Sherman in 1864, a turning point in the American Civil War. It is possible to construct the story's timeline to place Effie and John Hermon's marriage during the period of Congressional Reconstruction, which also forms the backdrop to the events preceding the action of 'The Five Orange Pips'. Reconstruction refers to the attempts to reform the eleven Confederate states after being readmitted to the Union following the Civil War; Congressional Reconstruction refers to the period (1866–70) when Republicans in Congress seized control of Reconstruction from President Andrew Johnson, who was set to readmit the Confederate states without requiring them to reform their race laws. The clear implication of Effie's estrangement from her 'race' is that her interracial marriage defied cultural norms if not the laws that preceded and followed the Reconstruction Era in Georgia.[15] One of Effie's misunderstandings is to assume that the attitudes prevailing in post-Civil War Georgia would be replicated in suburban Surrey: while it may stretch our credibility that Lucy would be assimilated into late nineteenth-century Norbury, that is clearly what Cuningham calls the story's didactic purpose.

'The Yellow Face', then, places racial prejudice within an epistemological frame: knowledge is not reliable or stable, but is continually subject to new information and insight. The implication is that we should remain cautious in judgement and sceptical of theories. Such a reading is supported by Doyle's own comments, in retrospect, on his West African odyssey in the early 1890s. His account in *Memories and Adventures* is mercifully free of the racist theorising of 'On the Slave Coast with a Camera', and he calls our attention to an important meeting with an unnamed American diplomat, the US Consul at Monrovia in Liberia, the 'most intelligent and well-read man whom I met on the Coast':

> My starved literary side was eager for good talk, and it was wonderful to sit on deck discussing Bancroft and Motley, and then suddenly realize that you were talking to one who had possibly been a slave himself, and was certainly the son of slaves. He had thought a good deal about African travel. 'The only way to explore Africa is to go without arms and with few servants. You would not like it in England if a body of men came armed to the teeth and marched through your land. The Africans are quite as sensitive.' ... This negro gentleman did me good, for a man's brain is an organ for the formation of his own thoughts and also for the digestion of other people's, and it needs fresh fodder.[16]

Owen Dudley Edwards has identified the Consul as Henry Highland Garnet (1815–82), a militant abolitionist who died not long after his appointment to Monrovia and his journey with Doyle. Edwards remarks that Doyle's three days with Garnet was 'perhaps the most momentous encounter he had yet sustained in the course of his life ... He had given him his first authentic voice outside his own range of experience, and the voice was black.'[17] We should not overstate the effect of the encounter on Doyle's literary performances: he wrote 'On the Slave Coast with a Camera' after meeting Garnet, and 'The Three Gables' a couple of years after recollecting the meeting in his autobiography. But Doyle's own retrospective account asserts that such encounters are intellectually nutritious, leading to growth and change. 'The Yellow Face' was his most productive response to that change – a humanistic text that celebrates the value of knowledge as a means towards empathy and sympathy.

Notes

1. The use of 'Masser' is inconsistent in the *Strand* texts: Dixie first addresses Holmes as 'Masser' and subsequently as 'Mister'. See Doyle, *The Case-Book of Sherlock Holmes*, ed. W. W. Robson, pp. 263–4.
2. Henry Cuningham, 'Sherlock Holmes and the Case of Race', p. 123. Cuningham unconvincingly seeks to acquit Doyle of racism by suggesting that he was merely invoking a tradition of stock characterisation that lived on in British and American culture for much of the twentieth century.
3. D. Martin Dakin, *A Sherlock Holmes Commentary*, p. 252.
4. Doyle, *The Case-Book of Sherlock Holmes*, ed. W. W. Robson, p. 264.
5. George Orwell, 'Rudyard Kipling' in *Collected Essays,* Vol. 2, p. 215; China Achebe, 'An Image of Africa'.
6. Lycett, *Conan Doyle*, p. 76.
7. Ibid., p. 77.
8. Conan Doyle, 'On the Slave Coast with a Camera'. For an elaboration of these points, see Jinny Huh, 'Whispers of Norbury', pp. 560–1.
9. 'On a Slave Coast with a Camera'.
10. Ibid.
11. Huh, 'Whispers of Norbury', p. 562.
12. 'On a Slave Coast with a Camera'.
13. Cuningham, 'Sherlock Holmes and the Case of Race', p. 113.
14. Doyle, *The Memoirs of Sherlock Holmes*, ed. Christopher Roden, pp. xxiv–xxv.
15. Ibid., p. xxiii.
16. Doyle, *Memories and Adventures*, pp. 55–6.
17. Owen Dudley Edwards, *The Quest for Sherlock Holmes*, p. 255. See also Huh, 'Whispers of Norbury', p. 551.

Chapter 14

The Heat of the Amazon Was Always in her Blood

For a man who never set foot there, South America seemed to exert an unusual degree of influence over Conan Doyle's imagination. His great post-imperial romance *The Lost World* was his most sustained exploration – in every sense of the word – of the imagined continent, and much can be read into his decision to locate a dinosaur-inhabited plateau in the centre of the Amazonian rainforest. For the British explorers under the leadership of Professor Challenger who set off in search of evidence of prehistoric life in the modern age, the interior of Brazil is one of the last remaining blank spaces on the map: only in such unexplored terrain can prehistory survive, untroubled by the twentieth century. The blank space exerts an irresistible appeal over the Challenger expedition, which comprises men who long to add to the world's knowledge, to their own celebrity and to their own wealth (they discover diamonds, inconveniently located in the lair of some particularly aggressive pterodactyls). Exploration in *The Lost World* is given a strikingly sexual twist: the novel's narrator, McArdle, repeatedly uses the word 'penetrate' to describe his mission, which for his part is motivated by the desire to impress a young woman called Gladys:

> we should return to London with first-hand knowledge of the central mystery of the plateau, to which I alone, of all men, would have penetrated. I thought of Gladys, with her 'There are heroisms all round us.' I seemed to hear her voice as she said it.[1]

As Louise Guenther has shown, South America was a highly sexualised continent in British culture in the long nineteenth century: its sexuality was both literal, with breathless accounts of its population of dusky and voluptuous beauties, and figurative, inviting exploration and exploitation by a virile commercial and imperial nation.[2]

Some of Doyle's other fictions exemplify this tendency. 'The Story of the Brazilian Cat', one of Doyle's most successful attempts at the horror genre which was first published in the *Strand* in 1898 (illustrated, like the Holmes stories, by Sidney Paget), features an aristocrat with the telling name of Everard King who has returned to his estate in rural Suffolk after 'an adventurous life in Brazil' where he collected both a wife and a large puma-like cat called Tommy.[3] Mrs King is de-sexualised: she is 'a tall, haggard woman' who treats the story's narrator with indifference bordering on contempt: 'Her actual words were, as a rule, courteous, but she was the possessor of a pair of particularly expressive dark eyes, and I read in them very clearly from the first that she heartily wished me back in London once more.'[4] In this story, the feminine sexuality of South America is transferred from the female Mrs King to the apparently male Tommy: he is 'as black and sleek as ebony', and 'huge, lithe' when 'fondled' by its owner.[5] Whenever he faces the cat, the narrator reveals that he cannot take his eyes from it. Everard King tricks the narrator into its cage in order to murder him for his inheritance, the cat attacking him in a strikingly sexual manner: 'One sharp, white hook tore through my trousers.' Facing almost certain death, he nonetheless feels a physical attraction: 'I found myself even at that moment admiring the sinuous grace of the devilish thing, its long, undulating, rippling movements, the gloss of its beautiful flanks, the vivid, palpitating scarlet of the glistening tongue which hung from the jet-black muzzle.'[6] The cat succeeds in wounding him and ripping off his trousers, but the narrator manages to escape, whereupon he faints, his mind drifting 'into strange, vague dreams, always with that black face and red tongue coming into them'.[7]

Despite her large expressive eyes, Mrs King is exceptional among Doyle's Latin American women for lacking sexual attractiveness. More representative is Beryl Garcia in *The Hound of the Baskervilles*, 'one of the beauties of Costa Rica' (159) who married Rodger Baskerville (the younger) in South America, and is forced to play the role of sister to her husband's assumed identity of Stapleton. As Beryl Stapleton, she is an incongruity in rural Devonshire, a point emphasised by Watson in his first encounter:

> I remembered that I had heard someone describe her as being a beauty. The woman who approached me was certainly that, and of a most uncommon type. There could not have been a greater contrast

between brother and sister, for Stapleton was neutral tinted, with light hair and grey eyes, while she was darker than any brunette whom I have seen in England – slim, elegant, and tall. She had a proud, finely cut face, so regular that it might have seemed impassive were it not for the sensitive mouth and the beautiful dark, eager eyes. With her perfect figure and elegant dress she was, indeed, a strange apparition upon a lonely moorland path. (69–70)

Beryl becomes the nearest thing in the novella to a love interest, as Sir Henry begins to pay court to her and is bemused by Stapleton's jealous reaction. But it is clear from Watson's description that her sexuality is far from that of the conventional English rose: she is 'darker' and more passionate and excitable than other young women in Watson's experience. Watson (and presumably Sir Henry) are attracted by her very extraordinariness. The extreme, feral sexuality of Tommy in 'The Brazilian Cat', and exotic, anomalous beauty of Beryl Garcia in *The Hound of the Baskervilles* are two very different expressions of the lure of the exotic that was exemplified in the period's culture by Latin American woman. This is replicated even more strongly, and insistently, in three late stories. One is Isadora Klein in 'The Three Gables', the fading society beauty whose love affair with Douglas Maberley caused the latter to waste away in broken-hearted depression. Holmes reports on her personal history:

> She was, of course, *the* celebrated beauty. There was never a woman to touch her. She is pure Spanish, the real blood of the masterful conquistadores, and her people have been leaders in Pernambuco for generations. She married the aged German sugar king, Klein, and presently found herself the richest as well as the most lovely widow upon earth. (*Case-Book*, 146)[8]

Aside from her wealth and beauty, Mrs Klein's principal attribute appears to be her sexual voracity:

> Then there was an interval of adventure when she pleased her own tastes. She had several lovers . . . But she is the '*belle dame sans merci*' of fiction. When her caprice is satisfied, the matter is ended, and if the other party in the matter can't take her word for it, she knows how to bring it home to him. (146)

As Guenther notes, British travel writing 'had long publicised the idea that Brazilian women's lustful appetites verged on depravity',[9] and Doyle drives the point home by drawing on some of the tropes associated with Eastern sexuality: Holmes and Watson confront her in 'an Arabian-nights drawing-room' (147) in her Grosvenor Square home. When haughty indifference fails to shake Holmes off, she turns to a 'charming coquettish intimacy', but Holmes is indifferent to her 'roguish and exquisite' (148) appearance.

Two other women in the late stories appear to fit this stereotype of the Latin-American femme fatale. The Peruvian Mrs Ferguson in 'The Adventure of the Sussex Vampire' (1924) and Mrs Gibson in 'Thor Bridge' are (like Isadora Klein) beautiful wives of wealthy Western men: Robert Ferguson is a successful tea-broker, and J. Neil Gibson is an American gold magnate and former senator of vast wealth. Both met their wives while in South America on business, and brought them to England to live domesticated lives in the Home Counties (West Sussex and Hampshire respectively). In both cases, however, the husband has begun to fall out of love – in Ferguson's case,

> the fact of her foreign birth and of her alien religion always caused a separation of interests and of feelings between husband and wife, so that after a time his love may have cooled towards her and he may have come to regard their union as a mistake. He felt there were sides of her character which he could never explore or understand. (*Case-Book*, 74)

Both stories also exemplify another cliché of the feral South American woman: in Guenther's words, 'to remove such a creature from her natural environment was to invite disaster'.[10] Guenther traces this trope back to Charlotte Bronte's *Jane Eyre*, a novel which hovers behind several of the Holmes stories, most obviously 'The Copper Beeches': Bertha Mason, Rochester's Jamaican-born first wife, was

> the boast of Spanish Town for her beauty . . . a fine woman . . . tall, dark and majestic. Her family wished to secure me because I was of a good race and so did she . . . my senses were excited; and being ignorant, raw, and inexperienced, I thought I loved her.[11]

A similar stereotype can also be found in 'The Second Stain', in which Eduardo Lucas is murdered by his wife who is 'of Creole origin', 'of an extremely excitable nature', and who 'has suffered in the past from attacks of jealousy which have amounted to frenzy' (*Return*, 305). But it is Mrs Ferguson in 'The Sussex Vampire' who most resembles Bertha, confined to her bedroom and forbidden from seeing her baby son who is kept in the charge of the nurse, a 'tall, gaunt woman' (84) called, significantly enough, Mrs Mason.

'The Sussex Vampire' and 'Thor Bridge' are also connected in a more fundamental way: both use the presence of exotic femininity in a narrative strategy of misdirection, or what we might call the art of the red herring. In both cases, the deception depends on the same set of cultural assumptions that Doyle appeared to indulge and reproduce in *The Hound of the Baskervilles* and 'The Three Gables'. Robert Ferguson's baby son is apparently being attacked by his own mother, who is seen sucking blood from his neck: her origin marks her as alien and exotic, and her presence is the obvious explanation for the outbreak of bizarre, psychotic or even supernatural violence in the rural domain of the Sussex wolds. This juxtaposition of the mundane and the extraordinary, the traditional and the exotic is signalled in the story's title and is evident throughout but it is particularly stark in Watson's first impressions of Cheeseman's, Ferguson's 'isolated and ancient farmhouse', in which an 'odour of age and decay pervaded the whole crumbling building'. Inside, Watson sees 'half-panelled walls' that 'may well have belonged to the original yeoman farmer of the seventeenth century', and above them 'there was hung a fine collection of South American utensils and weapons, which had been brought, no doubt, by the Peruvian lady upstairs' (80). But while the facts of the case suggest that the vampire of the story is Mrs Ferguson, this description is one of a series of clues that reveal what is really happening at Cheeseman's. The culprit is in fact Jacky, Ferguson's disabled son by his first marriage, who parasitically draws on his father's indulgent love while expressing jealous hatred and fear of anyone and everything else in his father's life. Holmes pointedly asks him whether he likes Mrs Mason, and Jacky's 'expressive mobile face shadowed over, and he shook his head' (85). Jacky experiments on the family dog with his murder weapon, an arrow (stolen from his parents' collection) dipped in curare 'or some other devilish drug' (87). But his principal victims are his stepbrother and stepmother – one he tries to kill, and the other he frames as an insane monster.

Although South America happens to be the source of the weapon, the evil behind the crime is not exotic but traditional and local. Jacky is, we discover, merely an extreme version of the spoiled brat, his relationship with his father corrupted into 'a distorted love, a maniacal exaggerated love for you, and possibly for his dead mother' (87). While his disability may help explain Ferguson's over-indulgence, it also stands as an emblem of the family's degeneration, a counterpart to the 'uneven floors sagged into sharp curves' of the 'crumbling building'. Just as Matilda Briggs in the solicitor's letter which begins the case is not a woman but a ship, so the Sussex

Vampire is not the hot-blooded South American, but a cold-blooded teenager from a well-to-do English family living in rural prosperity. This is a story of Englishness gone bad, not the irruption into the home counties of sinister, alien or supernatural forces. Far from being a bloodsucker, Mrs Ferguson is actually a source of new blood for the family, replenishing the stock that had become so degenerate as to produce an overindulgent father and a jealous, physically weakened son.

The misdirection strategy is obvious enough in 'The Sussex Vampire' but a little more nuanced in 'Thor Bridge'. Once more, our attention centres on a woman whose South American origin is not merely a biographical fact but her essential defining characteristic: Maria Gibson is the apparent victim of murder, and her identity and behaviour lies at the heart of the story's problem. Even before Holmes's client – Neil Gibson, a Cecil Rhodes-like American plutocrat – has arrived at Baker Street, one of Gibson's disgruntled employees, Bates, turns up in Baker Street to vilify his boss and to disclose Maria Gibson's victimisation by her husband. In doing so, Bates portrays her as having a stereotypically Latin temperament:

> She was a creature of the Tropics, a Brazilian by birth, as no doubt you know? . . . Tropical by birth and tropical by nature. A child of the sun and of passion. She had loved him as such women can love, but when her own physical charms had faded – I am told that they once were great – there was nothing to hold him. (28)

When Gibson tells his side of the story, he emphasises the same point but for a different purpose: rather than elicit sympathy for the dead woman, he needs to explain the collapse of their marriage:

> I met my wife when I was gold-hunting in Brazil. Maria Pinto was the daughter of a Government official at Manaos, and she was very beautiful. I was young and ardent in those days, but even now, as I look back with colder blood and a more critical eye, I can see that she was rare and wonderful in her beauty. It was a deep rich nature, too, passionate, wholehearted, tropical, ill-balanced, very different from the American women whom I had known. Well, to make a long story short, I loved her and I married her. It was only when the romance had passed – and it lingered for years – that I realized that we had nothing – absolutely nothing – in common. My love faded. If hers had faded also it might have been easier. But you know the wonderful way of women! Do what I might nothing could turn her from me. If I have been harsh to her, even brutal as some have said, it has been because I knew that if I could kill her love, or if it turned to

Figure 14 'She poured her whole wild fury out in burning and horrible words –' Illustration by Alfred Gilbert, *Strand Magazine*, March 1922.

hate, it would be easier for both of us. But nothing changed her. She adored me in those English woods as she had adored me twenty years ago on the banks of the Amazon. Do what I might, she was devoted as ever. (32–3)

What Gibson is doing here is seeking to justify his own conduct while trying to save the life of Grace Dunbar, the Gibsons' beautiful governess and the motive for Mrs Gibson's sexual jealousy. Holmes goes to some lengths to ensure Gibson spells out his sexual interest in Miss Dunbar, although Gibson suggests that there was justification for 'soul-jealousy' but not 'body-jealousy', implying that he loved the governess but had not succeeded in seducing her. Gibson's framing of his marital relationship is striking: he looks on her with 'colder blood', but her blood never cools:

She was crazy with hatred, and the heat of the Amazon was always in her blood. She might have planned to murder Miss Dunbar – or we will say to threaten her with a gun and so frighten her into leaving us. Then there might have been a scuffle and the gun gone off and shot the woman who held it. (35)

Gibson thus presents himself as rational and his wife as irrational, drawing on an identification of Latin American women with South America's natural environment, 'with its unpredictable tempests and vast, unmapped jungles of disturbing flora and dangerous fauna'.[12] More fundamentally, there is also a strong suggestion here of discredited Lamarckian theories of biological inheritance, which imagined that humans could pass on characteristics acquired in their lifetimes to their offspring, and which were particularly strong in British culture during the heyday of degeneration in the late nineteenth century: Maria Gibson's temperament is biologically determined, but by her Amazonian environment rather than her Spanish descent.

At this point, Holmes's investigation suggests two possible explanations: that Gibson murdered a woman he had married for her sexual attractiveness but who no longer satisfied his desire for youth and beauty, or that Grace Dunbar killed Maria Gibson in self-defence. The first scenario invokes the famed sexuality of South American women, while the second depends on the same stereotyped assumptions about their temperament and essential nature examined in 'The Sussex Vampire'. The latter explanation appears to be confirmed when Holmes and Watson interview the chief suspect, Grace Dunbar, in prison in Winchester. Watson's presentation of her invokes a diametrically opposed stereotype, that of the well-bred English rose – she is 'a brunette, tall, with a noble figure and commanding presence' with a 'strong, clear-cut and yet sensitive face, that even should she be capable of some impetuous deed, none the less there was an innate nobility of character which would make her influence always for the good' (41). This description invokes every cliché of the strong-yet-sensitive genteel English lady in order to impress upon us that she is both truthful and virtuous. So when she, too, analyses Maria Gibson's character, her words carry special weight:

> She hated me, Mr Holmes. She hated me with all the fervour of her tropical nature. She was a woman who would do nothing by halves, and the measure of her love for her husband was the measure also of her hatred for me. . . . I would not wish to wrong her, but she loved so vividly in a physical sense that she could hardly understand the mental, and even spiritual, tie which held her husband to me, or imagine that it was only my desire to influence his power to good ends which kept me under his roof. (42)

In one respect, Neil Gibson and Grace Dunbar are both correct: Maria is a woman deeply in love with her husband and consumed with jealous hatred of her rival. But the repeated emphasis on her 'tropical nature', her passion and her physicality at the expense of her mental capabilities directs our attention away from the possibility that she was clever, ingenious and patient. Without these qualities she could never have devised the stratagem of the pistol tied to a stone which would ensure the murder weapon would remove itself from the scene of the crime, so that in a single coup she would kill both herself and – she intended – her rival by framing her for murder. Holmes ignores all of the assumptions about tropical natures and approaches the case purely as an investigative problem: by assuming all those involved in the case have acted rationally, he realises immediately that Grace Dunbar would never have concealed the murder weapon in her own wardrobe, and that Maria Gibson was capable of careful and extended planning.

Maria Gibson's hot blood, then, is a myth: she is every bit as cold-blooded as her husband. But her cold-bloodedness is justified in part by the fact that she is so clearly a victim as well as a perpetrator. A loving wife and the mother of two children, she refuses to accept her husband's altered feelings; he then uses mental cruelty to force a change in her emotions, without success. Although he claims that Grace Dunbar's influence is reforming him, Neil Gibson makes no secret of his exploitative nature: 'I can make or break and it is usually break. It wasn't individuals only. It was communities, cities, even nations. Business is a hard game, and the weak go to the wall' (34). Neil Gibson's conduct and behaviour – Holmes treats him with particular disdain in Baker Street – shows that this story is a moral as well as logical problem. Gibson is accused of immorality by Bates, by Holmes and, in effect, by himself when he admits to his harshness and brutality towards Maria: violence and cruelty are not confined to the victim-perpetrator and conveniently tidied away when Holmes solves the case, but are a function of social hierarchy and economic power relations.

Nor is it any accident that the Gold King is American. Britain had exercised considerable political and economic power in South America throughout the nineteenth century to the point that large parts of the continent became part of what historians today describe as Britain's 'informal empire', but from the beginning of the twentieth century it was challenged and then overtaken by American commercial investment and state intervention. As in Joseph Conrad's geopolitical novel of South American finance, precious metals and revolution, *Nostromo* (1904), where the maker and unmaker of communities and nations is an American capitalist operating from San Francisco, 'Thor Bridge' offers us 'the greatest financial power in the world' (26) who operates a globalised economic power network from an estate in Hampshire. Neil Gibson's marriage is emblematic, almost allegorical, of a globalised world in which the weak go to the wall if they fail to meet the imperious demands of the modern-day capitalist conquistadores. Maria Gibson's reversal of the Latin American stereotype is her resistance to her husband's exploitative schemes: in effect, she tries to beat him at his own game. Thanks to Holmes, she fails, and Gibson is free to resume his sexual and financial depredations.

Notes

1. Doyle, *The Lost World*, p. 168.
2. Louise Guenther, 'The Artful Seductions of Informal Empire', pp. 208–28.
3. Doyle, *Round the Fire Stories*, p. 159.
4. Ibid., p. 161.
5. Ibid., pp. 165–6.
6. Ibid., pp. 176–8.
7. Ibid., p. 181.
8. Pernambuco is a state in north-east Brazil. Mrs King in 'The Brazilian Cat' also hails from the state, and returns there to take the veil after her husband is killed and eaten by Tommy.
9. Guenther, 'Artful Seductions', p. 224.
10. Ibid., p. 224.
11. Qtd in Guenther, 'Artful Seductions', p. 225.
12. Guenther, 'Artful Seductions', p. 224.

Part VI: War

Chapter 15

This Circle of Misery and Violence and Fear

'The Cardboard Box' is a strange story with an unusual textual history. First published in the *Strand Magazine* in January 1893, it was the only story of the series left out of the first English edition of *The Memoirs of Sherlock Holmes* (published by George Newnes later the same year). It made it into the first American edition, published by Harper in 1894, only to be removed from later American editions. Its disappearance from the *Memoirs* led to some significant cutting and pasting: a nineteen-paragraph exchange between Holmes and Watson in Baker Street was taken from the opening of 'The Cardboard Box' and moved to 'The Adventure of the Resident Patient' (1893), where it replaced one and a half paragraphs of introductory material, changing the setting of 'The Resident Patient' from a 'boisterous' autumn to a boiling summer (and causing some strange meteorological phenomena in the process). 'The Cardboard Box' remained suppressed for over two decades. Its inclusion in *His Last Bow* in 1917, making up the weight of what would otherwise have been a slim volume, is an anomalous intrusion of the nineteenth century into stories written in and often explicitly concerned with the twentieth: 'His Last Bow', for example, is set in 1914, features a motor car, and mentions aeroplanes, Zeppelins, and Marconi. 'The Cardboard Box' is also textually anomalous, and has created particular problems for Doyle's editors. Does it belong in *The Memoirs* or *His Last Bow*? Should the long passage attached to 'The Resident Patient' remain in that story, or revert to its original location? (Some collected editions of the Holmes stories allowed it to remain in both.) Behind these questions lies a much more fundamental one: why did Doyle have second thoughts about the story in 1893, before deciding to reinstate it to the Holmes saga in 1917?

Doyle himself gave conflicting, and unconvincing, explanations. In one letter he said that the story, in which Jim Browner murders his wife Mary Cushing and her lover Alex Fairbairn, and then takes a grotesque revenge on his sister-in-law, 'is rather more sensational than I care for'; in another he said that 'a tale involving sex was out of place in a collection designed for boys'. But elsewhere Doyle also said that the story was too 'weak' to be included in the *Memoirs*.[1] Critics have generally been sceptical of these claims: Christopher Roden, for instance, points out that there is plenty of material unsuitable for boys in other stories, and protests that there is nothing weak about 'The Cardboard Box'.[2] Certainly its major clue – a box, filled with coarse salt, containing two severed ears, one from a man, another from a woman – is as memorable as any in the saga, while the confession of guilt by Jim Browner is an almost naturalistic tale of sexual jealousy and human frailty. Moreover, Watson draws attention to the story's sensationalism in his introduction, but his apologetic explanation of his duty to present a record of the case, far from undermining its legitimacy, serves instead to whet the reader's appetite for the lurid details to come. Roden speculates that Doyle's decision was influenced 'by sensitivity within his family over the question of violence brought about by alcoholism'.[3] And given Charles Altamont Doyle's decades of drunken marriage and parenthood, and his unhappy end in a sanatorium, this is a tempting explanation – until we recall that alcoholics, including very violent ones, are rather common in the Holmes saga. Watson's older brother in *The Sign of Four* is a sad case of alcoholism, but more brutish ones include Toller in 'The Copper Beeches', Black Peter, and Sir Eustace Brackenstall in 'The Abbey Grange'.

No single explanation seems to suffice, leaving us to speculate with Roden as to whether some personal event occurred between serial and volume publication to change Doyle's view of his own story. But we also need to account for why Doyle saw fit to reuse substantial material from 'The Cardboard Box' in 'The Resident Patient'. The passage in question is one of the most impressive displays of Holmes's inferential logic: he appears to read Watson's mind, but then explains that he was merely observing Watson's eyes and facial expressions to infer his thoughts. In addition to his human subject, Holmes benefits from three items of data: Watson's new, framed portrait of General Charles Gordon, his unframed portrait of Henry Ward Beecher and his wound from his service in the Second Afghan War. Watson glances at the portraits, touches his wound and displays a series of contrasting facial expressions, enabling Holmes to deduce, correctly, that Watson was thinking first of the glory, and then of the folly of war. Doyle's reuse of this material suggests that he was sufficiently proud of it to want it preserved in the volume version, at the cost of an awkward fit to another story.

Doyle's presumably high opinion of the passage is, though, hard to reconcile with Holmes's own views. The literary source for the passage, acknowledged by Holmes, is Poe's 'The Murders in the Rue Morgue', in which Dupin infers the thought processes of the narrator during a stroll in central Paris: as Holmes observes, 'when I read you the passage in one of Poe's sketches in which a close reasoner follows the unspoken thoughts of his companion, you were inclined to treat the matter as a mere *tour-de-force* of the author' (*Memoirs*, 31). What is surprising here is that Holmes also deprecated Dupin's method, as we know from *A Study in Scarlet*: 'Dupin was a very inferior fellow. That trick of his of breaking in on his friends' thoughts with an apropos remark after a quarter of an hour's silence is really very showy and superficial' (21). Although Holmes shrugs off his own demonstration in 'The Cardboard Box' as merely 'superficial', his imitation of Dupin's tour de force demonstrates the enormous skill apparently at work – an almost superhuman sensitivity to non-verbal signals from human subjects. As a demonstration of what Holmes calls the science of deduction, this was simply too good to discard, whatever the problems with the rest of 'The Cardboard Box'.

This passage is not, however, an easily detachable instance of Holmes's inferential technique, as is evident not only from its uncomfortable fit in 'The Resident Patient' but also from its thematic links to the rest of 'The Cardboard Box'. One such link provides the basis to an ingenious reading of the story (and its suppression) by Christopher Metress, who argues that the story '*had* to disappear' because it threatened to undermine the whole rationalist project that the Holmes stories were brought into being to promote by 'celebrating the power of reason'.[4] 'The Cardboard Box' appears to follow the standard trajectory of a Holmes story: the client's unusual problem leads to an investigation, which seems to generate more complexity and mystery, before Holmes's solution delivers a rational, simple explanation. 'The Cardboard Box' is different, though, in two ways. First, Browner is himself an unofficial detective: he follows a series of clues to detect his wife's adultery; he pursues the guilty parties to a dramatic confrontation; he even parallels Holmes's thought-reading demonstration when he realises Sarah Cushing's jealous love for him: 'I looked into her eyes and I read it all there. There was no need for her to speak, nor for me either'

(48). Browner's investigations, however, lead not to knowledge and resolution, but to the brutal deaths of his wife and her lover Alec Fairbairn, and thereby to his own incarceration or execution, and possibly madness. Second, Holmes's reaction to reading Browner's confession is unprecedented:

> 'What is the meaning of it, Watson?' said Holmes, solemnly, as he laid down the paper. 'What object is served by this circle of misery and violence and fear? It must tend to some end, or else our universe is ruled by chance, which is unthinkable. But what end? There is the great standing perennial problem to which human reason is as far from an answer as ever.' (52)

No other cases of murder or mayhem seem to inspire Holmes to such soul-searching philosophical eloquence, so there must be something particularly powerful in Browner's confession. For Metress, it is the implication that the application of human reason does not necessarily lead to a vision of order, but may reveal instead a kind of labyrinth (implied by Holmes's metaphor of the circle), which may even be 'maliciously designed'.[5]

There are several objections that can be advanced against Metress's argument: in particular, it follows Rosemary Jann's influential reading of the Holmes saga as straightforwardly inscribing and celebrating positivistic science. But he is persuasive in showing that we cannot understand the anomalous status of 'The Cardboard Box' without examining the whole story, and the relationship between its constituent parts (the mind-reading demonstration, the investigation, Browner's confession and Holmes's philosophical coda). Metress is right to identify the coda as the most important clue in the unsolved mystery of the story's suppression, but this is also open to a rather different interpretation.

Holmes suggests that Browner's story is but one instance in a repeating pattern ('circle') of 'misery and violence and fear', suggesting that these conditions are constants in human experience. But Holmes may also mean that they constitute a vicious, mutually reinforcing circle: the misery of, say, poverty or alcoholism can lead to physical violence, and the fear of violence begets more misery. Holmes embeds this observation in a question: what is the purpose of these wholly negative emotions and behaviours and conditions in an ordered universe? He dismisses the notion of a random, Schopenhauerian universe as 'unthinkable': Holmes is no radical sceptic, but is making a secular enquiry into theodicy, or the problem of evil, which has long preoccupied philosophers of religion. If God is omnipotent, omniscient and benevolent, how can He

Figure 15 Illustration by Sidney Paget, *Strand Magazine*, January 1893.

permit the existence of evil? Holmes leaves God out of the question, but his suggestion of a universal order implies a purpose to creation. Also important is the fact that Holmes seems to accept that we cannot yet answer the question ('human reason is as far from an answer as ever'). This suggests that we can do no more than treat the story of Browner and the Cushing sisters as yet more evidence of the existence of evil – human enquiry into the purpose of evil remains inadequate, despite it having been examined by philosophers from Epicurus onwards.

Working backwards – as Holmes himself does in the case (42) – we come next to Browner's confession. Although we may not be able to explain why evil exists, Browner's narrative casts valuable light on how it manifests itself. On the face of it, the narrative is simple enough: Sarah Cushing's unrequited love for Browner turns to jealous hatred, so she interferes in his domestic arrangements, turning her sister Mary against her husband, which causes him to take again to the bottle. Sarah introduces into the household Alec Fairbairn, whose name betokens his handsome charm, and then creates opportunities at her own lodging house for Alec to meet Mary, causing more jealous rage on Browner's part. Browner by chance then sees his wife and Fairbairn in a cab, so he follows them: they take a pleasure boat, he sets off in pursuit, and beats them both to death before removing his grisly trophies to be used to torment Sarah in revenge. The facts of the confession are grim enough, but Browner's interpretation of his own actions is telling. He prefaces his account with an admission of his alcoholism, which he presents as an animalistic condition: 'I know that I went back to drink, like the beast that I was' (47). Relating the unplanned murder of his wife after shattering Fairbairn's skull with his heavy oak stick, he again reveals his bestial nature: 'I was like a wild beast then that had tasted blood' (51). Finally, in narrating the post-mortem amputation of their ears, he admits to feeling 'a kind of savage joy when I thought how Sarah would feel when she had such signs as these of what her meddling had brought about' (51–2). But Browner is clearly no animal, as his anguish after the murders shows: he has a conscience, and remains haunted by the faces of the two people he has killed. His self-ascribed bestiality suggests, then, that his savage passion (potentially exacerbated by drink) is part of his emotional character, sometimes held in check, sometimes not. Holmes's final comment thus provides a gloss on what might be considered an isolated case: Browner is not a universal type, but cases of this kind nonetheless recur.

When we come to Holmes's investigation, we find that even before Holmes has deduced Browner's role, he and Watson consider this to be a case involving savage passions: Holmes dismisses Lestrade's favoured explanation of a medical student's practical joke, prompting Watson to reflect that the 'brutal preliminary seemed to shadow forth some strange and inexplicable horror in the background' (37). The horror, however, swiftly becomes all too explicable – Susan Cushing (oldest of the three sisters, and recipient by mischance of the severed ears) foreshadows the solution by revealing that 'a little drink' would send Browner 'stark, staring mad' (39), and Holmes swiftly identifies jealousy as 'the motive for the crime' (44).

Finally, we come to the story's overture: Holmes's demonstration of apparent mind-reading. How does this seemingly light-hearted passage relate to the grim material that follows? And are the portraits of Beecher and Gordon purely incidental, or part of the story's thematic design? In the case of Beecher, there is the intriguing fact that his sister, the novelist Harriet Beecher Stowe, once received a severed ear in the post.[6] But it is more important that Beecher was, for Conan Doyle as for many Victorians, a hugely admirable figure, for his stand on Abolitionism and for the events which Holmes deduces to be on Watson's mind: Beecher's British speaking tour during the American Civil War (conducted at the behest of Abraham Lincoln himself) to build international support for the Union's cause. Conan Doyle may well have witnessed Beecher's famous oratory in action, in Portsmouth in 1886.[7] And although Beecher was linked to numerous mistresses, the Beecher-Tilton Scandal, which culminated in Beecher being sued for adultery in 1875, was inconclusive (the jury in the case failing to return a verdict). There can be no doubt from Holmes's deductions that Beecher was, for him and for Watson, a great man: 'I remember your expressing your passionate indignation at the way in which he was received by the more turbulent of our people' (32). In the context of the 1890s, Gordon was an even more admirable figure: he was, simply, the most eulogised figure of the late nineteenth century.

There is no need to go hunting for ingenious linkages between the mind-reading passage and the rest of the story, as Holmes himself supplies the connection: as he deduces, war occupies Watson's thoughts at the beginning of the story. The three wars in question – in America, Sudan and Afghanistan – were all ones that fascinated Conan Doyle, and it is hardly surprising that they should feature in Watson's thoughts and in the story. The siege of Khartoum (1884–5) and the fall of the European garrison commanded by Gordon was among the most traumatic military or political events of the period, costing Gladstone his second premiership and leading to the failed Gordon Relief Expedition – a campaign which forms the scenario for one of Conan Doyle's best war stories, 'The Green Flag', published less than six months after 'The Cardboard Box'. Doyle would remain preoccupied with the Sudan until the Khalifa Abdullahi's regime was destroyed by the British invasion at the end of the decade: his thriller *The Tragedy of the Korosko* (1897), serialised in the *Strand* (with illustrations by Sidney Paget) during the long interregnum between 'The Final Problem' and *The Hound of the Baskervilles*, tells of the primeval cruelty of the Dervishes, who kidnap a group of Western tourists holidaying in Upper Egypt, at the historical moment when Kitchener's forces had issued forth to destroy them. In fact, Doyle witnessed in 1896 some of their preparations as the hastily accredited correspondent of the *Westminster Gazette*, experiences which he would use in his short story 'The Three Correspondents', published the same year, although his journalism on this occasion was cut short by Kitchener himself, who told him that he would be unlikely to see very much and would be better off back in London. All this, however, was still in the future when Doyle wrote 'The Cardboard Box': in 1892, the death of General Gordon was part of Britain's unfinished imperialist business. Gordon's portrait is a reminder to its owner of the risks but also the necessity of war for a major imperial power.

Watson's contemplation of Beecher's unframed portrait – more unfinished business – leads him to an involved consideration of martial ethics as demonstrated during the American Civil War. Although Watson has no first-hand knowledge of this conflict, imagining it causes his lips to set, his eyes to sparkle and his hands to clench. Holmes says, 'I was positive that you were indeed thinking of the gallantry which was shown by both sides in that desperate struggle' (32). The opportunities presented by war for men to display what is best and noblest in their natures is a major theme of Doyle's fiction and non-fiction, from the historical novels *The White Company* (1891) and *Sir Nigel* (1906) to the future-war story 'Danger!' (1914), and from his Boer War pamphlet of 1902 to his First World War history, *The British Campaign in France and Flanders* (1916–20). He also examines the theme in a comic mode in the Brigadier Gerard stories, and in drama with *The Story of Waterloo* (1907). Doyle never tired of examining the rights and wrongs of the conduct of war, and was attached emotionally and strongly to the British army: as Douglas Kerr has observed, Doyle 'knew more about the army, and had seen it at closer quarters, than most civilians', and he 'loved it unconditionally, all his life, with a boy's love'.[8] But as 'The Cardboard Box' demonstrates, his love for military heroics was not confined to British forces: for Doyle, heroism was an absolute value, and not the exclusive prerogative of any single nation.

'The Cardboard Box' also points to another side of warfare. Under Holmes's gaze, Watson's face grows sadder and he shakes his head: 'You were dwelling upon the sadness and horror and useless waste of life' (32–3). The vast numbers of casualties – some estimates put deaths alone at over a million – made the American Civil War the emblematic 'waste of life' of the Victorian age: this rare acknowledgement that war may be a waste as well as a heroic opportunity is particularly appropriate in this context. And Watson's mental journey does not end there: the physical reminder of his wound from a *jezail* bullet during the Battle of Maiwand (1880) in the Second Anglo-Afghan War causes a smile to quiver on his lips which, Holmes comments, 'showed me that the ridiculous side of this method of settling international questions had forced itself upon your mind' (33). This sentiment takes us far from the moral universe of *The White Company* and closer to that of the vainglorious (but consistently entertaining) Etienne Gerard, who would replace

Holmes as a serial character in the *Strand* from December 1894 to December 1895. Watson's wound, received during a nasty imperial defeat – Kipling's surviving soldier in 'That Day' (*Barrack-Room Ballads*, 1892) recalls that 'along the line o' flight they cut us up like sheep'[9] – seems an unlikely stimulus to a reflection on the absurdities of conflict. It suggests, perhaps, a sense of superiority: Ayub Khan's victory at Maiwand was a pyrrhic one, as the Afghan losses – five times those of the British forces – weakened them so severely that the British force under Field Marshal Roberts was able comprehensively to defeat Khan at Kandahar a month later. Alternatively, it may suggest futility: the conflict also caused the British to finally realise that they could not control Afghanistan.

But how does this connect to the story of Jim Browner, his alcoholism and his disastrous ménage with Mary and Sarah Cushing? Browner is Doyle's portrait of the human animal stripped to reveal its primeval urges of lust and violence; his employment in the merchant navy is the only barrier to his exercising his bestial passions. The prelude in Baker Street suggests that the story will examine some aspect of war, but what follows is an examination of a waste of life in a distinctly suburban setting. That 'The Cardboard Box' is reaching for a higher purpose than simply telling a tale of grim detection is obvious from Holmes's philosophical coda, but the fact that we cannot reliably decipher that coda's significance suggests that there is something missing in the story – a more obvious connection between war, the base elements of humanity and the purpose of existence. Doyle's suppression of the story for nearly twenty-five years may be accounted for by a craftsman's sense of an imperfectly shaped work. But with the vast destruction of humanity on the Western Front at the forefront of his mind, a story which so precariously links human nature with the urge for violence may suddenly have acquired a new relevance.

Notes

1. Christopher Redmond, *Sherlock Holmes Handbook*, 2nd edn (Toronto: Dundurn Press, 2009), p. 20.
2. Christopher Roden, 'Introduction' in Doyle, *The Memoirs of Sherlock Holmes*, pp. xx–xxi.
3. Ibid, p. xxi.
4. Christopher Metress, 'Thinking the Unthinkable: Reopening Conan Doyle's "Cardboard Box"', *The Midwest Quarterly* 42.2 (2001), 183–98, p. 185.

5. Ibid., p. 195. Metress goes on to stretch the point by suggesting the story's human ears as labyrinthine symbols of its themes of outward order and inner inexplicability.
6. See Doyle, *The Memoirs of Sherlock Holmes*, ed. Christopher Roden, pp. 280–2.
7. Ibid., p. 281.
8. Kerr, *Conan Doyle*, p. 173.
9. Kipling, *Rudyard Kipling's Verse*, p. 497.

Chapter 16

Do We Progress?

James Mortimer, Holmes's client in *The Hound of the Baskervilles*, is no ordinary general practitioner. Consulting the *Medical Directory*, Watson finds him to be the author of several learned essays: 'Is Disease a Reversion?', winner of the Jackson Prize for Comparative Pathology, and 'Some Freaks of Atavism' and 'Do We Progress?', published in *The Lancet* and *Journal of Psychology* respectively. It thus hardly seems fair for Holmes to characterise him as a mere 'country doctor' (6). Mortimer's publication history is highly revealing, both about his own scientific world view and that of the novel. Keywords in the essays' titles – 'reversion', 'atavism' and 'progress' – clearly indicate that these are investigations in evolutionary biology. More specifically, Mortimer is interested in the possibility that human evolution can actually go into reverse, producing degenerate specimens of the human race, descending down the evolutionary ladder into the animal kingdom, or afflicted by genetic conditions that cause abnormalities ('freaks') or disease.

Blessed with a twenty-first-century view of such pseudoscience, we might conclude that Mortimer is a crank, an impression apparently confirmed by one of his first actions in the story – running his finger along Holmes's 'parietal fissure', while exclaiming, 'It is not my intention to be fulsome, but I confess that I covet your skull' (8). This causes even Watson to characterise him as 'strange'. Skulls, we discover, are Mortimer's 'special hobby'. He claims to be able to read skulls as accurately as Holmes can read typefaces, so that he can easily distinguish 'the skull of a negro from that of an Esquimaux' (32). Mortimer's 'special hobby' resembles that of a close contemporary, the sinister doctor in Conrad's 'Heart of Darkness' (1899), who eagerly measures Marlow's skull 'in the interests of science' before the latter's journey into the interior of Africa.[1] Mortimer, however, is a character in a very different kind of tale. Conrad's phrenologist is the scientific representative of a racist, imperialist ideology, exploiting the people and resources of a vast region. Mortimer, if he represents anything in *The Hound of the Baskervilles*, represents modern science.

We can say this with some confidence as the novella repeatedly validates Mortimer's views. Mortimer praises Holmes as 'the second highest expert in Europe' (9), the top position being held by the criminologist Alphonse Bertillon, pioneer of measurement as a means of documenting and categorising the criminal body, for whom Holmes had earlier (in 'The Naval Treaty') 'expressed his enthusiastic admiration' (*Memoirs*, 235). While Bertillon's biometric techniques were genuinely pioneering, and were only superseded as a means of identification by the adoption of fingerprinting at the beginning of the twentieth century, his theories rested on the belief that criminal behaviour was caused by faulty genes and was marked and readable on the human body.

The Hound of the Baskervilles presents a case study that confirms Mortimer's theories and Bertillon's. The convicted murderer Selden, being sheltered on Dartmoor after his escape from Princeton by his sister and brother-in-law, is glimpsed by Watson and Sir Henry Baskerville:

> there was thrust out an evil yellow face, a terrible animal face, all seamed and scored with vile passions. Foul with mire, with a bristling beard, and hung with matted hair, it might well have belonged to one of those old savages who dwelt in the burrows on the hill-sides. The light beneath him was reflected in his small, cunning eyes, which peered fiercely to right and left through the darkness, like a crafty and savage animal who has heard the steps of the hunters. (97)

Here is living, biological proof that answers the question posed in the title of Mortimer's essay, 'Do We Progress?' Selden is evidence of atavism, biological reversion to lower forms of life, signalled by the label of 'animal' being applied to him twice in three sentences. Importantly, Watson suggests he is a reversion in time as well as in development, to an age of 'savages' and humans as hunter-gatherers.[2] But Selden is not the only instance of biological atavism in the novella. Collectively, the various Baskervilles we meet or hear about demonstrate that immorality is genetically inherited: the villainous Stapleton is, we discover, an alias used by the son of Rodger Baskerville, the 'black sheep of the family' and scion 'of the old, masterful Baskerville strain' (23). This suggests that this Rodger was the heir of the 'wild, profane, and godless' (11) Hugo Baskerville's villainy, an impression supported by

Figure 16 '"Good heavens!" I cried, in amazement.' Illustration by Sidney Paget, *Strand Magazine*, March 1902.

the recurrence of the names Hugo and Rodger in the Baskerville family line.[3] Stapleton's true identity becomes clear to Holmes and Watson in one of the novella's most brilliant *coups de théâtre*, when they contemplate a portrait of Hugo Baskerville: Holmes conceals Hugo's hat with his arm and Watson records his amazement: 'The face of Stapleton had sprung out of the canvas' (139). This moment echoes the spectral portraits of Gothic fictions such as *The Castle of Otranto* (1764), but it also offers a vivid metaphor of the past intruding on the present. Holmes explains that Stapleton is 'an interesting instance of a throwback' (139), a genetic reversion, but he also suggests the re-emergence of the ancient past in the modern present.

This notion of temporal reversion is crucial to the novella's ideological significance. A fear that evolution could be thrown into reverse, and that this may already be occurring among sections of the population, was widespread in Britain and Europe when Doyle was writing. That Britons in particular were deteriorating was, by the turn of the century, held by many to be self-evident: the disagreement was over whether the causes were environmental or hereditary. Sir James Cantlie (1851–1926), a pioneer of first aid and of the study of tropical disease, and (like Mortimer) a surgeon at the Charing Cross Hospital (Mortimer from1882 to 1884, Cantlie from 1877 to 1888), was one of the most eminent figures to argue for environment. His first foray into the topic, a paper given in 1885 called 'Degeneration amongst Londoners', attributed physical decline particularly to the air quality of industrial cities. But others saw degeneracy as a genetic phenomenon, with the most notorious articulation of this theory coming from the Paris-based physician and social critic Max Nordau, whose *Degeneration* (*Entartung*, 1892) ran to seven editions in six months on first appearing in English in 1895. This extended the concept of biological reversion to Western culture, claiming that art and letters were, along with the human species, reverting to an uncivilised type. But Mortimer's theories, and Watson's description of Selden, go further than merely suggesting genetic degradation. By conjuring the fears of a return to a primeval past, the novella places the degeneration idea in a highly political context that reflects contemporary debates and Conan Doyle's own experiences as an observer and a participant in Britain's turn-of-the-century wars in Africa.

The novella presents a stark and highly ideological distinction between the forces of progress and civilisation, and the forces of primeval disorder. The former comprise Holmes, Watson, Mortimer and the American Sir Henry Baskerville, whose first words on seeing the gloomy ancestral home is to promise illumination from 'a thousand-candle-power Swan and Edison right here in front of the hall door' (57). The domain of progress is London, with its modern hotels, art galleries, steam engines and hansom cabs, post and messenger offices, shops selling exotic tobacco and Ordnance Survey maps, and newspapers carrying articles on free trade. On the side of primeval disorder are Stapleton, Selden and the hound itself. First presented to us from the pages of the eighteenth-century manuscript, the hound haunts the imagination of Sir Charles Baskerville and, according to Stapleton, the inhabitants of Grimpen and its environs. Although its spectral reappearance is the result of a very modern application of phosphorescent paint, that is not how it appears to Inspector Lestrade, who throws himself onto the ground in fright, or Watson, for whom the spectacle conjures up primal terrors: 'Never in the delirious dream of a disordered brain could anything more savage, more appalling, more hellish, be conceived than that dark form and savage face which broke upon us out of the wall of fog' (150–1). Again, Watson repeats a keyword: the hound is savage in more than one sense. It is a legacy – at least in the imagination of those who witness it – of an uncivilised age.

The domain of these forces of disorder comprises both Baskerville Hall, an 'ancient' (56) ivy-covered Gothic pile with sombre yew-lined avenues, rafters of 'age-blackened oak' (58), unlit passageways and venerable and occasionally spectral portraits of Sir Henry's ancestors – it is another of the many versions of the House of Usher that we can find in the Holmes saga – and the moor itself, a place where, the legend tells us, 'the powers of evil are exalted' during the hours of darkness (14). Despite Holmes's purchase of an Ordnance Survey map from Stanford's in London, the great Grimpen Mire defies modern cartography and is perilous to any living being that tries to cross it, from a pit pony screaming as it is sucked under, to Stapleton whose confidence in knowing a safe path through the mire turns out to be misplaced when he disappears, presumably drowned, at the climax of the novella. But if Baskerville Hall seems ancient to Watson, then the remnants of habitations on the moor are from a different era altogether. As Watson reports to Holmes, on the moor 'you have left all traces of modern England behind you, but on the other hand you are conscious everywhere of the homes and the work of prehistoric people':

> On all sides of you as you walk are the houses of these forgotten folk, with their graves and their huge monoliths which are supposed to have marked their temples. As you look at their grey stone huts against the scarred hillsides you leave your own age behind you, and if you were to see a skin-clad, hairy man crawl out from a low door, fitting a flint-tipped arrow on to the string of his bow, you would feel that his presence there was more natural than your own. (75)

The persistence of these ruins means that the contemporary moor remains unchanged from the place crossed by the evil Hugo and his entourage in the seventeenth century: 'Now it opened into a broad space in which stood two of those great stones, still to be seen there, which were set by certain forgotten peoples in the days of old' (13). After the deaths of the hound and its owner, Holmes and Watson approach Stapleton's base of operations in the great Grimpen Mire, through a landscape more primeval than prehistoric:

> the path zig-zagged from tuft to tuft of rushes among those green-scummed pits and foul quagmires ... Rank reeds and lush, slimy water-plants sent an odour of decay and heavy miasmatic vapour into our faces, while a false step plunged us more than once thigh-deep into the dark, quivering mire, which shook for yards in soft undulations around our feet. (155)

Like the Challenger expedition in *The Lost World*, here Holmes and Watson are, in effect, travelling back in time.

Critics have attached different kinds of significance to these vivid descriptions of the moor and the Mire. For some the Mire is a marker of the novella's Gothic genre, for others a link to an occluded subtext of Irish politics. Diana Barsham proposes a more topical resonance in South Africa, pointing out the similarities between the Mire and the base of the Boer commander Piet Cronje on the Modder River, as it is described in Doyle's *The Great Boer War* (1901):

> Already down there, amid slaughtered oxen and dead horses under a burning sun, a horrible pest-hole had been formed which sent its mephitic vapours over the countryside. Occasionally the sentries down the river saw amid the brown eddies of the rushing water the floating body of a Boer which had been washed away from the Golgotha above. Dark Cronje, betrayer of Potchefstroom, iron-handed ruler of natives, reviler of the British, stern victor of Magersfontein, at last there has come a day of reckoning for you! ... A visit to the laager showed that the horrible smells which had been carried across to the British lines, and the swollen carcasses which had swirled down the muddy river were true portents of its condition. Strong-nerved men came back white and sick from a contemplation of the place in which women and children had for ten days been living. From end to end it was a festering mass of corruption, overshadowed by incredible swarms of flies.[4]

Barsham's suggestion is supported by Doyle's recollection of the South African landscape in *Memories and Adventures*: 'It is a strange wild place, the veldt, with its vast green plains and peculiar flat-topped hills, relics of some extraordinary geological episode.'[5] In *The Hound of the Baskervilles*, Stapleton points out the Mire, fatal to men and ponies alike, as a 'great plain to the north here, with the queer hills breaking out of it' (66). As with the territory which Cronje commands, the sinister power of the moor lies not only in the landscape itself, but also in its capacity to conceal evil, as is evident in Watson's first observations of the 'wild place':

> Our wagonette had topped a rise and in front of us rose the huge expanse of the moor, mottled with gnarled and craggy cairns and tors. A cold wind swept down from it and set us shivering. Somewhere there, on that desolate plain, was lurking this fiendish man, hiding in a burrow like a wild beast, his heart full of malignancy against the whole race which had cast him out. It needed but this to complete the grim suggestiveness of the barren waste, the chilling wind, and the darkling

sky ... The road in front of us grew bleaker and wilder over huge russet and olive slopes, sprinkled with giant boulders. Now and then we passed a moorland cottage, walled and roofed with stone, with no creeper to break its harsh outline. (56)

The Great Boer War rhetorically positions the conflict as the forces of the twentieth century battling those of the seventeenth. Doyle describes the Boers as 'brave, hardy, and fired with a strange religious enthusiasm. They were all of the seventeenth century, except their rifles.'[6] But in his characterisation of 'dark Cronje',[7] who resembles what Barsham calls the sinister patriarchs of Doyle's early fiction, we have a villain who is, like Selden and Stapleton, a 'throwback' to a pre-civilised age, or even to a subhuman ancestry:

Cronje had suddenly become aware of the net which was closing round him. To the dark fierce man who had striven so hard to make his line of kopjes impregnable it must have been a bitter thing to abandon his trenches and his rifle pits. But he was crafty as well as tenacious, and he had the Boer horror of being cut off – an hereditary instinct from fathers who had fought on horseback against enemies on foot ... With furious speed he drew in his right wing, and then, one huge mass of horsemen, guns, and wagons, he swept through the gap between the rear of the British cavalry bound for Kimberley and the head of the British infantry at Klip Drift. There was just room to pass, and at it he dashed with the furious energy of a wild beast rushing from a trap ... This was no deer which they were chasing, however, but rather a grim old Transvaal wolf, with his teeth flashing ever over his shoulder.[8]

This animalistic Cronje is part of the grim, gloom-filled veldt of the South African war: in negotiations with Lord Kitchener, he 'disappeared with a snarl of contempt into his burrows'; his trenches are like dens, invisible and inaccessible until overrun by the forces of order.

The veldt is not the only African landscape to leave an imprint on Doyle's imagined Dartmoor. The late 1890s also saw Conan Doyle in Upper Egypt, first on a holiday which brought him to the borders of the Mahdiyya, the Islamist state founded by Mohammed al-Mahdi in 1881, then as a correspondent for the *Westminster Gazette* to report on Kitchener's preparations for the invasion of the Sudan. The main literary result from these experiences was *The Tragedy of the Korosko*, which tells of a group of tourists who are kidnapped by the Mahdiyya's forces, known to Victorians as the Dervishes, and subjected variously to violence and threats of rape or forced conversion. Like the Boers, the Dervishes are products of the pre-civilised past: the tourists find themselves in 'the rough clutch of the seventh century'.[9] And, as with Cronje, their regressive beliefs and conduct are determined by, or at least consistent with, the primitive landscape in which they are found: 'an expanse of savage and unrelieved desert' interspersed with 'fantastic hills' with 'their savage, saw-toothed crests' and, in places, the 'crumbling remains of ancient buildings, so old that no date could be assigned to them'.[10] The three ancient landscapes of these texts – desert, veldt and moor – are starkly different but, in Doyle's rhetorical construction, strikingly similar.

It is, perhaps, unsurprising that *The Hound of the Baskervilles* should share material with *The Great Boer War*. Doyle's work on the novella began a matter of weeks after his return from South Africa where he had worked in a private hospital in Bloemfontein – having attempted, unsuccessfully, to enrol in the Middlesex Yeomanry at the age of forty. The writing and serial publication of the novella was contemporaneous with the second half of the war, and of the later editions of *The Great Boer War* which, initially conceived as an eyewitness history of what was expected to be a short war, turned into an organic history of a conflict that dragged on far longer than anyone expected. And the conception of *The Hound of the Baskervilles* owed much to a friendship that developed on the journey back from South Africa with a journalist and minor writer of fiction, B. Fletcher Robinson, who had been covering the war for the *Daily Express* and whose idea for a story about a spectral hound was shared with Doyle on a golfing weekend in Cromer. (Robinson was credited in the *Strand* as a collaborator, but only earned the dedication in the volume version published later in 1902.) The influence on the novella of the South African war is no mere coincidence of timing and happenstance, but a deeply ideological connection that reveals Doyle's thinking on the problem of war and civilisation, and one which brings us back to the novella's preoccupation with genetics and inheritance.

The South African war revived long-standing late nineteenth-century concerns over the physical condition of British men. When Britain went to war against the Boers in 1899, its technological and economic superiority seemed to guarantee a swift victory. But the refusal of Boers to be defeated, and the British Army's obvious difficulty in eliminating resistance, caused anxious debate over what the journalist Arnold White, an imperialist and eugenicist whom Doyle knew, called the 'racial efficiency' of town-bred British men facing the hardy outdoorsmen of the veldt.[11] This was by no means the concern of a handful of pseudoscientific cranks and imperialist blowhards: so widespread were anxieties of racial deterioration as a factor in the Boer War's longevity that 1902 to 1904 saw the creation of a series of official enquiries into the matter culminating in The Inter-Departmental Committee on Physical Deterioration. This eventually rejected heredity as a factor in the physical condition of the population, and identified poor nutrition as the cause of what deterioration could be detected, but the question was, in the public sphere, unresolved and of great public concern when Doyle wrote *The Hound of the Baskervilles*. *The Great Boer War* presents a contradictory picture of the Boers – both atavistic and purified by their healthy, outdoor environment – and *The Hound of the Baskervilles* provides something of a mirror image in which the British population is divided between the racially and culturally progressives, associated with urban society, colonialism and science, and regressive forces associated with superstition and savagery. The novella thus provides an answer to Mortimer's question: history should move forwards, to greater and greater civilisation. We progress, but only by defeating in war the forces of darkness in and around us, and fighting for civilised values. Progress is not inevitable: it requires vigilance, discipline and military power, because on moors, on veldts and in deserts there are forces from the past waiting to pull us back from the twentieth century into an age of darkness.

Notes

1. Joseph Conrad, *Heart of Darkness*, p. 37.
2. For further explorations of this important theme in the novella, see James and John M. Kissing, 'Sherlock Holmes and the Ritual of Reason', Joseph A. Kestner, *The Edwardian Detective,* pp. 36–40, and David Grylls, 'The Savage Sub-Text of The Hound of the Baskervilles'.
3. The legend of the curse of the Baskervilles was recorded in 1742 by Hugo Baskerville, writing to his sons Rodger and John. The eighteenth-century Hugo begins the account by explaining that he comes 'in a direct line' from the seventeenth-century Hugo, and that he 'had the story' from his father, 'who also had it from his' (11). The legend itself is thus another Baskerville inheritance.
4. Doyle, *The Great Boer War*, pp. 335, 340; Barsham, *The Meaning of Masculinity*, pp. 222–3.
5. Doyle, *Memories and Adventures*, pp. 160–1.
6. Doyle, *The Great Boer War*, p. 66.

7. Ibid., p. 66.
8. Ibid., pp. 324–5.
9. Doyle, *The Tragedy of the Korosko*, p. 96.
10. Ibid., pp. 72, 214.
11. Richard A. Soloway, *Demography and Degeneration*, p. 41.

Chapter 17

The East Wind

'There's an east wind coming, Watson.'
 'I think not, Holmes. It is very warm.'
 'Good old Watson! You are the one fixed point in a changing age. There's an east wind coming all the same, such a wind as never blew on England yet. It will be cold and bitter, Watson, and a good many of us may wither before its blast. But it's God's own wind none the less, and a cleaner, better, stronger land will lie in the sunshine when the storm has cleared.' (*Last Bow*, 172)

Holmes's words to Watson at the end of 'His Last Bow' (1917) express an idea of warfare that sits uneasily with our contemporary perception of the First World War. Today we are accustomed to associate that war with the horrors of the Western Front: the battles of the Somme (1916) and Passchendaele (1917) loom large in our cultural memory as paradigms of unnecessary bloodshed and strategic incompetence. But this was not how Conan Doyle saw it – and he saw the Western Front at first hand, while both his brother, Brigadier-General Innes 'Duff' Doyle, and his son Kingsley were in the thick of the action. At the invitation of the War Office, Doyle toured the British, Italian and French Fronts in 1916, and the Australian Front in 1918, using his authority as Deputy Lieutenant of Surrey to don an improvised khaki uniform 'which was something between that of a Colonel and Brigadier, with silver roses instead of stars or crowns upon the shoulder-states'.[1] These experiences informed his massive history of the conflict, serialised in the *Strand Magazine* and published in volume form as *The British Campaign in France and Flanders* (1916–20), and on which he was hard at work at the same time as writing 'His Last Bow'. Doyle was especially proud of his unfolding history, claiming that his unique access to British generals ensured that he was 'the first to describe in print the full battle-lines'. Indeed, he was disappointed that it did not have more impact on reviewers:

> I was really the only public source of supply of accurate and detailed information. I can only suppose that they could not believe it to be true . . . my war history, which reflects all the passion and pain of those hard days, has never come into its own. I would reckon it the greatest and most undeserved literary disappointment of my life if I did not know that the end is not yet and that it may mirror those great times to those who are to come.[2]

Reading Doyle's later reflections on his wartime experiences in *Memories and Adventures*, it is hard to believe that the First World War carried off eighteen million people, including his son, whose death from Spanish influenza in 1918 was partly a result of his war wound. (Doyle's brother died on duty, also from influenza, the following year.) His recollection of his first visit to the front is characteristic of his view of the conflict: 'The crowning impression which I carried away from that wonderful day was the enormous imperturbable confidence of the Army and its extraordinary efficiency in organization, administration, material, and personnel.'[3] The Royal Navy's expansion was 'a miracle'.[4] The British commander, Douglas Haig, was in Doyle's eyes far from being the principal 'donkey' of later historiography: 'his face was remarkable for beauty and power . . . the long powerful jaw was the feature which spoke particularly of the never-to-be-beaten quality which saved the army when the line was broken in the first Ypres battle and was destined to save it again in April, 1918'.[5] The German forces, meanwhile, were 'the Boche' (348) or 'the Hun' (353), sulking off stage and occasionally sending volleys of ordnance towards the British lines.[6]

Doyle thus remained remarkably consistent in his view of Britain's wars as just, noble and necessary, despite the pain and tragedy of their consequences, and the First World War was no exception. Holmes's closing speech in 'His Last Bow' can be seen, therefore, as a particularly direct expression of its author's lifelong and deeply held opinions. Holmes portrays the coming war as unavoidable – literally an act of God – and simultaneously destructive and invigorating. He eloquently vocalises Conan Doyle's romantic view of war as an essentially chivalrous activity, violent and noble at the same time. As he put it in *The German War* (1914):

> War may have a beautiful as well as a terrible side, and be full of touches of human sympathy and restraint which mitigate its unavoidable horror. . . . From the old glittering days of knighthood, with

their high and gallant courtesy, through the eighteenth-century campaigns where the debonair guards of France and England exchanged salutations before their volleys, down to the last great Napoleonic struggle, the tradition of chivalry has always survived.[7]

Behind Holmes's words we can see Doyle's characteristic sense of the nation needing to pass a moral as well as physical test, one that he predicts will be passed. In *Memories and Adventures*, he showed the accuracy of the prediction: 'we had gained an immense reassurance. Britain had not weakened. She was still the Britain of old.'[8]

Holmes's speech is not merely an expression of Doyle's world view, however. 'His Last Bow' was written and published when the battles of the Western Front were at their height, and Germany was seeking to undermine Britain's resolve with a campaign of unrestricted submarine warfare, targeting merchant shipping (and hence Britain's lifeline to the rest of the world). As indicated by its subtitle in the *Strand* ('The War Service of Sherlock Holmes'), the story both describes and is an act of service to a nation in peril. Three years into the war, but situated just before its outbreak, the speech has a clear and simple message: the sacrifice is worthwhile. Indeed, so effective is the speech that it was repeated almost word-for-word by Basil Rathbone to Nigel Bruce in Universal's *Sherlock Holmes and the Voice of Terror* (1942), a loose adaptation of 'His Last Bow' made immediately after the United States declared war on Germany. In a different medium, during a different conflict and in a different country, Holmes again spoke directly to the need to motivate public opinion behind a war that would exert an enormous cost in blood and treasure.

'His Last Bow' is fiction but it is also propaganda. Conan Doyle had been engaged in propaganda work of one kind or another since 1902, when he deployed his considerable cultural capital to defend Britain's conduct of the 1899–1902 Anglo-Boer War to a sceptical and often hostile European continent. Doyle's incredulity at the government's failure to win the international battle of hearts and minds over the Boer War led him to mount a freelance campaign to argue the British case against critics like the South African novelist Olive Schreiner, the journalist W. T. Stead and the economist J. A. Hobson. The centrepiece of this effort was his pamphlet, *The War in South Africa: Its Cause and Conduct* (1902), which was translated into fourteen languages (including Hungarian, Kanarese and Braille) and earned Doyle his knighthood at the personal instigation of Edward VII. What Doyle did not realise was that an anonymous contribution of £500 pounds to defray translation and printing costs came not, as he suspected, from the King, but from the Foreign Office's secret service fund: the government had woken up, late in the day, to the propaganda value of having a writer like Doyle on its side.[9] Perhaps in recognition of its lassitude over the Boer War, in 1914 the government immediately recognised the need to fight and win an information war alongside the military one. And given his sympathies, it was hardly surprising that Doyle would choose, like Holmes, 'to lay his remarkable combination of intellectual and practical activity at the disposal of the Government' (*Last Bow*, 3). Doyle thus became a founding member of a remarkable group of major British authors recruited to support the war effort, and which first met in secret at Wellington House in London on 2 September 1914. The meeting was called by the politician and social thinker C. F. G. Masterman, just appointed the first head of the War Propaganda Bureau, who was evidently selected because of his connections to literary as well as political networks: the government's immediate impulse was to recruit novelists and poets to fight the information war. Besides Doyle, other attendees included J. M. Barrie, Arnold Bennett (who would go on to run part of the propaganda effort later in the war), G. K. Chesterton, John Galsworthy, Thomas Hardy, John Masefield and H. G. Wells. (Rudyard Kipling sent his apologies.) Doyle can even be partly credited with the very idea of the Wellington House group: it took a literary man to state the government's case in 1902, so literary men were recruited in 1914.

Doyle would go on to be a prolific author of war propaganda; indeed, he started even before the Wellington House meeting, with his pamphlet *To Arms!* (1914). He signed the 'Declaration of Authors' – the War Propaganda Bureau's first operation – that was published in *The Times* on 18 September. Then followed *The German War*, *The World War Conspiracy* (1914), *The Story of British Prisoners* (1915), *A Visit to Three Fronts: Glimpses of the British, Italian and French Lines* (1916), with Masterman's office translating some of his pamphlets and essays into European languages.[10] While the Bureau's principal audience was the American public and government – also being courted by the Germans – Doyle's war propaganda also served to stiffen British resolve by justifying its intervention in a European conflict and urging participation in defence of chivalric ideals.

Although he repeatedly invoked a long history of valorous conflicts with the French, this war was different because the Germans had shown they were not playing by the same rules. During the Napoleonic Wars, for example, in 'an agreement faithfully kept upon either side', the British promised not to use an ancient bridge so that the monument would not be attacked by the French. 'Could one imagine Germans making war in such a spirit as this? Think of that old French bridge, and then think of the University of Louvain and the Cathedral of Rheims. What a gap between them – the gap that separates civilisation from the savage!'[11] Later, Doyle would uncritically accept and recycle the atrocity propaganda contained in the Bryce Report of 1915, which claimed (amongst other outrages) that German soldiers had bayoneted a two-year-old Belgian child, holding the impaled corpse aloft as they marched and sang. In pamphlets, books and letters to editors, Doyle would declaim against submarine raids, Zeppelins, poison gas and the execution of Edith Cavell as violations of the unwritten rules of chivalric warfare.[12] More extraordinary (to a modern eye) were his allegations of a vast, deeply planned conspiracy mounted by the Prussian Junkers against the European family of nations:

> Yes, it was a deep, deep plot, a plot against the liberties of Europe, extending over several years, planned out to the smallest detail in the days of peace, developed by hordes of spies, prepared for by every conceivable military, naval, and financial precaution, and finally sprung upon us on a pretext which was no more the real cause of war than any other excuse would have been which would serve their turn by having some superficial plausibility. The real cause of war was a universal national insanity infecting the whole German race, but derived originally from a Prussian caste who inoculated the others with their megalomania.[13]

The purpose of pressing Holmes into war service is clear enough, but 'His Last Bow' is not propaganda of the official variety like *The German War*. As far as we can tell, no one instructed Doyle to write the story; he simply saw it as his patriotic duty. It can therefore be seen as an extension of his pamphlet on the South Africa War: an attempt by a concerned citizen to achieve a public good through private endeavour. We are accustomed to think of propaganda as overtly or covertly a governmental activity, but this view has been challenged by scholars who see propaganda as a complex collection of activities which include popular, spontaneous and unofficial cultural production alongside strategic, governmental discourse.[14] 'His Last Bow' falls into the former category. It is by some way the most overtly patriotic story in the Holmes saga, but is highly unusual in other respects. Watson, who appears at the story's end in disguise as a chauffeur, and who is en route to re-joining his 'old service' (171) – whose officers and soldiers presumably would have been rather surprised to find a veteran of the Second Afghan War among their number – does not narrate. Neither does Holmes (who would go on to narrate 'The Blanched Soldier' and 'The Lion's Mane'). 'His Last Bow' is, with 'The Adventure of the Mazarin Stone' (1921), one of the only stories with an extradiegetic narrator. This enables us to eavesdrop on the conversations between the German spy Von Bork and his boss, Baron Von Herling, Chief Secretary of the German legation, before the arrival of Holmes or Watson, in which the two Germans congratulate each other on having run rings around the sleepy British. The story is also unusual in that its principal mystery is not solved by Holmes: it *is* Holmes – specifically, who or where he is. After Von Herling departs, anxious to return to Germany as war is about to break out, Von Bork's star agent arrives to hand over his final, triumphant haul of intelligence: the codes used by the Royal Navy. Anyone familiar with Conan Doyle's biography would realise that the agent's name, Altamont, is an alias – an allusion to Charles Altamont Doyle, Conan Doyle's artistically gifted but alcoholic father. Despite dealing directly with an imminent world war, opening with ominous reference – 'the most terrible August in the history of the world ... God's curse hung heavy over a degenerate earth' (155) – 'His Last Bow' is also unusual in being a comic tale. For example, Altamont's end-of-the-pier Americanese – 'I'm not stayin' in this goldarned country all on my lonesome. In a week or less, from what I see, John Bull will be on his hind legs and fair rampin'' (163) – prompts Von Bork to joke that he 'seems to have declared war on the King's English as well as on the English King' (160).

By situating the story on the eve of war, and taking international espionage as its theme, 'His Last Bow' exploits but in some ways also subverts the conventions of one of the most popular genres of the prewar period. Variously named as 'invasion-scare' or 'future-war fiction', this genre (originating in the 1870s but enjoying a particular vogue in the late Victorian and Edwardian age) served a nakedly political purpose: to bring about a moral and physical rearmament of Britain in the face of what were portrayed as increasing geopolitical threats. Prior to the *Entente Cordiale* of 1904, the enemy was often French, and (until the Anglo-Russian Entente of 1907) occasionally Russian, but after the Tangier incident of 1905, in which Germany sought to drive a wedge between Britain and France, Germany became the fictional adversary which consistently threatened Britain's national security through a combination of innovative military technology and ingenuity in espionage and subversion. The genre's most famous practitioner was William Le Queux, whose success was built not on literary talent but on his alliances with both Britain's military establishment and its popular press (notably Alfred Harmsworth, founder of the *Daily Mail* and owner from 1904 of *The Times*). Like his fellow invasion-scare writers George Griffith, Robert Cromie and Louis Tracy, Le Queux was an occasional journalist who achieved his effects through a strong sense of verisimilitude – moving his invading armies through topographically specific regions of middle Britain – and also, on occasion, by deliberately blurring the line between fact and fiction. Le Queux's standout successes were *The Great War in England in 1897* (1894), first serialised in 1893 in Alfred Harmsworth's penny paper *Answers* (which the previous year has serialised Doyle's *The Doings of Raffles Haw*), and *The Invasion of 1910* (1906), serialised in Harmsworth's *Daily Mail* with an aggressive marketing campaign designed to stir up feelings of alarm: the *Mail* ran excerpts featuring journalistic-style accounts of German atrocities side by side with the newspaper's actual reportage.[15] Le Queux's patriotic but alarmist message, repeated in many of the 160 or so novels he wrote between 1891 and his death in 1927, was that Britain was simultaneously strong and weak: it was strong in its traditions and national character, but weak in having neglected its national defence and preparations for armed conflict.

The most famous of all invasion-scare novels remains *The Riddle of the Sands* (1903) by Erskine Childers, whom Doyle admired as a writer, and with whom he shared a concern about the need to modernise the British Army.[16] *The Riddle of the Sands* is certainly more sophisticated than Le Queux's invasion novels but contains the same basic message: Britain needs to combine its diplomatic and intelligence resources (personified by the urbane Foreign Office official Carruthers) and its practical know-how (represented by the unpolished yachtsman Davies) in a concerted strategy to build the nation's defences against the pressing threat of a German seaborne invasion.

Invasion-scare fiction was part of a broad movement of mobilisation of public opinion in favour of a more aggressive military stance in Europe and a significant increase in defence at home. Unsurprisingly, Conan Doyle played a role in this movement, advocating a Channel tunnel and civilian rifle training, and writing to *The Times* in 1912 urging a campaign for Britain's motorists to become unofficial guardians of its coastal defences. But his greatest contribution was to the invasion-scare genre itself. His short story 'Danger!', published in the *Strand* on the eve of war in July 1914, purports to be the log of Captain John Sirius, a naval officer of Norland, 'one of the smallest

Powers in Europe', who brings the Royal Navy and hence Great Britain to its knees with a flotilla of eight submarines. It opens with a statement typical of the invasion-scare genre:

> It is an amazing thing that the English, who have the reputation of being a practical nation, never saw the danger to which they were exposed. For many years they had been spending nearly a hundred millions a year upon their army and their fleet. Squadrons of Dreadnoughts costing two millions each had been launched. They had spent enormous sums upon cruisers, and both their torpedo and their submarine squadrons were exceptionally strong. They were also by no means weak in their aerial power, especially in the matter of seaplanes. Besides all this, their army was very efficient, in spite of its limited numbers, and it was the most expensive in Europe. Yet when the day of trial came, all this imposing force was of no use whatever, and might as well have not existed. Their ruin could not have been more complete or more rapid if they had not possessed an ironclad or a regiment.[17]

'Danger!' was followed in the *Strand* by twelve responses from admirals and historians on the technical plausibility and likelihood of Doyle's innovations and their impact. Several acknowledged Britain's dependence on maritime trade, but the admirals were in general dismissive, with Admiral Penrose Fitzgerald confidently declaring that 'any civilised nation' would not lower itself to 'torpedo unarmed and defenceless merchant ships'. Three months later German U-Boats sank three Royal Navy ships, and in 1915 the Cunard liner *Lusitania* was torpedoed, with the loss of 1,198 civilians.[18]

As the magazine publication of 'Danger!' shows, invasion-scare fiction drew its power from its direct and immediate relationship with geopolitical and technological realities: the *Strand*'s juxtaposition of expert commentary and imaginative fiction, like Le Queux's reportage of the German invasion in the *Daily Mail*, seemed to turn fiction into fact as well as vice versa. Invasion-scare fiction was, then, prophetic, and often overtly – and this made the genre particularly congenial to Doyle, that most psychically sensitive of the period's authors. Reflecting on this in *Memories and Adventures*, he wrote:

> I naturally began to speculate as to the methods of attack and of defence. I have an occasional power of premonition, psychic rather than intellectual, which exercises itself beyond my own control, and which when it really comes is never mistaken. ... On this occasion I saw as clearly as possible what the course of a naval war between England and Germany would be. I had no doubt at all that our greatest

danger – a desperately real one – was that they would use their submarines in order to sink our food ships, and that we might be starved into submission.[19]

Moreover, 'Danger!' can be credited not only with predicting one of the strategic developments of the war, but also with influencing it. When the German naval blockade of Britain was declared just seven months after Doyle's story was published, the German Fleet Commander was reported to have credited Doyle with originating the idea.[20]

As its title makes clear, 'Danger!' is a call to action, and so is of a piece with the invasion-scare genre which often made no secret of its function to change political and public opinion about defence expenditure, civilian preparedness and the necessity for more muscular foreign policies. In its opening passages, 'His Last Bow' seems to occupy similar territory: the two German agents, Von Herling and Von Bork, discuss their intelligence haul in a passage that could have come straight from the pages of a William Le Queux novel. It reproduces the familiar charge that Britain is physically unprepared – its defences are weak, its citizens are complacent about the future and its vulnerability to espionage is demonstrated by the ability of hostile spies to operate almost in plain sight: 'And all the time this quiet country-house of yours is the centre of half the mischief in England, and the sporting squire – the most astute secret-service man in Europe. Genius, my dear Von Bork – genius!' (157) Von Herling assures Von Bork that 'so far as the essentials go – the storage of munitions, the preparation for submarine attack, the arrangements for making high explosives – nothing is prepared' (158). Von Bork then shows his boss his archive of secret intelligence: 'Each pigeon-hole had its label, and his eyes, as he glanced along them, read a long series of such titles as "Fords", "Harbour-defences", "Aeroplanes", "Ireland", "Egypt", "Portsmouth Forts", "The Channel", "Rosyth", and a score of others. Each compartment was bristling with papers and plans.' Von Bork adds:

> 'And all in four years, Baron. Not such a bad show for the hard-drinking, hard-riding country squire. But the gem of my collection is coming and there is the setting all ready for it.' He pointed to a space over which 'Naval Signals' was printed. (159)

Nor have they confined their malevolent activities to espionage: 'How then can England come in, especially when we have stirred her up such a devil's brew of Irish civil war, window-breaking Furies, and God knows what to keep her thoughts at home?' Here is another element familiar from the invasion-scare genre. Britain's enemies sap the national resolve by supporting and provoking enemies within: fifth columns of subversives, domestic terrorists, disloyal immigrants. Such forces had been supported and provoked by hostile foreign powers in invasion-scare fiction since at least Le Queux's *The Great War in England in 1897*, in which the Franco-Russian invasion is accompanied by an anarchist revolt in the East End of London.[21]

However, Altamont's arrival and his unmasking as Holmes then overturns the genre's conventions: although appearances may sometimes be to the contrary, Britain is morally, intellectually and therefore militarily superior to Germany. Altamont reveals that Von Bork's informant network is being wrapped up by the British authorities, and they are now on Altamont's trail; he hands over his final intelligence haul, which turns out to be the *Practical Handbook of Bee Culture*, by Sherlock Holmes. It is only then that we discover that Holmes has come out of retirement at the urging of first the Foreign Secretary and then the Prime Minister: Von Bork is so formidable an enemy that Holmes has abandoned his colonies of bees on the South Downs in order to defend the realm against the machinations of the German master spy. Holmes then takes considerable pleasure in telling Von Bork that much of the intelligence in his collection has been fabricated, and the German forces are about to encounter some unwelcome surprises. This is not what readers will have come to expect from invasion-scare fiction, which entertained them with fantasies of their own peril while seeking to change public opinion (and hence official policy) by forcing them to imagine the consequences of inaction and complacency. The propaganda purpose of 'His Last Bow' is reassurance, not raising fear: it seeks to inspire patience and resolve, not a reversal of policy.

The story's function of reassurance is achieved most directly by its examination of British and German national character. Von Bork and Von Herling discuss 'these Englanders', with the former observing that a 'more docile, simple folk could not be imagined' (156). Von Herling, anticipating the story's outcome, disagrees: 'It is that surface simplicity of theirs which makes a trap for the stranger. One's first impression is that they are entirely soft. Then you come suddenly upon something very hard, and you know that you have reached the limit, and must adapt yourself to the fact' (156). Von Herling explains that he speaks from personal knowledge, after he was identified as the source of a leak to the German Chancellor: 'There was nothing soft about our British hosts on that occasion, I can assure you' (156). But Von Herling also misreads the British character, predicting that Britain will leave France and Belgium to their fates, and exchange honour for peace: 'Honour is a mediaeval conception' (158). Von Herling's final comment in the story is that Martha, Von Bork's last remaining servant, 'might almost personify Britannia ... with her complete self-absorption and general air of comfortable somnolence' (161), and this shows that he too has accepted Von Bork's complacent view. But the story is a demonstration that the Germans' inability to detect the national steel beneath Britain's 'surface simplicity' leads to the failure of their espionage and, ultimately, will lead to their defeat in war. As Holmes observes, having bound Von Bork hand and foot when the latter threatens to call for help:

> if you did anything so foolish you would probably enlarge the too-limited titles of our village inns by giving us 'The Dangling Prussian' as a sign-post. The Englishman is a patient creature, but at present his temper is a little inflamed and it would be as well not to try him too far. (171)

Figure 17 'He was gripped at the back of his neck by a grasp of iron, and a chloroformed sponge was held in front of his writhing face.' Illustration by Arthur Gilbert, *Strand Magazine*, September 1917.

The story's message is consistent with Conan Doyle's own opinions on Germany's war motives and its inability to understand Britain's national character: 'it is clear that the delusions as to our degeneration in character had really persuaded the Germans that the big cowardly fellow would stand by with folded arms and see his little friend knocked about by the bully'.²² As for the German character, we have Holmes's observation that Von Bork's sportsmanship is 'one quality which is very rare in a German', as well as the imagery of Von Bork and Von Herling conversing, 'the two glowing ends of their cigars might have been the smouldering eyes of some malignant fiend looking down in the darkness' (155). More telling, though, are their attitudes: Von Bork is weary of experiencing British 'good form' and 'playing the game' (156), while Von Herling proclaims that 'we live in a utilitarian age' (158). Conan Doyle studied the German language and for 'a long time' he 'never seriously believed in the German menace'.²³ But by 1917 he was prepared to press Sherlock Holmes into service against a stereotyped enemy – vainglorious, unimaginative and entirely convinced by what Von Herling calls *'real-politik'* (158).

The most reassuring aspect of 'His Last Bow' is the presence of Sherlock Holmes himself. By 1917, Holmes had become firmly established in national mythography as a peculiarly British kind of genius – so much so that he is repeatedly invoked, for example, by Robert Baden-Powell in his astonishingly popular manual for citizen mobilisation, *Scouting for Boys* (1908). Published in a year in which fears of German invasion and subversion reached a crescendo, Baden-Powell shadowed Le Queux's calls for a step change in national readiness: The scouts' motto is 'BE PREPARED, which means you are always to be in a state of readiness in mind and body to do your DUTY'.²⁴ Baden-Powell identified Holmes's powers of observation and deductive reasoning (what *Scouting for Boys* labels as 'Sherlock-Holmesism') as vital skills for the Boy Scout, to be imitated or acquired.²⁵ Holmes was, therefore, a particularly valuable figure for wartime propaganda, a quintessence of the national genius for empirical observation and patient, rational enquiry, as is evident in his review of how he built his case against Von Bork:

> It has cost me two years, Watson, but they have not been devoid of excitement. When I say that I started my pilgrimage at Chicago, graduated in an Irish secret society at Buffalo, gave serious trouble to the constabulary at Skibbareen and so eventually caught the eye of a subordinate agent of Von Bork, who recommended me as a likely

man, you will realize that the matter was complex. Since then I have been honoured by his confidence, which has not prevented most of his plans going subtly wrong and five of his best agents being in prison. I watched them, Watson, and I picked them as they ripened. (168–9)

For British counter-intelligence, ripeness is all. Baden-Powell urged his young disciples to imitate Holmes and be prepared, but in 'His Last Bow' Holmes's message to a war-weary nation is a different one. Far from the jeremiads of the invasion-scare genre and Doyle's own warnings against submarines and strategic complacency, Holmes reveals that the nation was prepared all along, and that the dividend would shortly be paid in the form of a British victory.

Notes

1. Doyle, *Memories and Adventures,* p. 345.
2. Ibid., pp. 334–5.
3. Ibid., p. 347.
4. Ibid., p. 353.
5. Ibid., p. 357.
6. Ibid., pp. 348, 353.
7. Doyle, *The German War,* pp. 80–1.
8. Doyle, *Memories and Adventures,* p. 395.
9. Lycett, *Conan Doyle,* p. 272.
10. See Jain Anurag, *British Propaganda of the First World War,* pp. 154–5.
11. Doyle, *The German War,* p. 81.
12. Anurag, *British Propaganda of the First World War,* pp. 189–206.
13. Doyle, *The German War,* p. 62.
14. See, for example, Stephane Audoin-Rouzeau and Annette Becker, *14–18,* pp. 108–12.
15. See I. F. Clarke, *Voices Prophesying War,* pp. 58–9, 122–4.
16. For Doyle's recollection of debating the use of cavalry with Childers, see *Memories and Adventures,* p. 214. For correspondence, see Lycett, *Conan Doyle,* p. 341.
17. Arthur Conan Doyle, *Danger! And Other Stories,* pp. 1–2.
18. See Clarke, *Voices Prophesying War,* p. 91, and Daniel Stashower, *Teller of Tales,* pp. 300–3.
19. Doyle, *Memories and Adventures,* p. 321.
20. Lycett, *Conan Doyle,* p. 349; Stashower, *Teller of Tales,* pp. 302–3. Stashower convincingly suggests that the report should be seen as 'demoralizing propaganda'.
21. William Le Queux, *The Great War in England in 1897.* See also David Stafford, 'Spies and Gentlemen', p. 501.

22. Doyle, *Memories and Adventures*, pp. 312–13.
23. Ibid., p. 311.
24. Robert Baden-Powell, *Scouting for Boys*, p. 48.
25. Ibid., p. 141. Baden-Powell goes on to recommend that scouts read *The Adventures of Sherlock Holmes* and *The Memoirs of Sherlock Holmes* (pp. 146, 148).

Part VII: Secrecy

Chapter 18

That Secret History of a Nation

'The Bruce-Partington Plans', in which the design of a new and devastating type of submarine is stolen from Woolwich Arsenal and sold to a foreign spy, came at an ominous moment in British history. When it was first published in the December 1908 issue of the *Strand Magazine*, the war that would consume Conan Doyle's attention – and several members of his family – was still more than five years away. But Germany had already become Britain's principal geopolitical adversary: Britain entered strategic *ententes* with France (1904) and Russia (1907), alliances which would endure into – and help precipitate – the First World War; a naval arms race, centred on Dreadnought-class battleships but including the new, disruptive technologies of submarines and torpedoes, was in full swing; and Germany was widely believed to be conducting espionage in Britain on an unprecedented scale.

Britain at this time became gripped by what historians now call 'spy fever': vast numbers of German agents, often posing as waiters or barbers, were believed to be diligently collecting intelligence on coastal defences, roads and railways, and the strength and disposition of the armed forces: for example, in 1908 Lord Roberts, Britain's most highly decorated war hero, announced to Parliament that Germany had infiltrated 80,000 trained soldiers into the British Isles.[1] What was remarkable about this moral panic was not just that it was so exaggerated, but that it largely derived from fiction. As well as conjuring fears of the shape of wars to come, invasion-scare fiction also developed into the genre of espionage fiction which, after the First World War, supplanted it in British popular culture.[2] Kipling's *Kim* (1901), which tells how an Irish street urchin in Lahore becomes one of British Intelligence's most valuable agents in its cold war with the Russian Empire, is often credited as a foundational text of the genre, along with the late-imperial romances of John Buchan which updated the adventure fiction of imperial expansion with the geo-political tensions of an age of imperial contestation.[3] But as David Stafford has shown, it was William Le Queux, E. Phillips Oppenheim and others of their ilk who developed many of the tropes and themes that now seem so familiar from spy fiction.

Le Queux is a particularly significant figure because of his real-world activities as well as his career as an author. One of his most influential contacts was the head of army counter-intelligence, James Edmonds, whose advice convinced the British government of the need to radically reform its intelligence bureaucracy, creating the Secret Service Bureau (forerunner of MI5 and MI6) in 1909. Edmonds relied not on evidence or intelligence of German espionage and subversion but gossip and testimony from members of the public. And such fears were deliberately stoked by Le Queux, who was determined to shake British officialdom out of its complacency and arm itself physically, legally and morally against the German espionage threat. His *Spies of the Kaiser* (1909) was first serialised in the *Weekly News* which, as Nicholas Hiley has pointed out, also appointed a 'Spy Editor' and positioned Le Queux's serial alongside headlines screaming 'FOREIGN SPIES IN BRITAIN./ £10 given for information./ Have you seen a spy?'[4] When the text came out in volume form, Le Queux's preface, 'If England Knew', asserted as a matter of fact the presence of over five thousand 'agents of the German Secret Police at this moment working on behalf of the Intelligence Department in Berlin'.[5] Le Queux was no doubt satisfied to receive dozens of letters from concerned members of the public identifying German agents, which he lost no time in transmitting to Edmonds at the War Office.

To defeat the German menace at home, Le Queux needed to make domestic counter-espionage acceptable in a country where spies were traditionally viewed with considerable distaste as being both under-hand and troublingly associated with despotic foreign powers.[6] Just as the rearmament of Continental powers necessitated the development of Britain's coastal defences, so the practice of espionage by those same Continental powers meant that Britain could not simply stand by and watch as foreign spies penetrated the homeland in order to establish fifth columns in case of invasion, and more immediately to report back on the state of Britain's preparedness. Le Queux achieved his aim by emphasising the consequences of successful espionage, as well as presenting Britain's counter-intelligence specialists as a new breed of heroes. (Le Queux's Duckworth Drew, hero of *Secrets of the Foreign Office* (1903), is clearly a forerunner of James Bond.) But while German agents were widely believed to be collecting their intelligence simply by observation, the novels frequently seek to make their plots more exciting and urgent by including the theft and recovery of secrets, as indicated by the number of popular novels published from 1900 to 1914 with the word 'secret' in the title.[7]

As the arms race between Britain and Germany gathered pace, it was hardly surprising that technological innovations should be a major focus of the spies and counter-spies. This is exemplified by Le Queux's *Spies of the Kaiser*, a collection of fourteen linked short stories, in which the amateur detective Ray Raymond and his narrator-sidekick Jack Jacox find German agents in every corner of the British Isles busily stealing secrets, copying plans and reconnoitring military establishments. In the first story, 'How the Plans of Rosyth Were Stolen', Raymond investigates the theft of the plans of the new submarine dockyard at Rosyth, which were kept in an apparently impregnable safe, keys to which were accessible to only two of the base's most trusted and loyal employees. Raymond links the theft to the death, apparently by suicide, of a young clerk in London; a document is found in his pocket which turns out to be an exact copy of one of the Rosyth plans. The clerk's fiancée reveals that he had been perturbed in the days leading up to his death, and foretold that he would be in the newspapers before long. Raymond's investigations show that the clerk had stumbled across a German espionage plot, run from the clubhouse of the Dunfermline Golf Club, and directed from Knightsbridge by Germany's master spy, Hermann Hartmann.

As this summary makes clear, there can be little doubt that Le Queux read 'The Bruce-Partington Plans', published just months before *Spies of the Kaiser*. The latter's second story, 'The Secret of the Silent Submarine', further confirms that Conan Doyle was a major influence on one of the most politically effective fictions of the Edwardian period. Indeed, the relationship between Doyle's and Le Queux's fictions was close and reciprocal: Doyle drew on the invasion-scare and espionage genres in stories like 'Danger!' and 'His Last Bow', while Le Queux based his amateur detectives on Holmes and Watson, and appropriated specific details from Doyle. In 'The Bruce-Partington Plans', Mycroft Holmes requests his brother's help to solve the mystery of Cadogan West, a clerk at Woolwich Arsenal who was found dead on the tracks just outside Aldgate Station on the London Underground. In his pocket were seven of the plans for the Bruce-Partington submarine, 'the most jealously guarded of all Government secrets'. As Mycroft explains, the submarine is so efficient and covert that 'naval warfare becomes impossible within the radius of the Bruce-Partington's operation'

(*Last Bow*, 42): the submarine is a guarantee of both peace and of continued British naval superiority. Unfortunately for the government, ten papers have been stolen from Woolwich; the three still unaccounted for are the 'most essential' (43). Sensing that the value of the plans could only be realised by selling them to a foreign power, Holmes seeks from his brother 'a complete list of all foreign spies or international agents known to be in England' (48). Mycroft reports that only three are worth consideration: Adolph Meyer, Louis La Rothière and Hugo Oberstein.

Although the story is supposedly set in November 1895, its publication in the context of Anglo-German tensions and an alliance with France means that it is no surprise that the Teutonic-sounding Oberstein, and not the presumably Francophone La Rothière, is the story's principal villain. Breaking into Oberstein's house, Holmes and Watson discover that he was communicating with the thief using the alias Pierrot; Holmes poses as Pierrot to entrap the culprit, Colonel Valentine Walter, the younger brother of West's head of department at Woolwich, who needed money to repay a Stock Exchange debt. Walter reveals that West followed him to a rendezvous with Oberstein, where West was killed in a struggle, the two men throwing the corpse onto the roof of a passing train. With Walter's help, Holmes then sets a further trap. He lures Oberstein to Charing Cross with a promise of further plans of the submarine, and Watson celebrates the result:

> It is a matter of history – that secret history of a nation which is often so much more intimate and interesting than its public chronicles – that Oberstein, eager to complete the coup of his lifetime, came to the lure and was safely engulfed for fifteen years in a British prison. In his trunk were found the invaluable Bruce-Partington plans, which he had put up for auction in all the naval centres of Europe. (66)

At this point, however, Doyle and Le Queux part company. Oberstein may have been convicted for the common-law offences of murder or manslaughter, but he could not have been convicted for espionage as the offence at the time did not exist in British law. The Official Secrets Act 1889 criminalised the disclosure of sensitive information, but not its acquisition by foreign powers, and changing the law was Le Queux's clear aim in *Spies of the Kaiser*, in which Raymond and Jacob repeatedly catch the spies red-handed but watch impotently as one after the other is released back into society. All of that changed with the 1911 Official Secrets Act – a vindication of Le Queux's political campaign.

Figure 18 'Do you mean to say that anyone holding these three papers, and without the seven others, could construct a Bruce-Partington submarine?' Illustration by Arthur Twidle, *Strand Magazine*, December 1908.

Watson's reference to 'secret history' identifies one of the main pleasures of espionage fiction – the sense that we become privileged observers of the real but hidden workings of state power. This secret history lies behind the official world of parliamentary debates and press reports, both of which feature in the opening pages of 'The Bruce-Partington Plans'. Setting the scene, Watson reports that the newspapers contained 'news of a revolution, of a possible war, and of an impending change of government' (37); on receiving Mycroft's telegram concerning Cadogan West, Watson locates the relevant newspaper account which tells the bare facts of the body's discovery and the apparently trivial detail that his pockets contained 'a small packet of technical papers' (41). Mycroft's inside knowledge and Holmes's investigations then take us behind the public facts. Mycroft knows the true significance of the papers, which have been carefully withheld from public knowledge: 'Fortunately it has not come out. The Press would be furious if it did' (42). Significantly, Holmes discovers that the spy and the thief have been communicating in code in the agony columns of the *Daily Telegraph*; even the most routine and quotidian part of a daily newspaper is, underneath the surface, an arena for covert activity affecting the destiny of nations.

Commanding one of the most privileged positions of all in government, Mycroft is the repository of all of the British state's secret histories, as Holmes makes clear: 'he is the central exchange, the clearing-house ... All other men are specialists, but his specialism is omniscience' (39). What Holmes describes here is a sort of one-man Cabinet Office, a link between departments working on the full range of the government's business – clearly Mycroft's official role has expanded enormously since 'The Greek Interpreter', when he was employed by the government merely for his financial acumen: 'he audits the books in some of the Government departments' (*Memoirs*, 195). The implications of Mycroft's government role have appealed to writers and directors adapting Holmes for the screen: in Billy Wilder and I. A. L. Diamond's movie *The Private Life of Sherlock Holmes*, Mycroft is a government spymaster who is responsible for Britain's race to stay ahead of Germany in submarine technology, a conceit repeated and emphasised in Steven Moffat and Mark Gatiss's *Sherlock*, in which Holmes himself eventually becomes something akin to an MI6 agent. In fact, while the suggestion that Holmes has an intelligence role might seem fanciful, there are suggestions in several stories that he has undertaken espionage missions, perhaps with his brother's connivance. In 'The Empty House', for instance, Holmes reveals that he obtained Mycroft's financial support after his confrontation with Moriarty in Switzerland; he then spent the next two years touring notable trouble spots on the fringes of the British Empire, including Lhasa (destination of the Younghusband Expedition, which had set off shortly before Conan Doyle wrote the story, a military and political mission which aimed to ensure that Tibet did not enter the Russian sphere of influence in Asia), Persia (where Russia, Germany and Britain all entertained imperialist ambitions), and Khartoum, where Holmes 'paid a short but interesting visit to the Khalifa ... the results of which I have communicated to the Foreign Office' (*Return*, 12). In 'The Bruce-Partington Plans', Holmes rejects Mycroft's suggestion that taking on the case might result in an official honour – 'I play the game for the game's own sake' – although Watson reveals that his defeat of Oberstein leads to an audience at Windsor and the gift of 'a remarkably fine emerald tie-pin' (67). But this cannot be the only covert service that he supplied to the nation, as we discover in 'The Three Garridebs' that in June 1902 'Holmes refused a knighthood for services which may perhaps some day be described' (*Case-Book*, 89). Watson's reticence suggests that these services were of a secret variety.

The period's shifting geopolitical alliances are reflected by one of the espionage genre's most prominent tropes – that of a diplomatic document which is stolen and must be recovered, or which needs to be concealed from hostile eyes. The document is often a secret treaty or communication which, if revealed to the public, would catastrophically upset the delicate European diplomatic balance, or infuriate a public into demanding war. Le Queux's *Whose Findeth a Wife* (1897), for example, concerns the recovery of an Anglo-German treaty which has the potential to push Russia into war, while E. Phillips Oppenheim's *A Maker of History* (1905) begins with a young Englishman in a German forest accidentally witnessing the signing of a secret treaty between the Kaiser and the Tsar, after which he is pursued by agents determined to ensure he does not reveal his knowledge; when the treaty is revealed to the French, they agree to a strategic alliance with Britain.

Although Conan Doyle is rarely credited with being an originator of spy fiction, one of the earliest stories to make use of the theft of a secret treaty that could imperil European peace was 'The Naval Treaty', first published in the *Strand* in October and November 1893. Holmes's client is a young diplomat, Percy Phelps, whose uncle, Lord Holdhurst, is Foreign Minister. No doubt due to this nepotism, Phelps 'rose rapidly to a responsible position' (*Memoirs*, 217) – so much so that Lord Holdhurst entrusted to him 'the original of that secret treaty between England and Italy, of which, I regret to say, some rumours have already got into the public Press'. The Foreign Minister underlines the secrecy and significance of the treaty's contents: 'It is of enormous importance that nothing further should leak out. The French or Russian Embassies would pay an immense sum to learn the contents of these papers' (218). The treaty is nonetheless stolen, and Holmes eventually discovers the thief to be Joseph Harrison, Phelps's prospective brother-in-law, who (Holmes presumes) would have taken the treaty 'to the French Embassy, or wherever he thought a long price was to be had' (247–8). With these scant details, Doyle helped established several of the espionage elements of the invasion-scare genre: Britain is embroiled in delicate great power diplomacy; it negotiates a treaty with one or several European powers, the details of which could upset the balance of power in Europe; the treaty or documents pertaining to it are stolen; the most senior ministers in government appoint a specialist to retrieve the stolen secrets before Europe lurches into war. However, these features are not entirely Doyle's inventions. For a start, 'The Naval Treaty' is another of Doyle's variations on Poe's 'The Purloined Letter': in both stories, a stolen document is presumed to have been spirited away but actually remains hidden in an enclosed private space where much of the action takes place. Doyle's story also resembles Le Queux's *The Great War in England in 1897*, published in book form in 1894 but serialised the previous year in Alfred Harmsworth's popular magazine *Answers*. Le Queux's novel was one of the first to combine the invasion/future-war scenario with international espionage: the spy Count von Beilstein is instructed by his Russian employers to steal a secret treaty recently agreed between Britain, Austria and Italy. He succeeds in doing so by exploiting his friendship with a young Foreign Office diplomat, and this intelligence coup is the catalyst for the subsequent European war and invasion of Britain.[8] Doyle and Le Queux can, then, both be credited with developing the features of the espionage fiction so familiar to us today – the foreign spymaster, recruiting naive or impecunious Britons to steal documents or report on defences; the resourceful British secret agent, deployed by the government on dangerous overseas missions to retrieve secrets or at home to unmask the spies; the risk of global catastrophe if he should fail.

By the time Doyle returned to the genre in 1904 with 'The Second Stain', yet another reworking of 'The Purloined Letter', many of these elements would already have become familiar to Edwardian readers. 'The Second Stain' begins with lightly fictionalised portraits of the highest levels of government: Holmes's clients are none other than the Prime Minister, Lord Bellinger, and the Secretary for European Affairs, Trelawney Hope.[9] This story had, appropriately enough, already been foreshadowed in Watson's introduction to 'The Naval Treaty', in which he announced that 'The Second Stain' 'deals with interests of such importance, and implicates so many of the first families in the kingdom, that for many years it will be impossible to make it public' (213). This immediately situates the story in the espionage genre, which frequently featured senior ministers as the taskmasters of the protagonists; Le Queux's *Secrets of the Foreign Office*, for instance, published a year before 'The Second Stain', opens with the Foreign Secretary, the Marquess of Macclesfield, sending his intelligence officer Duckworth Drew to discover if the European powers are negotiating against Britain's interests. The document in 'The Second Stain' is not a treaty but a letter 'from a certain foreign potentate who has been ruffled by some recent Colonial developments of this country', and which was 'written hurriedly and upon his own responsibility entirely' (*Return*, 295). The problem is not what it means diplomatically but its likely political effect: 'it is couched in so unfortunate a manner, and certain phrases are of so provocative a character, that its publication would undoubtedly lead to a most dangerous state of feeling in this country' (294). Doyle thus updates the details to include topical but coded references to Kaiser Wilhelm II, whose telegram to the Boer President Paul Krueger in 1896, perceived as a provocative intervention in Britain's sphere of influence, inflamed British public opinion against Germany.

As well as demonstrating fiction's capacity for appropriating the news, the letter's reported contents show Doyle reflecting the altered geopolitical reality: where France had been the presumed enemy in 'The Naval Treaty', 'The Second Stain' was first published in the *Strand* in December 1904, shortly after the *Entente Cordiale* was agreed between Britain and France in April of that year. Indeed, 'The Second Stain' (like Oppenheim's *A Maker of History*) can be read as something of a celebration of the new-found amity with France: the murder of Eduardo Lucas, the spy responsible for the plot to steal the letter, is solved not by Holmes but by the Parisian police, described significantly enough by Lestrade as '[o]ur French friends' (307). With Germany now firmly outside Britain's strategic alliances, the story acknowledges increased tensions by emphasising the gravity of the consequences in the event of its disclosure: 'its publication might very easily – I might almost say probably – lead to European complications of the utmost moment. It is not too much to say that peace or war may hang upon the issue' (292). Doyle also brought in from the emerging espionage genre the figure of the professional intelligence agent, allied not to a particular country but buying (or stealing) and selling secrets to the highest bidder. But here Doyle again reflects geopolitical rivalries when Holmes identifies three potential suspects, two of whom would still be active in 'The Bruce-Partington Plans': the names of Oberstein, La Rothiere and Eduardo Lucas each indicate a Continental origin but cover a range of rival powers.[10]

Holmes's investigation reveals three plots at work. Of greatest concern to his clients is Eduardo Lucas's plot to steal the letter from the foreign potentate, and thereby put in jeopardy the delicate balance of power in Europe. He achieves this through a second plot: he blackmails Trelawney Hope's wife with an indiscreet letter she had written many years previously, and which would jeopardise her marriage. But Lucas himself becomes the victim of a third plot – the revenge of his crazed and jealous wife, Mme Henri Fournaye, who wrongly believes Lady Hilda Trelawney Hope to be her husband's lover. Catherine Belsey has shown that the story connects sexuality and politics, with two letters (one political, one sexual) which 'symbolically parallel' each other. The secrets of espionage and high diplomacy are matched by the secrets of the bedroom, but the important point for Belsey is that both remain secrets: 'the text is symmetrically elusive concerning both sexuality and politics'.[11] Belsey aims to deconstruct the story by showing that its inability to relate the contents of the letters reveals the limits of its realism. But the story's reticence is entirely appropriate given that its entire preoccupation is with secrecy. It purports to tell the secret history behind events which we can recognise as the Krueger Telegram and the *Entente Cordiale* but does so within a frame of official secrecy: at the story's outset, Watson tells how he secures Holmes's agreement to publication on condition that his account should be 'carefully guarded'; Watson asks 'the public' to 'understand' his 'reticence' if he appears 'somewhat vague in certain details' (291). Watson then refuses to disclose the decade, let alone the year or dates on which the events took place. This partly misdirects us from the highly topical nature of the story's frame of reference, but it also (*pace* Belsey) brings us into a game of verisimilitude by effectively redacting the narrative in line with the requirements of government.

Christopher Metress develops Belsey's argument, revealing the story's 'duplicitous' nature, which is encapsulated in its title and repeated insistently through a remarkable collection of doublings (two stains, two letters, two scandals, two husbands, two wives) and 'a masterly suggestive sequence of doubled scenes'.[12] Metress shows that the story's intricate structure works on a 'both/and' rather than 'either/or' logic, with a fundamental dichotomy between diplomacy (which seeks to conceal) and detection (which seeks to reveal). The story conceals and reveals. But we can go further than Metress and see that the story conceals when it appears to be revealing. This is evident in Holmes's request to know the contents of the potentate's letter. Lord Bellinger initially refuses: 'That is a State secret of the utmost importance, and I fear that I cannot tell you, nor do I see that it is necessary.' When Holmes then declines to take the case, the Prime Minister appears to relent, only to fail to disclose the identity or nationality of the author, or anything about what he actually wrote: all he will say is that its 'manner' is 'unfortunate', there are 'certain phrases' of a 'provocative . . . character' (295). Holmes works out the author's identity, but instead of asking he writes the name on a piece of paper for Lord Bellinger to confirm – a bizarre ruse, given that there are only four people in the room, two of whom know the secret already: after Holmes's correct deduction, the secret remains unknown only to Watson, the reader's representative in the room. The pleasures of secret histories are enhanced, not frustrated, by such reticence: our knowledge of the inner workings of the state, like the suggestions of what goes on in the bedroom, are all the more powerful for being limited and fragmentary.

Notes

1. Stafford, 'Spies and Gentlemen', pp. 489–509.
2. Ibid., p. 505.
3. See Michael Denning, *Cover Stories*, pp. 11–13.
4. Hiley, 'The Failure of British Espionage against Germany', p. 844. See also David French, 'Spy Fever in Britain, 1900–1915', p. 357.
5. William Le Queux, *Spies of the Kaiser*, p. x.
6. Stafford, 'Spies and Gentlemen', pp. 506–7.
7. Le Queux alone was responsible for *Of Royal Blood. A Story of the Secret Service* (1900), *Secrets of the Foreign Office* (1903), *The Secret of the Square* (1907), *Revelations of the Secret Service* (1911) and *A Secret Sin* (1914), while Oppenheim produced *The Secret . . .* (1907) and *Mr Marx's Secret* (1909).
8. William Le Queux, *The Great War in England in 1897*.
9. Lord Bellinger is sometimes assumed to have been based on W. E. Gladstone, and Sidney Paget's illustrations for the story clearly show that he took Gladstone as his model. However, Lord Bellinger, twice prime minister, may equally be a portrait of the Marquess of Salisbury, three times prime minister and for much of the same time also foreign secretary.
10. For an assessment of this point against the background of the *Strand*'s more general coverage of current affairs, see Jonathan Cranfield, 'From Baskerville to the Moon'. By making Lucas the culprit, Doyle also permitted himself a joke at the expense of the well-known Edwardian travel writer and belle-lettrist E. V. (Edward) Lucas. The name La Rothiere presumably derives from the Battle of La Rothière (1814), which would have been familiar to Doyle from his research into the Napoleonic Wars. Note that La Rothiere appears without an accent in 'The Second Stain', but as La Rothière in 'The Bruce-Partington Plans'.
11. Belsey, *Critical Practice*, p. 116.
12. Christopher Metress, 'Diplomacy and Detection in Conan Doyle's "The Second Stain"', pp. 41–3.

Chapter 19

Oaths and Secrets

Organised criminality and violence appear frequently in the Holmes stories. *A Study in Scarlet* imagines Brigham Young's nascent Mormon state as a tightly knit conspiratorial organisation, exerting uncompromising control over its membership even beyond its notional borders. An ideological conspiracy of a very different kind lies behind the surreal menace of 'The Five Orange Pips', in which the Ku Klux Klan enforces its organisational rules through fear-inducing symbols, followed by swift and merciless punishment. The clues in this story reveal the organisation's global reach: at their home in Horsham, the Openshaws receive letters from the Klan postmarked Pondicherry, Dundee and East London; Holmes discovers that the murderers of John Openshaw are led by the captain of the barque *Lone Star*, registered in Savannah, Georgia. The Sicilian Mafia is behind the theft of the Borgia Pearl in 'The Adventure of the Six Napoleons' (1904), and 'The Red Circle' features another Italian crime syndicate. The protagonists of 'The Golden Pince-Nez' turn out to be Russian Nihilists, one hiding from his former comrades, the other on a mission to save her lover from Russian tyranny. Theft and fraud by organised gangs are the centre of 'The Red-Headed League', 'The Engineer's Thumb', 'The Resident Patient', 'The Greek Interpreter' and 'The Dancing Men', while the greatest crime syndicate of all is overseen by Professor James Moriarty, as we discover in 'The Final Problem', 'The Empty House' and *The Valley of Fear*.

The figure of Moriarty, 'organiser of half that is evil and of nearly all that is undetected in this great city' (*Memoirs*, 252), embodies a conspiratorial, totalising view of criminality that contrasts with that of most of the other sixty Holmes stories, in which criminality and human folly come in many and various forms. Moriarty's spider's web with 'a thousand radiations' (252) implies that crimes are not random or accidental but coordinated and concerted; their patterns are evidence of human agency and control. Moriarty's crimes are of a different order to the crimes that Holmes imagines to be taking place in the 'scattered houses' of 'the smiling and beautiful countryside' as he travels to Winchester with Watson in 'The Copper Beeches':

> But look at these lonely houses, each in its own fields, filled for the most part with poor ignorant folk who know little of the law. Think of the deeds of hellish cruelty, the hidden wickedness which may go on, year in, year out, in such places, and none the wiser. (*Adventures*, 280)

Compared to this bleak vision of random mayhem, Moriarty's web of crime is reassuringly planned and ordered: once Holmes removes the spider at its centre, crime can be brought back under control.

Organised conspiracies may be more readily detectable than unplanned violence or individual acts of folly. A criminal network has to communicate in order to function, and if one can read the signs – as Holmes of course is adept at doing – then the conspiracy can be detected, exposed and disrupted. Some of Holmes's most celebrated cases turn on his success in understanding the codes and procedures necessary to execute a conspiracy, as in 'The Dancing Men' in which Holmes deciphers Abe Slaney's messages, written in a symbolic code developed by the Chicago crime gang to which Slaney belonged. Similarly, in 'The Five Orange Pips', the Openshaws are baffled by the contents of three letters sent to their home in Horsham, but Holmes understands their contents to be a coded warning by connecting the orange pips and the letters K. K. K. to his knowledge of American secret societies, codified in the entry in the American Encyclopaedia which he reads to Watson:

> Ku Klux Klan. A name derived from a fanciful resemblance to the sound produced by cocking a rifle. This terrible secret society was formed by some ex-Confederate soldiers in the Southern States after the Civil War, and it rapidly formed local branches in different parts of the country, notably in Tennessee, Louisiana, the Carolinas, Georgia, and Florida. Its power was used for political purposes, principally for the terrorizing of the negro voters, and the murdering or driving from the country of those who were opposed to its views. Its outrages were usually preceded by a warning sent to the marked man in some fantastic but generally recognized shape – a sprig of oak leaves in some parts, melon seeds or orange pips in others. On receiving this the victim might either openly abjure his former ways, or might fly from the country. If he braved the matter out, death would unfailingly come upon him, and usually in some strange and unforeseen manner. So perfect was the organization of

the society, and so systematic its methods, that there is hardly a case upon record where any man succeeded in braving it with impunity, or in which any of its outrages were traced home to the perpetrators. (*Adventures*, 117)

We have seen that Conan Doyle's stories of espionage purport to reveal the hidden wiring of state power; these stories of organised crime do something similar for non-state criminal networks, which are concealed from the view of the average *Strand* reader but which exert a palpable influence over the real world through theft, fraud, subversion and terrorism. Holmes's successful efforts to decipher criminal communications are one method of exposing these organisations' methods and aims; another is the testimony of witnesses to the gangs' activities brought into the story by Holmes's investigation. One such witness is Emilia Lucca in 'The Red Circle', whose husband Gennaro, 'driven half mad by the injustices of life' (*Last Bow*, 112), unwisely joins a secret society in Naples. She claims the Red Circle 'was allied to the old Carbonari' (literally 'charcoal makers'), a cellular network of covert organisations founded during the Napoleonic Wars and dedicated to the unification of Italy under a republican government. However, her description of the Red Circle's protection rackets and blackmail operations in New York is more suggestive of a Mafia-type criminal organisation, and the evidence shows that Doyle had in mind the Camorra ('Camorra' is struck through in the manuscript and 'Carbonari' is substituted).[1] Emilia explains that the Red Circle's membership rituals were used not only for induction and mutual recognition, but also to instil fear and ensure discipline: 'The oaths and secrets of this brotherhood were frightful; but once within its rule no escape was possible' (112). After Emilia and Gennaro flee to New York, the latter has a fateful meeting:

> What was his horror one evening to meet in the streets the very man who had initiated him in Naples, the giant Gorgiano, a man who had earned the name of 'Death' in the South of Italy, for he was red to the elbow in murder! He had come to New York to avoid the Italian police, and he had already planted a branch of this dreadful society in his new home. All this Gennaro told me, and showed me a summons which he had received that very day, a Red Circle drawn upon the head of it, telling him that a lodge would be held upon a certain date, and that his presence at it was required and ordered. (112)

The Red Circle, which blows up its enemies with dynamite, is one of several organisations that critics have suggested should be seen as substitutes for Fenian organisations such as Clan-na-Gael, a network which operated from the United States and was behind the Fenian dynamite campaign on the British mainland in the early 1880s, and the Irish Republican Brotherhood (IRB), forerunner of the twentieth-century IRA. Owen Dudley Edwards, for example, suggests that the use of 'brotherhood' in 'The Red Circle' is a sign that Doyle had the IRB in mind.[2] Discussing other stories, Catherine Wynne goes further, suggesting that Moriarty's network is another Fenian substitute, and cites as evidence the apparently Irish names of Moriarty and his deputy, Colonel Sebastian Moran.[3] Such connections are tempting, given Doyle's partial Irish ancestry, his glimpse of Fenians on a visit to Ireland in his childhood, and his complex engagement with Irish politics, his loyalties switching from Unionism to supporting Home Rule.[4] However, such readings are both strained and incomplete, leaving out other important influences. Emilia's reference to a lodge is suggestive of Freemasonry, a world which Doyle knew from the inside, having joined Phoenix Lodge no. 257 in Portsmouth in 1887, the year in which Sherlock Holmes first entered into print. Intriguingly, Doyle resigned from the lodge in the same year as the publication of 'The Red Circle'. More importantly, 'The Red Circle' draws on a long history of literary and historical interest in Italian secret societies, which would have been familiar to Doyle from his researches into the Napoleonic Wars, if nothing else.

In fact, the influence here of one of Doyle's favourite authors, Wilkie Collins, has been entirely overlooked. The colourful villain Count Fosco in *The Woman in White* (1859–60) enters the novel as Sir Percival Glyde's accomplice, assisting Glyde in his plan to enrich himself through marriage and legacy tampering. But Fosco turns out to be involved in more far-reaching conspiracies, and his membership of an Italian secret society, The Brotherhood (itself based on the Carbonari), reveals *The Woman in White* to be a far more plausible source for 'The Red Circle' – and several of Doyle's other secret societies – than the IRB. Another member of Collins's Brotherhood, Professor Pesca, reveals that he joined in a moment of intense personal vulnerability, just as Gennaro joined the Red Circle:

> I, in my younger time, under provocation so dreadful that I will not tell you of it, entered the Brotherhood by an impulse, as I might have killed myself by an impulse. I must remain in it, now – it has got me, whatever I may think of it in my better circumstances and my cooler manhood, to my dying day.

He goes on to reveal The Brotherhood to be a particularly covert and uncompromising organisation:

> We are warned, if we betray the Brotherhood, or if we injure it by serving other interests, that we die by the principles of the Brotherhood – die by the hand of a stranger who may be sent from the other end of the world to strike the blow – or by the hand of our own bosom-friend, who may have been a member unknown to us through all the years of our intimacy. . . . A man who has been false to the Brotherhood is discovered, sooner or later, by the Chiefs who know him – Presidents or Secretaries, as the case may be. And a man discovered by the Chiefs is dead. *No human laws can protect him.*[5]

The Woman in White is also a source for *The Valley of Fear*, Doyle's most sustained exploration of the mechanics of organised criminal conspiracies. Pesca reveals to Collins's hero, Walter Hartright, that his arm bears a branded symbol, 'deeply burnt in the flesh and stained of a bright blood-red colour' which marks him for life as a member of The Brotherhood. Hartright adds: 'I abstain from describing the device which the brand represented. It will be sufficient to say that it was circular in form, and so small that it would have been completely covered by a shilling coin.'[6] A similar brand is found on the right forearm of the corpse discovered at Birlstone Manor House – 'a curious brown design, a triangle inside a circle' (*Valley*, 30) – while beside the body there is a card with the message 'V. V. 341'. The symbol appears to confirm the identification of the body as that of John Douglas, the American tenant of Birlstone Manor, as he was seen by the butler to have the symbol branded onto his arm. (The dead man has been shot in the face with a sawn-off shotgun, leaving him otherwise unrecognisable.) Holmes concludes that Douglas is still alive and concealed within the Manor, that the dead man was the assailant and bore the same branded symbol on his arm, that V. V. stands for Vermissa Valley, a coal-mining district in the United States, and 341 is the number of the lodge of the Ancient Order of Freemen in the valley. Douglas's narrative then reveals the symbol to be the mark of membership of the Scowrers, a powerful labour organisation in the valley that is somewhere between crime syndicate, trade union and (by its connection to the Ancient Order of Freemen) masonic lodge.

Here, critics like Dudley Edwards and Wynne are on much firmer ground in identifying a link between violent Irish secret societies and Doyle's fiction. The Scowrers are closely based on the Molly Maguires, a violent, oath-bound labour syndicate with roots in secret Catholic agrarian groups in Ireland, and which was widely believed to have exerted a reign of terror over the anthracite coalfields of Pennsylvania in the 1860s and 1870s. Sixteen men, mostly mine officials, were killed, and twenty members of the Molly Maguires were tried and hanged.[7] As was his custom with historical fiction, Doyle researched the subject thoroughly, but it is clear that his major source was Allan Pinkerton's *The Molly Maguires and the Detectives* (1877), as he acknowledged in a collected edition of the long Holmes stories in 1929: *The Valley of Fear* 'had its origin through my reading a graphic account of the Molly McQuire [sic] outrages in the coalfields of Pennsylvania, when a young detective drawn from Pinkerton's Agency acted exactly as the hero is represented as doing'.[8] The book – another possible source for 'The Red Circle', which also features a Pinkerton's detective – purports to be the inside story of the breaking up of the syndicate, but has been judged by Kevin Kenny, a historian sceptical about the Molly Maguires' reputation for terroristic violence, to be 'semifictional'.[9] It tells the story of Pinkerton's agent James McParlan,

Figure 19 'He nearly fainted at the sudden shock of it, but he bit his lip and clenched his hands to hide his agony. "I can take more of that," said he.' Detail from illustration by Frank Wiles, *Strand Magazine*, March 1915.

who from 1873 to 1876 infiltrated the Molly Maguires in the identity of a tramp called James McKenna, culminating in the arrest of the chief members of the syndicate, after which McParlan fled to Philadelphia. Pinkerton describes in detail McParlan's initiation into the Ancient Order of Hibernians, a masonic-like Catholic order (a Catholic response to Ulster's Orange Order) which was a parent organisation for the Molly Maguires, and his rise to authority as secretary of the Hibernians' Shenandoah Lodge. McParlan is the model for *The Valley of Fear*'s Birdy Edwards, the Pinkerton's agent who, in the guise of John McMurdo, infiltrates the Scowrers and brings their wicked leader Boss McGinty and eight accomplices to the scaffold, before escaping to England in the guise of John Douglas. The distinctive hierarchy of the Scowrers – Division Master, Bodymaster, Brother – come from Pinkerton, as does Edwards's first meeting with Bodymaster McGinty, based (as Dudley Edwards has pointed out) on Pinkerton's account of McParlan's meeting with a Pottsville tavern proprietor and leading Molly called Pat Dormer.[10]

Doyle carefully removed most traces of the Irishness of the Molly Maguires when he turned the syndicate into the Scowrers, as he revealed to his editor at the *Strand*, Herbert Greenhough Smith: 'I change all names so as not to get into possible Irish politics.'[11] In another letter to Smith, he insisted that the Molly Maguires must on no account be identified: 'It was an Irish organization and the Irish are exceedingly touchy upon the point . . . It would be a *most serious error* to be definite in the matter.'[12] Only John McMurdo remains Irish: 'with his glib Irish tongue . . . He could talk of the sweet valleys of County Monaghan from which he came, of the lovely distant island, the low hills and green meadows of which [sic] seemed the more beautiful when imagination viewed them from this place of grime and snow' (95). But McMurdo is of course an imposter and, as Wynne notes, his apparently true identity of Edwards does not sound especially Irish.[13] Doyle replaced the trappings of Irish nationalism with language and rituals drawn from Freemasonry: the Ancient Order of Hibernians becomes the Ancient Order of Freemen, and Edwards's initiation into the Scowrers, which does not derive from Pinkerton, has a distinctly Masonic quality of trial and ritual. The ceremony begins with the adoption of Masonic dress:

> The three of them then removed his coat, turned up the sleeve of his right arm, and finally passed a rope round above the elbows and made it fast. They next placed a thick black cap right over his head and the upper part of his face.

McGinty then tests Edwards with a kind of catechism, which he passes: 'We know, brother, by your sign and your counter sign, that you are indeed one of us.' The final test is an ordeal of fear and pain: his arm is branded, and 'he felt two hard points in front of his eyes, pressing upon them so that it appeared as if he could not move forward without a danger of losing them. None the less, he nerved himself to step resolutely out' (115).

Doyle draws on his inside knowledge of Freemasonry to develop an alternative, apparently apolitical flavour of clandestinity in the Scowrers' operations. At the end of the novella, he compounds this apparent depoliticisation by placing the Scowrers within a larger frame – the vast operations of Professor Moriarty, whom Holmes believes to have been employed by the Scowrers to locate Birdy Edwards and advise on how he could be eliminated, before being forced to 'step in himself with a master touch' (169). Far from being evidence of Moriarty's 'alignment with, or adhesion to, American and, by extension Irish secret societies – in particular Fenianism and its counterpart, Clan-na-Gael' as Wynne unconvincingly contends, Moriarty's involvement seals the novella's removal from Irish politics.[14] Doyle wrote *The Valley of Fear* in three months (February to April 1914) in the midst of a political and constitutional crisis over Home Rule. The Government of Ireland Bill, which would have created a new parliament in Dublin and abolished the colonial administration, was making its slow and painful way through the British Parliament where between 1912 and May 1914 it was passed by the Commons and rejected by the Lords three times; in May 1914 the government used the new Parliament Act, which enshrined the supremacy of the Commons over the Lords, to enact the bill (although it became law, it was effectively suspended by Asquith's government after the outbreak of the First World War). Simultaneously, the Unionist community in Ulster began arming and mobilising, raising the spectre of civil war: they created the paramilitary Ulster Volunteer Force (UVF) in 1913, and while Doyle was writing *The Valley of Fear*, the so-called Curragh Mutiny in March 1914 saw officers of the British Army in Ireland resign rather than take on the UVF.[15] Although Doyle had become in public a supporter of Home Rule – on imperialist rather than Irish nationalist grounds, as he saw devolved government as the best route to keeping the empire intact – he was clearly anxious to keep Holmes separate from contentious politics.

And yet in his attempts to depoliticise the novella's events in America, he sent Holmes into equally contentious terrain closer to home. Removing one context amplified another: the Scowrers are Masonic but they are also a labour union. Their function is to maintain control over the Vermissa Valley region by terrorising the mine owners and officials, and subduing the police; they use their control to maintain protection rackets, silence dissent and enforce restrictive labour practices. While Doyle endeavours to paint the Scowrers as a primarily criminal enterprise, the contest in the valley is between labour and capital, as well as between crime and order. Edwards tells Morris, a dissident Scowrer, that 'some would say it was war . . . A war of two classes with all in, so that each struck as best it could' (128). McGinty curses the Coal and Iron Constabulary as 'the paid tool of the capitalists' (111) and 'a capitalist outrage' (133). Edwards (as McMurdo) ironically describes himself as having 'all the millions of the capitalists at his back' (155). He later rationalises the murder of a mine official: 'Sure, it is like a war . . . What is it but a war between us and them, and we hit back where we best can?' (143).

The Valley of Fear's first readers could not have missed the contemporary resonances of a story of industrial unrest, political subversion and class conflict: as Joseph Kestner has observed, the novella's 'labour unrest is that of early Georgian Britain as much as it is of America'.[16] The years between 1910 and 1914 were marked in Britain (including Ireland) by a dramatic deterioration in industrial relations, as workers responded angrily to stagnant wages and a rising cost of living, resulting in 'social unrest on a scale beyond anything that had occurred since the first half of the nineteenth century'.[17] There were more strikes, and more working days lost – forty million in 1913 – than in any previous period.[18] It is still striking just how much violence – on both sides – characterised the period's industrial relations, as strikers resorted to sabotage and intimidation, and the government responded with civil and military force. A prolonged strike in the Rhondda Valley coalfields in 1910–11 turned increasingly violent, culminating in the Tonypandy riots. The year 1911 saw the first national rail strike and a general transport strike in Liverpool; responding with characteristic belligerence, Winston Churchill repeatedly called on the army (cavalry as well as infantry) to aid the police, and summoned a Royal Navy armoured cruiser to the Mersey; two strikers were shot dead in Liverpool and two in Llanelli. In 1912 a million coal miners used a 37-day strike to obtain a minimum wage for the first time. In 1913, dock workers struck for six weeks in Leith, and a dock strike and lockout in Dublin which lasted for nearly six months is probably the most significant industrial unrest in Irish history.[19] The Miners Federation, National Union of Railwaymen and the National Transport Workers' Federation formed the 'Triple Alliance' in early 1914, a prelude to greater organisation and militancy: writing in 1935, the journalist George Dangerfield famously proposed that had war not broken out, Britain would have been in the grip of a general strike by September 1914.[20] These events took place against the background of rapidly growing union membership, which more than doubled from two million in 1901 to over four million in 1914, and a stronger political voice: the 1906 election, in which Conan Doyle stood unsuccessfully for the Liberal Unionists (allied to the Conservative Party), saw not only a Liberal Party landslide but also the election of twenty-nine MPs from the Labour Party, which had recently been formed by the unions to represent their interests in Parliament. Working men and working women – the number of women in unions doubled between 1905 and 1913 – had unprecedented political power in the era, and *The Valley of Fear* signals unease at its effects, on behalf of the largely white-collar, middle-class readership of the *Strand*.

These unsettling social and political developments – physical-force Irish republicanism, secret agency, the growing political power of women and industrial workers – resurface in 'His Last Bow' where, once more, they are presented as the product of an organised conspiracy, rather than as the structural effects of social and political forces. Set in August 1914 – the eve of the First World War, but also the moment of publication of *The Valley of Fear* – the story revives the myth of the vast, criminal conspiracy: 'Agents were suspected or even caught', Holmes recalls, 'but there was evidence of some strong and secret central force' (*Last Bow*, 168). This time, however, the author of all ill is not Professor Moriarty but the German secret service. Baron Von Herling makes clear that Germany has sown the seeds of domestic disorder in order to ensure Britain's removal from the military sphere when it executes the Schlieffen Plan: 'How then can England come in, especially when we have stirred her up such a devil's brew of Irish civil war, window-breaking furies, and God knows what to keep her thoughts at home?' (158). Although Conan Doyle's politics were in some respects progressive for his age, this story sounds the note of what Jonathan Cranfield has dubbed the 'twentieth-century Victorian', disturbed by changes he does not fully understand, and nostalgic for a past age of simpler virtues and reliable certainties. Moreover, 'His Last Bow' shows Doyle no longer warily avoiding Irish politics, personified by Holmes's alter ego Altamont, 'a real bitter Irish-American'. Clearly, something changed between the writing of *The Valley of Fear* and 'His Last Bow', and that was probably the Easter Rising of 1916. 'All changed, changed utterly', in W. B. Yeats's words:[21] the Rising removed Home Rule from the agenda, and set Irish nationalism and British imperialism on a collision course. These developments were clearly on Doyle's mind at the time, as he wrote furiously to the *Belfast Telegraph* while working on 'His Last Bow', condemning Sinn Fein for its record:

> It has brought about the destruction of part of its own capital city . . .
> It has, so far as it could, thrown away the fruits of fifty years of patient Constitutional reform.
> It only remains for it now to open a civil war against a perfectly united Empire which has shown that it can put five million men in the field, and would do so again before it would consent to having a foreign representative between it and the oceans of the world. When it has achieved this result its cycle of insanity will be complete. Meanwhile I would ask whether any British party has ever in the whole course of history injured Ireland so much in so short a time.[22]

But 'His Last Bow' is the exception, not the rule, in Doyle's engagement with Irish politics. The secret societies in the Holmes stories reflect only in part the manifestations of physical-force republicanism and nationalism. Organised conspiracies represent not one ideology but a range of late Victorian and Edwardian anxieties, from Nihilism to Suffragism to the empowerment of the working class. Rather than seeking to understand the world that was changing around him, by attributing these developments to 'some strong and secret central force', Doyle attempted to explain them away.

Notes

1. See Doyle, *His Last Bow*, ed. Owen Dudley Edwards, p. 207.
2. Ibid., pp. 207–8.
3. Catherine Wynne, *The Colonial Conan Doyle*, pp. 49–56.
4. Doyle estimates that his visit to Ireland took place in 1866, when he would have been six or seven years old: see *Memories and Adventures*, pp. 12–13. For Doyle's shifting views on Home Rule, see Doyle, *Letters to the Press*, pp. 158–9; 164–5.
5. Wilkie Collins, *The Woman in White*, pp. 536–7.
6. Ibid., p. 537.
7. Kevin Kenny, *Making Sense of the Molly Maguires*, p. 3.
8. Qtd in Doyle, *The Valley of Fear*, ed. Owen Dudley Edwards, p. xxxii.
9. Kenny, *Making Sense of the Molly Maguires*, p. 3.
10. Allan Pinkerton, *The Molly Maguires and the Detectives*, pp. 73–81; *Valley*, ed. Dudley Edwards, p. 198.

11. Conan Doyle to Greenhough Smith, 6 February 1914. Qtd in *Uncollected Sherlock Holmes*, p. 135.
12. Ibid., pp. 135–6.
13. Wynne, *Colonial Conan Doyle*, p. 42.
14. Ibid., p. 42.
15. For the historical background, see Simon Heffer, *The Age of Decadence*, pp. 804–16.
16. Kestner, *Sherlock's Men*, p. 161.
17. Hugh Armstrong Clegg, *A History of British Trade Unions Since 1889*, vol. II, p. 24.
18. Ibid., p. 24.
19. For details of the industrial unrest from 1911 to 1914, see Clegg, *History of British Trade Unions*, pp. 26–71, and Heffer, *The Age of Decadence*, pp. 651–706.
20. George Dangerfield, *The Strange Death of Liberal England*, p. 396.
21. W. B. Yeats, 'Easter 1916', in Yeats, *The Poems*, pp.180–2.
22. Doyle, *Letters to the Press*, p. 251.

Chapter 20

The Giant Rat of Sumatra

The late story 'Thor Bridge' opens with a celebrated passage in which Watson reveals the existence of 'a travel-worn and battered tin dispatch-box with my name, John H. Watson, MD, Late Indian Army, painted upon the lid' (*Case-Book*, 23) in the vaults of the Charing Cross branch of Cox and Co. bank. This was a real bank, founded in 1758 and which specialised as an army agency, responsible for army logistics and payments to officers and men: for its military customers it would have taken care not only of salaries but also of tax, insurance and bills, and it had branches across British India as well as the British Isles. For a former Indian Army doctor, therefore, it would have been a logical choice for placing an account, and its branch at 16–18 Charing Cross was, during the First World War, one of the busiest banks in the world, open all hours for men returning from the front.[1] Its wartime expansion could not be sustained and it was taken over by Lloyd's Bank in 1923, the year after 'Thor Bridge' was published in the *Strand*, although Lloyd's later sold its Indian operations which eventually became Cox and Kings travel agent, and which flourishes to this day.

Watson anchors the opening of this story to a fact, one that would have been recognisably true to many of its original readers. He then asks us to believe that this fictional tin box is 'crammed with papers' which document the untold adventures of Sherlock Holmes. These fall into three categories. The first are the 'unfinished tales' and 'unfathomed cases' – records of Holmes's 'complete failures' that lack a 'final explanation' and so, while being of possible interest to students, would 'hardly fail to annoy the casual reader' (23). Then there are cases 'which involve the secrets of private families to an extent which would mean consternation in many exalted quarters if it were thought possible that they might find their way into print'. To spare the blushes of the nobility, Holmes will ensure that 'these records will be separated and destroyed now that my friend has time to turn his energies to the matter' (23). Finally, the box contains records 'of cases of greater or less interest which I might have edited before had I not feared to give the public a surfeit which might react upon the reputation of the man whom above all others I revere' (23). This third category includes not only 'Thor Bridge' but also 'The Adventure of the Creeping Man' (1923) and, we might presume, other stories in the final sequence presented in volume form in *The Case-Book of Sherlock Holmes*.

The tin dispatch-box is on one level simply a ruse to explain why, long after Holmes's supposed retirement, new stories keep emerging. It is also a method of creating verisimilitude – the art of making fiction seem like fact. Doyle not only locates the box in a real and familiar place, but also contends that some stories cannot or should not be told – either because they are too dull, or because their details are too sensitive. The conceit here is a familiar one from the nineteenth-century realist novel: what is narrated is true, even if dates, names and places have been altered or redacted to preserve the sensibilities of those involved. The author poses as a selector of material, not an inventor: as Watson later says in a similar passage at the beginning of 'The Veiled Lodger', 'it will be clear that I have a mass of material at my command. The problem has always been, not to find, but to choose' (208). For all their outré effects (to use one of Holmes's favourite words), anchoring the stories in what purports to be reality connects them more firmly to our experiences and thereby increases their power. Similar techniques can be seen at work in some of Doyle's favourite authors, such as Wilkie Collins's use of legal instruments in *The Woman in White*, or the specificity of Poe's topographical detail in his Dupin stories. On a deeper level, however, in the opening of 'Thor Bridge' Watson is telling us something important about the originality of the Holmes saga: nowhere else in English literature can we find allusions to such a large corpus – nearly one hundred stories – of untold narrative.[2]

What, then, is the purpose of these untold stories? For a start, we can conclude that Watson's tripartite categorisation is unreliable. His first category of 'unfathomed cases' may lack final solutions but they certainly do not, as he claims, appear to be devoid of interest. He offers three examples. The first is the story of Mr James Phillimore, 'who, stepping back into his own house to get his umbrella, was never more seen in this world'. The second is 'that of the cutter *Alicia* which sailed one spring morning into a small patch of mist from where she never again emerged, nor was anything further ever heard of herself and her crew'. The third features 'Isadora Persano, the well-known journalist and duellist, who was found stark staring mad with a matchbox in front of him which contained a remarkable worm, said to be unknown to science' (23). In fact, he contradicts himself with the second example, as he admits that it is '[n]o less remarkable' than the first. A disappearing man and a disappearing ship are intriguing enough, but the third case sounds positively outlandish. For a start, Persano has a female forename, recalling the world-famous dancer Isadora Duncan, who by the early 1920s was busily scandalising the Western world with her Communist politics and bisexual liaisons, but is given a male personal pronoun. Like his female namesake, Persano evidently courts notoriety, but the circumstances of his mental collapse are both extraordinary and oddly indefinite. We might speculate that the worm has some kind of hallucinogenic property, like the African root in 'The Devil's Foot' which is similarly intractable to modern scientific enquiry, but why should the worm in the matchbox be 'said to be unknown to science'? It either is or is not. The indeterminate judgement suggests that scientific investigation was incomplete or undisclosed, meaning that it is not just the worm that is unknown.

Watson furnishes no examples of his second category of stories too sensitive to be published, although he elaborates in the opening of 'The Veiled Lodger' when discussing the contents of 'the long row of yearbooks which fill a shelf' and 'dispatch cases filled with documents' (208) concerning Holmes's unpublished cases (Doyle presumably had forgotten about the tin box in the bank). These would be 'a perfect quarry for the student not only of crime, but of the social and official scandals of the late Victorian era'. We are once again in the territory of secret history, but of the domestic rather than governmental variety. Watson goes on to narrate a brief story of his own:

> I may say that the writers of agonized letters, who beg that the honour of their families or the reputation of famous forebears may not be touched, have nothing to fear. The discretion and high sense of professional honour which have always distinguished my friend are still at work in the choice of these memoirs, and no confidence will be abused. I deprecate, however, in the strongest way the attempts which have been made lately to get at and to destroy these papers. The source of these outrages is known, and if they are repeated I have Mr Holmes's authority for saying that the whole story concerning the politician, the lighthouse, and the trained cormorant will be given to the public. There is at least one reader who will understand. (208)

This passage remains consistent with Watson's practice of nondisclosure – it merely hints at the story's events. In fact, there are two untold or barely told stories here. The first concerns the attempts to destroy the papers – but Watson says nothing about who is making the attempt, how, and which papers are concerned. The second, which – if it could be told – would connect a prominent person, a remote or marginal place and a highly unusual bird (although cormorants have historically been trained in the Far East as aids to fishermen), is also presumably connected to the first, but evidently has its own narrative coherence. Mentioning these untold stories has an explicit purpose, as a warning to 'at least one reader' – that is, whoever is trying to destroy the papers. Nor are they entirely incidental to the fully narrated story that follows. This is the sad tale of Eugenia Ronder, a circus performer whose plot to murder her violent, tyrannical husband miscarries when Sahara King, the lion which would be blamed for the killing, escapes from its cage and mauls Eugenia herself, mutilating her face horrifically. For 'The Veiled Lodger' is really a collection of stories, each told in a different way. Watson's prologue gives way to the narrative of Holmes's client Mrs Merrilew, who is concerned at the health of her mysterious, mutilated lodger; Holmes then locates in his commonplace books his record of Ronder's death, known at the time as 'the Abbas Parva tragedy' after the (fictitious) Berkshire village in which it took place, and summarises the events for Watson's benefit; Holmes and Watson then interview Eugenia herself, who retells the story from her perspective, revealing the crucial details of the murder plot. 'The Veiled Lodger' is, clearly, a story about stories. Eugenia wishes to reveal for the first time the true story in order to correct the existing narrative: 'I wanted to find one man of judgement to whom I could tell my terrible story, so that when I am gone all might be understood' (215). She is confident in her choice because she has read about Holmes's exploits in Watson's narratives, and permits Watson to use the story and thereby establish it as official history. But she also reveals that she lied to the police during the original investigation and will not speak to them to reveal the truth now: 'I could not stand the scandal and publicity which would come from a police examination' (215). This point invites us to recall Watson's prologue, and suggests a class dimension to Watson's reticence – the scandals of circus performers may be revealed, but those affecting the rich and famous must remain untold.

However, there are several canonical stories which deal with the family secrets of the nobility, such as 'The Noble Bachelor', or even royalty ('The Beryl Coronet', 'The Illustrious Client'), often preceded by an apology from Watson in which he announces that sufficient time has passed for the story to be disclosed, albeit with details that have been omitted or changed. Perhaps the most intriguing example is 'The Creeping Man', which reworks Stevenson's *The Strange Case*

Figure 20 'He did not rise, but sat upon a floor like some strange Buddha.' Illustration by Frank Wiles, *Strand Magazine*, February 1927.

of Dr Jekyll and Mr Hyde (1886). Professor Presbury is a wealthy and famous scientist who, at the age of sixty-one, attempts to rejuvenate his body with a serum derived from Himalayan monkeys in order to become more attractive to the much younger Alice Morphy, with whom he is infatuated. Watson supplies a rather strange prologue to this strange case in which he sets out the reasons for making the story public:

> Mr Sherlock Holmes was always of opinion that I should publish the singular facts connected with Professor Presbury, if only to dispel once for all the ugly rumours which some twenty years ago agitated the University and were echoed in the learned societies of London. There were, however, certain obstacles in the way, and the true history of this curious case remained entombed in the tin box which contains so many records of my friend's adventures. Now we have at last obtained permission to ventilate the facts which formed one of the very last cases handled by Holmes before his retirement from practice. Even now a certain reticence and discretion have to be observed in laying the matter before the public. (*Case-Book*, 50)

This is certainly a Gothic and rather grotesque tale but, on the face of it, is no more scandalous than many others in the saga. The oblique references to 'ugly rumours', 'certain obstacles' and the need for continued 'reticence and discretion', however, point us to read rather more sceptically or imaginatively. Does the scandal lie in the professor's serum-induced nocturnal wanderings around his handsome home in 'Camford' (a conflation of Cambridge and Oxford)? His daughter's experience of waking to see her father, vampire-like, trying to gain entrance to her bedroom from outside might suggest that it does. Or might there be some scandal in the revelation from Presbury's supplier, Lowenstein of Prague, that he has one other client in England? Either way, Watson's admission that he is not telling the full story reminds us that there is no clear line between the second and third categories he proposes in 'Thor Bridge', that is between those stories which must remain in the vault and those which can safely be told.

It seems appropriate that Watson's explanation for not telling stories should itself be misleading and incomplete. The untold stories perform a range of functions in the saga, and these evolve over time. In *A Study in Scarlet*, several stories are implied by the comings and goings which Watson records at his new shared lodging in Baker Street:

> One morning a young girl called, fashionably dressed, and stayed for half an hour or more. The same afternoon brought a grey-headed, seedy visitor, looking like a Jew pedlar, who appeared to me to be much excited, and who was closely followed by a slip-shod elderly woman. On another occasion an old white-haired gentleman had an interview with my companion; and on another, a railway porter in his velveteen uniform. (17)

These clients help build the character of Holmes and establish his professional credentials: he is in touch with all sorts and conditions of men, from the fashionable to the seedy, from the young to the elderly, showing that, like a medical professional, he does not discriminate. His references to earlier (fictional) cases in the criminal literature – 'There was the case of Von Bischoff at Frankfort last year. . . . Then there was Mason of Bradford, and the notorious Muller, and Lefevre of Montpellier, and Samson of New Orleans' (11) – complete the picture of a knowledgeable specialist. This continues in *The Sign of Four*, in which we learn that Holmes has been consulted by a French detective, François Le Villard, on a case concerning a will, that he previously advised Mary Morstan's employer on 'a little domestic complication' (12), and had previously set the police 'on the right track' in the Bishopsgate jewel case (44). As well as helping to construct character, Holmes's un-narrated casework is another route to verisimilitude. These apparently incidental details create an illusion of reality: Holmes is a successful and effective consultant, his services are therefore much in demand, and so he must have a historical caseload that exceeds what Watson is able to narrate.

As the saga unfolds, the untold cases become a useful device to explain or justify the existence of those stories which are narrated to us: the Holmes stories are told not in a linear sequence, but alternate between historical accounts and more recent or current adventures. Two stories in *The Memoirs of Sherlock Holmes* exemplify this: 'The Gloria Scott' and 'The Musgrave Ritual' are both drawn from Holmes's archives, and tell of his earliest cases (his first and third, to be precise). 'The Musgrave Ritual' is introduced to us as merely one of several narrative possibilities to be found in 'a large tin box' which Holmes retrieves from his bedroom:

> He lifted bundle after bundle in a tender, caressing sort of way. 'They are not all successes, Watson,' said he, 'but there are some pretty little problems among them. Here's the record of the Tarleton murders and the case of Vamberry, the wine merchant, and the adventure of the old Russian woman, and the singular affair of the aluminium crutch, as well as a full account of Ricoletti of the club foot and his abominable wife. And here – ah, now! this really is something a little *recherché*.' (114)

Holmes's tin box, like Watson's, is clearly more than a device for verisimilitude. By this point in the saga, we can see that we are being teased with intriguing summaries of cases we would want to read, if only Holmes would provide the material to his chronicler. Indeed, we can see that here Doyle is playing a game, inviting or challenging us to construct or decode the significance of an aluminium crutch or a club foot. By the time we reach the final sequence in *The Case-Book of Sherlock Holmes*, the game-playing has become sometimes comic, and occasionally outrageous. The very late story 'The Retired Colourman', for example, has Holmes preoccupied with 'this case of the two Coptic Patriarchs, which should come to a head to-day', while 'The Mazarin Stone', a most curious story with third-person narration that appears to be an adaptation of Doyle's short Holmes play *The Crown Diamond* (1921), has Holmes taunting the larger-than-life villain Count Sylvius with the contents of his notebook:[3]

> 'It's all here, Count. The real facts as to the death of old Mrs Harold, who left you the Blymer estate, which you so rapidly gambled away.'
> 'You are dreaming!'

'And the complete life history of Miss Minnie Warrender.'
'Tut! You will make nothing of that!'
'Plenty more here, Count. Here is the robbery in the train-de-luxe to the Riviera on February 13, 1892. Here is the forged cheque in the same year on the Credit Lyonnais.'
'No, you're wrong there.'
'Then I am right on the others!' (*Case-Book*, 13–14)

'The Sussex Vampire' begins with a reference to what may be the most celebrated untold story in the saga. Holmes receives a letter from Morrison, Morrison and Dodd, a firm of solicitors in London which 'specializes entirely upon the assessment of machinery', to the effect that Robert Ferguson will seek Holmes's advice on a matter concerning vampires. The letter concludes with a comment that the firm has 'not forgotten your successful action in the case of Matilda Briggs'. This prompts a reminiscence from Holmes: 'Matilda Briggs was not the name of a young woman . . . It was a ship which is associated with the giant rat of Sumatra, a story for which the world is not yet prepared' (*Case-Book*, 72).

What can we deduce from this passage? The ship's name may be an allusion to the *Marie Celeste*, the American merchant ship found deserted near the Azores in 1872, and the subject of Doyle's early horror story 'J. Habakuk Jephson's Statement' (1884): the *Marie Celeste*'s captain was Benjamin Briggs, and his daughter was named Sophia Matilda.[4] The giant rat of Sumatra cannot fit into Watson's first category of failed investigations, as the letter tells us that the case was successfully concluded. There is nothing to suggest that the sensitivities of wealthy or important people are concerned, although the involvement of a firm of City solicitors indicates significant commercial interests relating to the ship. But the fact that the story cannot yet be told means that it does not belong in the third category of cases which can safely be removed from the tin box in Charing Cross and published in the *Strand*. The passage suggests a fourth category: stories that are so astonishing, grotesque or macabre that they must wait for a change in society – that is surely the implication of Holmes's striking turn of phrase ('the world is not yet prepared'). The story of the giant rat must be unimaginably strange if it cannot yet be told in a volume that includes deadly jellyfish, a jealous boy who frames his stepmother as a vampire, and a university professor who transforms himself into a Himalayan monkey.

However, unimaginable is not quite the right word here. Watson's assertions that the published canon represents only a portion of the truth – assertions that increase in frequency in the later stories – gesture to the narrative possibilities that lie outside the saga's frame, a world about which we hear rumours but are never actually shown. While Doyle's imagination is often judged by critics to be running down in the 1920s, Watson's increasingly frequent references to non-canonical texts transfer the privilege of imagination to the reader. Along with the worm unknown to science and the trained cormorant, the giant rat of Sumatra invites readers to give scope to their imaginations. And many have accepted the invitation: the giant rat appears in numerous adaptations of the Holmes saga, from the Universal Sherlock Holmes movie *Pursuit to Algiers* (1945), in which Nigel Bruce's Watson appears to tell the story on board a ship in the Mediterranean, to a 2014 episode of the BBC's *Sherlock* in which the phrase is a coded reference to a North Korean bomb-plot. At least three novels – by 'Franklin W. Dixon' (the pseudonym used by the various authors of the Hardy Boys series of young adult novels), Rick Boyer and Steve Seitz respectively – have the phrase in their titles.

The untold stories stimulate new narratives, only some of which find their way into print, or on to stage or screen, but there is one example of Doyle accepting his own challenge. The existence of 'The Adventure of the Second Stain' was first revealed over a decade before its publication in 1904. In his prologue to 'The Naval Treaty', Watson confirms that, like the story of the giant rat of Sumatra, 'The Second Stain' cannot yet be told. The available clues suggest it fits into the second category of untold stories, those that concern sensitive issues among the elite, as it

> deals with interests of such importance, and implicates so many of the first families in the kingdom, that for many years it will be impossible to make it public. No case, however, in which Holmes was ever engaged has illustrated the value of his analytical methods so clearly or has impressed those who were associated with him so deeply. I still retain an almost verbatim report of the interview in which he demonstrated the true facts of the case to Monsieur Dubuque, of the Paris Police, and Fritz von Waldbaum, the well-known specialist of Dantzig, both of whom had wasted their energies upon what proved to be side issues. The new century will have come, however, before the story can be safely told. (*Memoirs*, 213)

Even though he would go on to kill Holmes in the subsequent story, the potential of this story's title was irresistible when Doyle revived Holmes a decade later. We have already seen that 'The Second Stain' follows an elegant and intricate structure, and this foreshadowing shows that Doyle wrote it within a self-imposed constraint of its description in 'The Naval Treaty': 'The Second Stain' needed both to satisfy the intriguing premise of its title, to concern the 'first families' in a potentially scandalous tale, and bring in Continental Europe.

These invitations and challenges make the Holmes stories, and the later ones in particular, exemplary texts for what the literary theorist Roland Barthes in his classic essay *S/Z* called the 'scriptable' (writerly) text:

> the writerly text is *ourselves writing*, before the infinite play of the world (the world as function) is traversed, intersected, stopped, plasticized by some singular system (Ideology, Genus, Criticism) which reduces the plurality of entrances, the opening of networks, the infinity of languages.[5]

Behind this opaque language is a simple but profound point: whereas most literary texts are limited in their scope of meaning by a constraining system such as an ideological world view, a minority of texts invite or even require us to create meaning, to interpret the text in our own way or in a multitude of ways. On Dartmoor, discovering the tracks of the missing racehorse in 'Silver Blaze', Holmes cries: 'See the value of imagination.' As he explains, imagination is a vital tool for the detective: 'We imagined what might have happened, acted upon the supposition, and find ourselves justified' (*Memoirs*, 18). The Sherlock Holmes saga is an unfolding, writerly text, with much material placed just outside the narrative frame, containing secrets that are alluded to but not disclosed. We need, like Holmes and Watson on Dartmoor, to imagine what might have happened, but we can never really know if what we find is justified.

Notes

1. See Lloyds Banking Group, 'Cox's & King's, Army Agents'.
2. For a list of the ninety-six untold stories, see *The Arthur Conan Doyle Encyclopaedia*: <https://www.arthur-conan-doyle.com/index.php?title=Category:Untold_Stories> (accessed 18 October 2017).
3. *The Crown Diamond* can be found in *The Uncollected Sherlock Holmes*, pp. 247–64, with a useful prefatory discussion by Richard Lancelyn Green discussing the play's relationship with 'The Mazarin Stone'.
4. Paul Begg, *Mary Celeste*, pp. 24–8.
5. Roland Barthes, *S/Z*, p. 5. Michael Atkinson also views the Holmes saga more generally as a potentially scriptable text. See *The Secret Marriage*, p. 172.

Figure 21 'The death of Sherlock Holmes.' Illustration by Sidney Paget, *Strand Magazine*, December 1893.

Conclusion

The Problem of Finality

'You will be amused to hear that I am at work upon a Sherlock Holmes story. So the old dog returns to his vomit.'[1]
Arthur Conan Doyle to Herbert Greenhough Smith

Sherlock Holmes, who died in Switzerland in May 1891, returned to the world on 23 October 1899. The location for his rebirth was, somewhat surprisingly, the Star Theatre in Buffalo, New York. Early the following month, Holmes moved to New York where he could be found in Manhattan's Garrick Theatre on 236 separate occasions, before making his way across the United States. In September 1901, Holmes went back to Great Britain, arriving (like so many travellers from the US) at Liverpool, before reaching London on 9 September 1901. He was so much in demand that on 1 February 1902 he received an audience with King Edward VII and Queen Alexandra. In 1902 he was again in New York, was seen travelling across northern England in 1903, and for the next thirty years popped up repeatedly in various American towns and cities.[2]

Holmes was reborn in the medium of theatre. *Sherlock Holmes: A Drama in Four Acts*, credited to Arthur Conan Doyle and William Gillette and starring the latter, was a highly successful play, running to more than 1,300 performances across Britain and the US. It reached an even wider audience in 1916 when it became a motion picture – long thought lost, but recovered in 2014 – and in 1935 a radio play, both with Gillette in the title role. The text itself was largely Gillette's creation (though he based it on elements of Doyle's *A Study in Scarlet*, 'A Scandal in Bohemia' and 'The Final Problem'), but the original idea was Doyle's: he wrote a five-act version of a Holmes play in 1897, which he offered to the two greatest actors of the age, Henry Irving (who turned it down) and Herbert Beerbohm Tree (who insisted on too many changes). The American producer Charles Frohman brought

Gillette into the project, who (if the legends are true) went to the effort of dressing up as Holmes when meeting Doyle for the first time at South Norwood station.[3] Doyle's text was effectively discarded in favour of Gillette's new version.

In *Memories and Adventures*, Doyle portrays his relationship with Holmes as primarily commercial, and Holmes's success was merely the effect of supply and demand in the literary marketplace: 'It was still the Sherlock Holmes stories for which the public clamoured, and these from time to time I endeavoured to supply'(99).[4] But for an author ambitious to succeed in what he considered to be the higher calling of historical fiction, 'being entirely identified with what I regarded as a lower stratum of literary achievement' was a problem which could only by solved by sending Holmes to his death in Switzerland, 'even if I buried my banking account along with him'. But 'the temptation of high prices made it difficult to get one's thoughts away from Holmes' (100), so Holmes was revived three times: first for the stage – 'I was charmed both with the play, the acting and the pecuniary result' (102) – then for the *Strand* with *The Hound of the Baskervilles* in 1901–2, and thirdly, in 1903, for both the American *Collier's* and the *Strand*.[5] Doyle's income from these revivals made him, along with Kipling, one of the highest paid authors in the world.

The accepted version of events is that Doyle revived Holmes reluctantly and only when offered astronomical sums: he told a friend in 1896 that

> I couldn't revive him if I would, at least not for years, for I have had such an overdose of him that I feel towards him as I do towards *pâté de foie gras*, of which I once ate too much, so that the name of it gives me a sickly feeling to this day.[6]

But Doyle's eagerness to see his creation on stage suggests that his well-known antipathy towards his own creation was not quite as heartfelt as he liked to suggest. And Doyle and Gillette's *Sherlock Holmes* also suggests another, more conceptual problem with Holmes's death and resurrection. Although Holmes's confrontation with Moriarty is at the heart of the play, neither is killed: in the last act, Holmes engineers Moriarty's arrest, discovers that he is in love with Alice Faulkner (loosely based on Irene Adler from 'A Scandal in Bohemia'), and the curtain falls on the loving couple in an embrace.[7] *Sherlock Holmes*, then, seems to take place in a different imaginative universe from 'A Scandal in Bohemia' and 'The Final Problem' – a universe in which Holmes and Moriarty never travel to Switzerland, and in which Holmes is no longer 'the most perfect reasoning and observing machine that the world has seen' with a 'cold, precise, but admirably balanced mind' (*Adventures*, 5), but an ardent lover.

To contemporary audiences, no doubt, the theatre was such a different medium from the short story that Holmes's rebirth and character reformation would have caused little cognitive dissonance. But when Doyle chose to revive Holmes in print, he did not have this luxury, so *The Hound of the Baskervilles* (subtitled 'Another Adventure of Sherlock Holmes' in the *Strand*) was presumably set before Holmes's death. A much greater challenge came when Doyle revived Holmes in 1903. Somehow Doyle had to explain how and why Holmes escaped death at the Reichenbach Falls. Holmes relates the chain of events to Watson after his dramatic reappearance:

> I have some knowledge . . . of *baritsu*, or the Japanese system of wrestling, which has more than once been very useful to me. I slipped through his grip, and he with a horrible scream kicked madly for a few seconds and clawed the air with both his hands. But for all his efforts he could not get his balance, and over he went. (*Return*, 9)

Realising that Moriarty's accomplices were still on his trail, Holmes relates how he climbed the sheer cliff-face, so that no tracks would be visible and anyone arriving at the scene would have assumed both men had fallen to their deaths. He later fled on foot, arriving in Florence from where he obtained Mycroft's assistance in changing his identity and travelling across three continents.

Extraordinary though it is, Holmes's explanation is consistent with the details set out in 'The Final Problem', suggesting that we should salute Doyle's ingenuity in creating a coherent and (within its own narrative logic) credible solution to the problem of reversing Holmes's apparent demise. But a close examination of 'The Final Problem' suggests that Doyle had plenty of space in which to work, in that this is a story characterised by contradictions and, as Michael Atkinson has shown, by gaps and absences: it is hardly a detective story at all, or rather it is a kind of inversion of the genre in which the detective is the quarry pursued by the criminal, who is scrutinising the detective's traces in order to solve his own problem.[8] The story's action begins after a mournful prologue in which Watson reveals that he is writing 'the last words in which I shall ever record the singular gifts by which my friend Mr Sherlock Holmes was distinguished' (*Memoirs*, 249). Holmes arrives in Watson's consulting room on 24 April 1891 announcing that he has been 'a little pressed of late' (250), on account of having finally come face-to-face with Professor Moriarty and his gang. Fearing attack from air guns, Holmes closes the shutters and announces that he will have to leave via the garden wall. 'It's not an airy nothing, you see', he says while showing his bleeding knuckles: 'On the contrary, it is solid enough for a man to break his hand over' (*Memoirs*, 250–1). This exchange sets the pattern for the rest of the story: Holmes asserts that his fears are real, but we receive remarkably little by way of corroboration. Despite Professor Moriarty being 'the Napoleon of crime' and 'the organizer of half that is evil and of nearly all that is undetected in this great city' (252), Holmes concedes that 'no one has heard of him' (251). But Holmes immediately contradicts himself: Moriarty is actually rather famous. 'His career has been an extraordinary one. He is a man of good birth and excellent education, endowed by Nature with a phenomenal mathematical faculty' (251–2). Moriarty's treatise on the Binomial Theorem won him a professorship and 'mathematical celebrity'. Clearly some people have heard of him. And we cannot explain this contradiction simply by assuming that he was famous in academia and operated entirely secretly in the underworld, as Holmes drops the intriguing comment that '[d]ark rumours gathered round him in the University town, and eventually he was compelled to resign his Chair and to come down to London' (252).

Holmes reveals that he deduced Moriarty's existence from an analysis of patterns of crime, and on that scientific hypothesis set out to find the evidence: 'at last the time came when I seized my thread and followed it, until it led me, after a thousand cunning windings, to ex-Professor Moriarty' (252). Holmes was unable to obtain any evidence of Moriarty's criminality, until he made one small error so that Holmes, finally, has his man:

> I have woven my net round him until now it is all ready to close. In three days, that is to say on Monday next, matters will be ripe, and the Professor, with all the principal members of his gang, will be in the hands of the police. . . . Now, if I could have done this without the knowledge of Professor Moriarty, all would have been well. But he was too wily for that. He saw every step which I took to draw my toils round him. Again and again he strove to break away, but I as often headed him off. I tell you, my friend, that if a detailed account of that silent contest could be written, it would take its place as the most brilliant bit of thrust-and-parry work in the history of detection. Never have I risen to such a height, and never have I been so hard pressed by an opponent. He cut deep, and yet I just undercut him. This morning the last steps were taken, and three days only were wanted to complete the business. (253)

This explanation is remarkable in its vagueness. We are given no clue as to Moriarty's mistake, the nature of the evidence Holmes obtained, and what actually happened during the 'silent contest' between the two men. Holmes then relates his confrontation with Moriarty in Baker Street, a narrative which begins in a particularly dreamlike fashion: 'I must confess to a start when I saw the very man who had been so much in my thoughts standing there on my threshold. His appearance was quite familiar to me' (254).[9] This passage at least provides some definition to Holmes's account: we have a celebrated description of Moriarty's appearance and character, which incidentally inspired T. S. Eliot's poem 'Macavity: the Mystery Cat' (1939), and a splendid dialogue, full of menace and bravado. But we are still left with the unsettling impression that we only have Holmes's word for it all: in most other cases dealing with manifestations of sheer villainy, such as 'The Speckled Band' or 'The Illustrious Client', Watson provides eyewitness testimony. In 'The Final Problem', Watson's reporting never implicates Moriarty in any criminality – all of that comes from Holmes. Holmes claims to have recently survived three attempts on his life – being nearly run over on a crossing in the West End, narrowly avoiding a brick falling from a roof, and being attacked by a ruffian. After the second incident, Holmes says he called the police, who investigated and suggested that it was merely the result of poorly secured building materials on a windy day. Most striking of all is Watson's narrative of the climactic struggle in Switzerland, which again is reported second-hand via Holmes, in the form of a statement written by Holmes and left at the scene, on the unlikely basis that Moriarty waited for him to write a valedictory before their death-grapple; Holmes's death is apparently confirmed by a vaguely described 'examination by experts' which 'leaves little doubt that a personal contest between the two men ended, as it could hardly fail to end in such a situation, in their reeling over, locked in each other's arms' (267). It would appear that Moriarty has gone out of his way to conduct his criminal enterprises, and ensure his own and Holmes's destruction, without providing any evidence that Watson can actually narrate.

Holmes's accounts to Watson on the subject of Moriarty strain credibility. Prior to 'The Final Problem', Holmes did not supply so much as a hint that his cases were connected, let alone that many of them were the work of a single organisation headed by a criminal genius. Moriarty's superhuman brilliance, together with Holmes's fears of persecution, are, as Atkinson has pointed out, more suggestive of paranoia than genuine threat. Indeed, Moriarty is remarkably invisible to everyone other than Holmes in this story. Watson glimpses him only once, when he and Holmes depart Victoria Station on the Continental express.

> 'Ah, there is Moriarty himself.'
> The train had already begun to move as Holmes spoke. Glancing back I saw a tall man pushing his way furiously through the crowd and waving his hand as if he desired to have the train stopped. It was too late, however, for we were rapidly gathering momentum, and an instant later had shot clear of the station. (259)

If Holmes is an unreliable reporter in this story, then even this is hardly evidence of Moriarty's existence, let alone his evil intent: all Watson sees is a tall man failing to catch a departing train. So is Moriarty merely a figment of Holmes's imagination? That in fact is the premise of Nicholas Meyer's 1974 novel *The Seven-Per-Cent Solution*, which recasts Holmes as a paranoid drug addict who is victimising an innocent university lecturer to the extent that he is persuaded to seek treatment from Sigmund Freud in Vienna. And there is some internal evidence for doubting Holmes's account, although it is discounted as unreliable: Watson claims that he is writing the story 'to lay the facts before the public exactly as they occurred' in response to 'the recent letters in which Colonel James Moriarty defends the memory of his brother' (249). But the point here is more that Holmes's apparent death is so distanced from the reader by a long chain of narration and a lack of corroboration that any number of scenarios could be constructed to explain his survival.

'The Final Problem', then, is a story with remarkably little finality: it is provisional, suggestive, incomplete. In this, it is more representative of the Holmes saga as a whole than we might suppose. Doyle made repeated attempts to bring Holmes to an end, from *The Sign of Four* when Watson's forthcoming marriage is clearly intended to be the final act, to Holmes's retirement to the Sussex Downs (announced in 'The Second Stain' and reinforced in Watson's prologue to *His Last Bow*), to the volume publication of *The Case-Book of Sherlock Holmes*, in which Conan Doyle's preface expresses the fear 'that Mr. Sherlock Holmes may become like one of those popular tenors who, having outlived their time, are still tempted to make repeated farewell bows to their indulgent audiences' (3). In this preface, Doyle admits that 'it was not difficult for me to respond to the flattering demand' for more Holmes stories after bringing Holmes to an end in 'The Final Problem': 'I did the deed, but, fortunately, no coroner had pronounced upon the remains' (4). Indeed, no remains were recovered on which a coroner could pronounce, but fortune may have had nothing to do with it.

Despite his protestations, ending the Holmes saga was clearly something that Conan Doyle found too difficult to achieve. This suggests that Holmes's many resurrections were not the result of commercial considerations alone: Holmes invites revival because, as John Gray has proposed, there is something mythic about his combination of rationalism and modernity on the one hand and the endurance of magic (Holmes's unerring ability to guess the truth) on the other.[10] But there is also the intrinsic quality of the stories, which contain layers of mystery, inviting sequels and alternative explanations. Far from being superior exercises in commodified mass-market fiction, as even Conan Doyle himself often claimed – 'He takes my mind from better things'[11] – the Holmes stories are multi-layered, allusive and, above all, imaginatively stimulating. The fact that these stories present so many opportunities to create meaning explains why they have been subject to an astonishing number and range of adaptations in almost every medium and genre, from relatively faithful radio, film and television adaptations to cartoons to pornographic fan-fiction. Doyle and Gillette's *Sherlock Holmes* initiated a long tradition of major performers taking the role of Holmes: at the time of writing, there are three enormously successful television or movie franchises featuring household names. And the curious phenomenon of Sherlockian criticism, initiated by Ronald Knox in the 1920s and taken up by Dorothy L. Sayers and others in the 1930s, persists to this day, applying the techniques of the higher criticism of biblical texts to what Sherlockians call 'the canon': *The Baker Street Journal* in the US and *The Sherlock Holmes Journal* in Britain have been published since 1946 and 1952 respectively.

There are many reasons for Sherlock Holmes's longevity, but chief among them is the stories' often surprising complexity and indeterminacy. Detective fiction, and the Holmes stories in particular, are often viewed reductively as articulations of particular ideological or value systems, such as empiricism and scientific positivism, bourgeois materialism, or the surveillance society. Catherine Belsey influentially declared in 1980 that Doyle's 'overt project' was 'total explicitness, total verisimilitude in the interests of a plea for scientificity'.[12] Also in 1980, Stephen Knight proposed that 'the central audience for the cerebral detective story' was 'the bourgeois professional intelligentsia' who dictated the genre's form and content, while Ronald R. Thomas sees detective fiction as an adjunct of the modern, bureaucratised state which required formal and informal policing to maintain discipline and control.[13] But the Holmes stories resist being placed in such ideological straitjackets. They are allusive and elusive, constantly suggesting connections to other literary works, to historical events and to social phenomena, while avoiding simplicity and closure by offering us anomalies, incomplete solutions and un-decoded secrets.

Notes

1. Herbert Greenhough Smith, 'Some Letters of Conan Doyle', p. 393.
2. For details of Holmes's theatrical career, see Amnon Kabatchnik, *Sherlock Holmes on the Stage*, pp. 14–17, and Rosemary Cullen and Don B. Wilmeth, Introduction to William Hooker Gillette, *Plays*, pp. 15–16.
3. Kabatchnik, *Sherlock Holmes on the Stage*, p. 14.
4. Doyle, *Memories and Adventures*, p. 99
5. Ibid., pp. 200–2.
6. *The New Annotated Sherlock Holmes*, p. xxxiii.
7. Even this gave Doyle another cause for disdain: he claimed that after Gillette cabled him to ask 'May I marry Holmes?', he replied, 'You may marry or murder or do what you like with him': *Memories and Adventures*, p. 102.
8. Atkinson, *Secret Marriage*, pp. 141–51.
9. Atkinson highlights this passage as a potential indicator of Holmes's paranoia, or a suggestion that Moriarty is some kind of doppelgänger. See *Secret Marriage*, p. 142.
10. John Gray, 'Sherlock Holmes and the Romance of Reason'.
11. Doyle, *A Life in Letters*, p. 300.
12. Belsey, *Critical Practice*, p. 114. She acknowledges however that the presence of 'shadowy, mysterious and often silent women' occasionally appears to subvert their rationalist aim.
13. Knight, *Form and Ideology in Crime Fiction*, p. 62; Ronald R. Thomas, *Detective Fiction and the Rise of Forensic Science*, pp. 4–5.

Bibliography

Achebe, Chinua, 'An Image of Africa: Racism in Conrad's "Heart of Darkness"', *Massachusetts Review* 18 (1977), pp. 782–94.
Anurag, Jain. *The Relationship Between Ford, Kipling, Conan Doyle, Wells and British Propaganda of the First World War*, unpublished PhD thesis, Queen Mary, University of London, 2009.
Arata, Stephen, *Fictions of Loss in the Victorian Fin de Siècle* (Cambridge: Cambridge University Press, 1996).
The Arthur Conan Doyle Encyclopaedia. Available at <https://www.arthur-conan-doyle.com/index.php?title=Sir_Arthur_Conan_Doyle:Complete_Workshttps://www.arthur-conan-doyle.com/index.php?title=Category:Untold_Stories> (last accessed 18 October 2017).
Atkinson, Michael, *The Secret Marriage of Sherlock Holmes and Other Eccentric Readings* (Ann Arbor: University of Michigan Press, 1996).
Audoin-Rouzeau, Stephane and Annette Becker, *14–18: Understanding the Great War* (Hill & Wang, 2003).
Baden-Powell, Robert S., *Scouting for Boys: A Handbook for Instruction in Good Citizenship*, 6th edn (London: C. Arthur Pearson, 1913).
Barsham, Diana, *Conan Doyle and the Meaning of Masculinity* (Aldershot: Ashgate, 2000).
Barthes, Roland, *S/Z*, trans. Richard Miller (London: Cape, 1975).
Begg, Paul, *Mary Celeste: The Greatest Mystery of the Sea* (Harlow: Pearson Education, 2007).
Belsey, Catherine, *Critical Practice* (London and New York: Methuen, 1980).
Bhabha, Homi K., *The Location of Culture* (London: Routledge, 1994).
Brantlinger, Patrick, *Rule of Darkness: British Literature and Imperialism 1830–1914* (Ithaca, NY: Cornell University Press, 1988).
Cain, Lynn, *Dickens, Family, Authorship: Psychoanalytic Perspectives on Kinship and Creativity* (Aldershot: Ashgate, 2008).
Campbell, Charles S., *Anglo-American Understanding, 1898–1903* (Baltimore: Johns Hopkins Press, 1957).
Cannadine, David, *The Decline and Fall of the British Aristocracy* (London: Penguin, 2005).

Cantlie, James, 'Degeneration amongst Londoners' (London: Field & Tuer, The Leadenhall Press, E.C., Simpkin, Marshall & Co.; Hamilton, Adams & Co., 1885). Available at <http://www.victorianlondon.org/publications/degeneration.htm> http://www.victorianlondon.org/publications/degeneration.htm (last accessed 18 October 2017).

Carey, John, *The Intellectuals and the Masses: Pride and Prejudice Among the Literary Intelligentsia 1880–1939* (London: Faber & Faber, 1992).

Chakravarty, Gautam, *The Indian Mutiny and the British Imagination* (Cambridge: Cambridge University Press, 2005).

Childers, Erskine, *The Riddle of the Sands: A Record of Secret Service* (Harmondsworth: Penguin, 1978).

Clarke, Clare, *Late Victorian Crime Fiction in the Shadows of Sherlock* (Basingstoke: Palgrave Macmillan, 2014).

Clarke, I. F., *Voices Prophesying War: Future Wars 1763–3749* (Oxford and New York: Oxford University Press, 1992).

Clegg, Hugh Armstrong, *A History of British Trade Unions Since 1889, Vol. II: 1911–1933* (Oxford: Clarendon Press, 1984).

Cline, C. L., Introduction to C. L. Cline (ed.), *The Owl and the Rossettis: Letters of Charles A. Howell and Dante Gabriel, Christina, and William Michael Rossetti* (University Park and London: Pennsylvania State University Press, 1978).

Collins, E. J. T., 'Introduction', in E. J. T. Collins (ed.), *The Agrarian History of England and Wales, Vol. VII 1850–1914* (Cambridge: Cambridge University Press, 2000).

—, 'The Great Depression, 1875–1896' in E. J. T. Collins (ed.), *The Agrarian History of England and Wales, Vol. VII 1850–1914* (Cambridge: Cambridge University Press, 2000).

Collins, Wilkie, *The Moonstone*, ed. J. I. M. Stewart (London: Penguin, 1986).

—, *The Woman in White*, ed. Harvey Peter Sucksmith (London: Oxford University Press, 1975).

Conrad, Joseph, *Heart of Darkness*, ed. Paul O'Prey (London: Penguin, 1985).

—, *A Set of Six* (London: Methuen, 1908).

Cornish, William Rodolph, George Norman Clark, Geoffrey de N. Clark, *Law and Society in England 1750–1950* (London: Sweet & Maxwell, 1989).

Cranfield, Jonathan, 'Arthur Conan Doyle, H. G. Wells and the *Strand Magazine*'s Long 1901: From Baskerville to the Moon', *English Literature in Transition, 1880–1920* 56.1, 2013, pp. 3–32.

—, *Twentieth-Century Victorian: Arthur Conan Doyle and the Strand Magazine, 1891–1930* (Edinburgh: Edinburgh University Press, 2016).

Criminal Law Amendment Act 1885 (48 and 49 Vict.) (London: Eyre and Spottiswoode, 1885).

Crozier, Ivan, 'Introduction: Havelock Ellis, John Addington Symonds and the Construction of Sexual Inversion', in Havelock Ellis and John Addington Symonds, *Sexual Inversion: A Critical Edition*, ed. Ivan Crozier (Basingstoke: Palgrave Macmillan, 2008).

Cullen, Rosemary and Don B. Wilmeth, 'Introduction', in William Hooker Gillette, *Plays* (Cambridge: Cambridge University Press, 1983).
Cuningham, Henry, 'Sherlock Holmes and the Case of Race', *The Journal of Popular Culture*, 28 (1994), pp. 113–25.
Dakin, D. Martin, *A Sherlock Holmes Commentary* (Newton Abbott: David and Charles, 1972).
Dangerfield, George, *The Strange Death of Liberal England* (New York: Smith and Has, 1935).
Denning, Michael, *Cover Stories: Narrative and Ideology in the British Spy Thriller* (London: Routledge and Kegan Paul, 1987).
Dickens, Charles, *Dombey and Son* (Harmondsworth: Penguin Books, 1984).
Doyle, Arthur Conan, *The Adventures of Sherlock Holmes*, ed. Richard Lancelyn Green (Oxford: Oxford University Press, 1993).
—, *Arthur Conan Doyle: A Life in Letters*, ed. Jon Lellenberg, Daniel Stashower and Charles Foley (London: Harper Perennial, 2008).
—, *The British Campaign in France and Flanders*, 6 vols (London: Hodder & Stoughton, 1915–20).
—, *The Case-Book of Sherlock Holmes*, ed. W. W. Robson (Oxford: Oxford University Press, 1993).
—, *Danger! and Other Stories* (London: John Murray, 1918).
—, *The German War. Some Sidelights and Reflections* (London, New York, Toronto: 1914).
—, *The Great Boer War* (London: Smith, Elder, 1901).
—, *His Last Bow*, ed. Owen Dudley Edwards (Oxford: Oxford University Press, 1993).
—, *The Hound of the Baskervilles*, ed. W. W. Robson (Oxford: Oxford University Press, 1993).
—, *Letters to the Press* (London: Martin Secker & Warburg, 1986).
—, *The Lost World* (London: Penguin Books, 2007).
—, *The Memoirs of Sherlock Holmes*, ed. Christopher Roden (Oxford: Oxford University Press, 1993).
—, *Memories and Adventures* (London: Hodder & Stoughton, 1924).
—, *Micah Clarke* (London and New York: Longmans, Green, 1889).
—, 'Mr Stevenson's Methods in Fiction', *National Review*, January 1890.
—, *The Mystery of Cloomber* (London: Ward & Downey, 1896).
—, *The New Annotated Sherlock Holmes*, ed. Leslie S. Klinger, vol. 1 (New York: Wessex Press, 2005).
—, 'On the Slave Coast with a Camera', *British Journal of Photography* 29 (31 March and 7 April 1882), pp. 185–7, 202–3. Text available at <https://www.arthur-conan-doyle.com/index.php?title=On_the_Slave_Coast_with_a_Camera> (last accessed 13 December 2017).
—, *The Poison Belt . . . Being an account of another adventure of Prof. George E. Challenger, Lord John Roxton, Prof. Summerlee and Mr E. D. Malone, the discovers of 'The Lost World'*, 2nd edn (London: Hodder & Stoughton, 1913).

—, *The Return of Sherlock Holmes*, ed. Richard Lancelyn Green (Oxford: Oxford University Press, 1993).
—, *Round the Fire Stories* (London: Greenhill Books, 1985).
—, *The Sign of Four*, ed. Christopher Roden (Oxford: Oxford University Press, 1993).
—, *Sir Nigel* (London: Smith, Elder, 1906).
—, *A Story of Waterloo. A Drama in One Act* (London: Samuel French, 1922).
—, *A Study in Scarlet*, ed. Owen Dudley Edwards (Oxford: Oxford University Press, 1993).
—, *Through the Magic Door* (London: Smith, Elder, 1907).
—, *The Tragedy of the Korosko* (London: Smith, Elder, 1898).
—, *The Uncollected Sherlock Holmes*, comp. Richard Lancelyn Green (London: Penguin, 1983).
—, *The Valley of Fear*, ed. Owen Dudley Edwards (Oxford: Oxford University Press, 1993).
—, *The White Company* (London and Sydney: Pan, 1976).
Eagleton, Terry, *Literary Theory: An Introduction*, 2nd edn (Oxford: Blackwell, 1996).
Edwards, Owen Dudley, *The Quest for Sherlock Holmes: A Biographical Study of Arthur Conan Doyle* (Edinburgh: Mainstream, 1983).
Eldridge Miller, Jane, *Rebel Women: Feminism, Modernism and the Edwardian Novel* (London: Virago Press, 1994).
Ellis, Havelock and John Addington Symonds, *Sexual Inversion: A Critical Edition*, ed. Ivan Crozier (Basingstoke: Palgrave Macmillan, 2008).
Ellmann, Richard, *Oscar Wilde* (London: Hamish Hamilton, 1987).
Ensor, R. C. K., *England 1870–1914* (Oxford: Clarendon Press, 1936).
Freeman, Nicholas, *1895: Drama, Disaster and Disgrace in Late Victorian Britain* (Edinburgh: Edinburgh University Press, 2011).
French, David, 'Spy Fever in Britain, 1900–1915', *The Historical Journal* 21.2 (June 1978), pp. 355–70.
Gaboriau, Emile, *File No. 113* (London: G. Routledge, 1887).
Gagnier, Regenia, *The Insatiability of Human Wants: Economics and Aesthetics in Market Society* (Chicago: University of Chicago Press, 2000).
Glazzard, Andrew, 'Inside the Empty House: Sherlock Holmes, For King and Country', *Public Doman Review*, 1 August 2014. Available at <http://publicdomainreview.org/2014/01/08/inside-the-empty-house-sherlock-holmes-for-king-and-country> (last accessed 5 March 2018). https://publicdomainreview.org/2014/01/08/inside-the-empty-house-sherlock-holmes-for-king-and-country/
Godwin, William, *Caleb Williams*, ed. Pamela Clemit (Oxford: Oxford University Press, 2009).
Gray, John, 'Sherlock Holmes and the Romance of Reason', *A Point of View*, BBC Radio 4, 17 August 2012.

Grylls, David, 'The Savage Sub-Text of The Hound of the Baskervilles', in Sam Naidu (ed.), *Sherlock Holmes in Context* (London: Palgrave Macmillan, 2017).
Guenther, Louise, 'The Artful Seductions of Informal Empire', in Matthew Brown (ed.), *Informal Empire in Latin America: Culture, Commerce, and Capital* (Maldon, MA, Oxford, Carlton Victoria: Blackwell, 2008).
Haggard, H. Rider, *Rural England: Being an Account of Agricultural and Social Researches Carried Out in the Years 1901 and 1902*, 2 vols (London: Longmans, Green, 1906).
Havers, Michael, Edward Grayson and Peter Shankland, *The Royal Baccarat Scandal* (London: Souvenir Press, 1988).
Heffer, Simon, *The Age of Decadence* (London: Random House, 2017).
Hiley, Nicholas, 'The Failure of British Espionage against Germany, 1907–1914', *Historical Journal* 28 (1985), pp. 835–62.
Hornung, E. W., *Raffles: The Amateur Cracksman*, ed. Richard Lancelyn Green (London: Penguin, 2003).
Howkins, Alun, *Reshaping Rural England: A Social History 1850–1925* (London: HarperCollins Academic, 1991).
Huh, Jinny, 'Whispers of Norbury: Sir Arthur Conan Doyle and the Modernist Crisis of Racial (Un)Detection', *MFS Modern Fiction Studies* 49.3 (2003), pp. 550–80.
Jann, Rosemary, *The Adventures of Sherlock Holmes: Detecting Social Order* (New York and Don Mills, Ontario: Twayne Publishers, 1995).
Kabatchnik, Amnon, *Sherlock Holmes on the Stage: A Chronological Encyclopedia of Plays Featuring the Great Detective* (Plymouth: Scarecrow Press, 2008).
Kenny, Kevin, *Making Sense of the Molly Maguires* (New York and Oxford: Oxford University Press, 1998).
Kerr, Douglas, *Conan Doyle: Writing, Profession, and Practice* (Oxford: Oxford University Press, 2013).
Kestner, Joseph A., *The Edwardian Detective, 1901–1915* (Aldershot: Ashgate, 2000).
—, *Mythology and Misogyny* (Madison: University of Wisconsin Press, 1989).
—, *Sherlock's Men: Masculinity, Conan Doyle, and Cultural History* (Aldershot: Ashgate, 1997).
Kipling, Rudyard, *Rudyard Kipling's Verse*, Inclusive Edition, 1885–1918 (London, New York, Toronto: Hodder & Stoughton, n.d.).
Kissing, James and John M., 'Sherlock Holmes and the Ritual of Reason', *Nineteenth-Century Fiction* 17 (March 1963), pp. 353–62.
Knight, Stephen, *Form and Ideology in Crime Fiction* (London and Basingstoke: Macmillan, 1980).
Le Queux, William, *The Great War in England in 1897* (London: Tower Publishing, 1894).

—, *Spies of the Kaiser. Plotting the Downfall of England* (London: Hurst and Blackett, 1909).
—, *Whose Findeth a Wife* (London: Ward, Lock, 1897).
Lloyds Banking Group, 'Cox's & King's, Army Agents (1758–1923)'. Available at <http://www.lloydsbankinggroup.com/Our-Group/our-heritage/our-history/lloyds-bank/coxs--kings-army-agents> (last accessed 18 October 2017).
Lycett, Andrew, *Conan Doyle: The Man Who Created Sherlock Holmes* (London: Weidenfeld & Nicolson, 2007).
McBratney, John, 'Racial and Criminal Types: Indian Ethnography and Sir Arthur Conan Doyle's *The Sign of Four*', *Victorian Literature and Culture* 33.1 (2005), pp. 149–67.
McCrea, Barry, *In the Company of Strangers: Family and Narrative in Dickens, Conan Doyle, Joyce, and Proust* (New York and Chichester: Columbia University Press, 2011).
McDonald, Peter D., *British Literary Culture and Publishing Practice, 1880–1914* (Cambridge: Cambridge University Press, 1997).
McKie, David, *Jabez: The Rise and Fall of a Victorian Rogue* (London: Atlantic Books, 2005).
McLaren, Angus, *Sexual Blackmail: A Modern History* (Cambridge, MA and London: Harvard University Press, 2002).
Marshall, Alfred, *Principles of Economics: An Introductory Volume*, 8th edn, (London: Macmillan, 1949).
Masterman, C. F. G., *The Condition of England* (London: Methuen, 1909).
Metress, Christopher, 'Diplomacy and Detection in Conan Doyle's "The Second Stain"', *English Literature in Transition, 1880–1920*, 37.1, 1994, pp. 39–51.
—, 'Thinking the Unthinkable: Reopening Conan Doyle's "Cardboard Box"', *The Midwest Quarterly* 42.2 (2001).
Meyer, Nicholas, *The Seven-Per-Cent Solution: Being A Reprint From The Reminiscences of John H. Watson M.D., as edited by Nicholas Meyer* (Hodder & Stoughton, 1975).
Miller, Karl, *Doubles: Studies in Literary History* (London: Oxford University Press, 1967).
Moretti, Franco, *Signs Taken for Wonders: On the Sociology of Literary Forms* (London and New York: Verso, 2005).
Morton, James, *The First Detective: The Life and Revolutionary Times of Vidocq* (London: Ebury Press, 2012).
Nayder, Lillian, 'Victorian Detective Fiction', in William Baker and Kenneth Womack (eds), *A Companion to the Victorian Novel* (Westport, CT and London: Greenwood Press, 2002).
Nordau, Max, *Degeneration*. Translated from the Second Edition of the German Work, Popular Edition (London: William Heinemann, 1898).
Oppenheim, E. Phillips, *A Maker of History* (London: Ward, Lock, 1905)
Orwell, George, *The Collected Essays, Journalism and Letters of George Orwell. Volume 2: My Country Right or Left, 1940–1943*, ed. Sonia Orwell and Ian Angus (Harmondsworth: Penguin Books, 1970).

Perkin, Harold, *The Rise of Professional Society: England since 1880* (London and New York: Routledge, 1989).
Pinkerton, Allan, *The Molly Maguires and the Detectives*. New and Enlarged Edition (New York: G. W. Dillingham, 1897).
Poe, Edgar Allan, *Selected Writings*, ed. David Galloway (Harmondsworth: Penguin, 1978).
Ponsonby, Arthur, *The Decline of Aristocracy* (London: T. Fisher Unwin, 1912).
Poovey, Mary, *Genres of the Credit Economy* (Chicago: University of Chicago Press, 2008).
Porter, Dennis, *The Pursuit of Crime: Art and Ideology in Detective Fiction* (New Haven: Yale University Press, 1981).
Reade, Winwood, *The Martyrdom of Man*, 8th edn (London: Trübner & Co., 1884).
Ridley, Jane, *Bertie: A Life of Edward VII* (London: Vintage, 2013).
Robb, George, *White-Collar Crime in Modern England: Financial Fraud and Business Morality, 1845–1929* (Cambridge: Cambridge University Press, 1992).
Rudolph, Donna Keyse and G. A. Rudolph, *Historical Dictionary of Venezuela*, 2nd edn (Lanham, MD and London: Scarecrow Press, 1996).
Showalter, Elaine, *Sexual Anarchy: Gender and Culture at the Fin de Siècle* (London: Bloomsbury, 1991).
Shpayer-Makov, Haia, 'Explaining the Rise and Success of Detective Memoirs in Britain', in Clive Emsley, Haia Shpayer-Makov (eds), *Police Detectives in History, 1750–1950* (Aldershot: Ashgate, 2006).
Slander of Women Act 1891 (54 & 55 Vict.) (London: Eyre and Spottiswoode, 1891).
Smith, Herbert Greenhough, 'Some Letters of Conan Doyle With Notes and Comments', *Strand Magazine* LXXX (October, 1930), pp. 390–5.
Soloway, Richard A., *Demography and Degeneration: Eugenics and the Declining Birthrate in Twentieth-Century Britain* (Chapel Hill, NC: UNC Press Books, 2014).
Stafford, David A. T., 'Spies and Gentlemen: The Birth of the British Spy Novel, 1893–1914', *Victorian Studies* 24.4 (Summer, 1981), pp. 489–509.
Stashower, Daniel, *Teller of Tales: The Life of Arthur Conan Doyle* (London: Allen Lane, 2000).
Stead, W. T., *Wanted: A Sherlock Holmes! A Chance for Amateur Detectives* (London: *Review of Reviews* Office, 1895).
Stevenson, Robert Louis, 'A Humble Remonstrance' in *Memories and Portraits* (New York: Scribners, 1895), pp. 275–99.
Stevenson, Robert Louis and Fanny Van de Grift Stevenson, *More New Arabian Nights: The Dynamiter* (New York: Henry Holt, 1885).
Stone, Lawrence, *Road to Divorce: England 1530–1987* (Oxford: Oxford University Press, 1990).
Summerscale, Kate, *The Suspicions of Mr Whicher, Or the Murder at Road Hill House* (London: Bloomsbury, 2008).

Sutherland, John, *Who Betrays Elizabeth Bennett: Further Puzzles in Classic Fiction* (Oxford: Oxford University Press, 1999).

Thomas, Peter, *Detection and its Designs: Narrative and Power in Nineteenth-Century Detective Fiction* (Athens: Ohio University Press, 1998).

Thomas, Ronald R., *Detective Fiction and the Rise of Forensic Science* (Cambridge: Cambridge University Press, 1999).

Thompson, F. M. L., *The Cambridge Social History of Britain, 1750–1950* (Cambridge: Cambridge University Press, 1990).

Todorov, Tzvetan, 'The Typology of Detective Fiction', in Tzvetan Todorov, *The Poetics of Prose* (Ithaca, NY: Cornell University Press, 1977).

Trodd, Anthea, *Domestic Crime in the Victorian Novel* (Basingstoke: Macmillan, 1989).

Veblen, Thorstein, *The Theory of the Leisure Class*, ed. Martha Banta (Oxford: Oxford University Press, 2009).

Wells, H. G., *Tono-Bungay*, ed. John Hammond (London: J. M. Dent, 1994).

Wilde, Oscar, *The Importance of Being Earnest*, ed. Russell Jackson (London: Bloomsbury, 2015).

—, *The Picture of Dorian Gray*, ed. Robert Mighall (London: Penguin, 2003).

Wilson, Edmund, '"Mr Holmes, They Were the Footprints of a Gigantic Hound"', in Philip A. Shreffler (ed.), *The Baker Street Reader: Cornerstone Writings about Sherlock Holmes* (Westport, CT and London: Greenwood Press, 1984).

Wynne, Catherine, *The Colonial Conan Doyle: British Imperialism, Irish Nationalism and the Gothic* (Westport, CT: Greenwood Press, 2002).

Yeats, W. B., *The Poems* (rev. edn), ed. Richard J. Finneran (New York: Macmillan, 1989).

Index

Abu Klea (battle), 67
Achebe, Chinua, 'Image of Africa, An', 139, 141
Afghanistan, 64–5, 126, 165, 167
Africa, 140–5
agricultural depression (1875–96), 24–8
Albert Edward, Prince of Wales ('Bertie') *see* Edward VII
alcoholism, 15, 83, 85, 88–9, 160, 162, 163–4, 167
Alexandra, Queen, 229
American Civil War, 8, 144–5, 164–6, 207
Andaman Islands, 126, 132–5
Anglo-Boer War (1899–1902), 5, 64, 103, 120–1, 174–7, 181–2
Anglo-Russian Entente, 184, 195
Answers, 185, 202
Arata, Stephen, 68, 117
Argentina, 34–5
aristocracy, 4–5, 22–4, 54–9, 65–9, 85–6, 96–8, 109–11
Asquith, H. H., 213
Atkinson, Michael, 51, 231, 233
Atlanta (Georgia), 144
Ayub Khan, 167

baccarat, 67
Baden-Powell, Robert, *Scouting for Boys*, 190–1
Baker Street Journal, 235
Balfour, Jabez, 35

Barnes, Julian, *Arthur and George*, 48
Barrie, J. M., 182
Barsham, Diana, 76, 93, 174–5
Barthes, Roland, *S/Z*, 227
Beck, Adolf, 48
Beecher, Henry Ward, 160, 164–6
Belfast Telegraph, 216
Bell, Joseph, 50
Belsey, Catherine, 203–4, 236
Bennet, Charles Augustus, Earl of Tankerville, 104
Bennett, Arnold, 182
Bertillon, Alphonse, 170
Bhabha, Homi, 135
Bibighar Massacre, 128
Blackwood's Magazine, 126
Bloom, Harold, 51
Boer War *see* Anglo-Boer War (1899–1902)
Boyer, Rick, 226
Braddon, Mary, *Aurora Floyd*, 105, 109
Brantlinger, Patrick, 21, 126–8
British Intelligence, 8, 196, 200, 202
British Journal of Photography, 140–1
British Medical Journal, 117
Bronte, Charlotte, *Jane Eyre*, 150
Bruce, Nigel, 181, 226
Bryce Report, 183
Buchan, John, 195–6
Bynoe, Charles Augustus, 103–4

Cain, Lynn, 92
Cantlie, Sir James, 171–2
Carey, John, 36, 46
Carpenter, Edward, 118
Cassell's Magazine, 116
Cavell, Edith, 183
Chakravarty, Gautam, 126
Chamberlain, Joseph, 25
Chaucer, Geoffrey, 'Pardoner's Tale, The', 30
Chesterton, G. K., 182
Childers, Erskine, *Riddle of the Sands, The*, 185
Churchill, Winston, 214
Clan-na-Gael, 209
Collier's Weekly, 63, 230
Collins, Wilkie, 7
  Moonstone, The, 30, 43, 58, 125–6, 130–1
  No Name, 105
  Woman in White, The, 209–10, 219
Congo Free State, 141
Conrad, Joseph, 139
  'Heart of Darkness', 169–70
  'Il Conde', 116
  Nostromo, 36n, 155
Conservative Party, 215
Cox and Co. (bank), 218
Cranfield, Jonathan, 46
Criminal Appeal Act 1907, 48
Criminal Law Amendment Act 1885, 104, 117
Criminal Tribes Act 1871, 134
Cromie, Robert, 185
Cronje, Piet, 174–5
Cuningham, Henry, 144–5
Curragh Mutiny, 213

Daily Express, 25, 176
Daily Mail, 13, 89, 185, 186
Daily Telegraph, 200
Dangerfield, George, 215
degeneration, 151–2, 154, 167–75

Dickens, Charles
  Bleak House, 43, 104, 109
  David Copperfield, 58
  Dombey and Son, 91–2
  Little Dorrit, 35
divorce law reform, 5, 85–90
Divorce Law Reform Union, 88
Dixon, Franklin W., 226
Douglas, Lord Alfred, 'Two Loves', 116
Doyle, Arthur Conan
  experiences in Egypt, 175
  experiences in South Africa, 176
  finances, 31, 34, 230
  political activities, 209, 215
  wartime propaganda activities, 179–83
  WORKS
  'Abbey Grange, The Adventure of the', 3–4, 5, 6, 23, 45, 85–90, 160
  Adventures of Sherlock Holmes, The, 11, 14–15, 18, 36, 92–3
  'Beryl Coronet, The Adventure of the', 30, 63, 221
  'Black Peter, The Adventure of', 31, 34–8, 45, 49n, 84, 97, 160
  'Blanched Soldier, The Adventure of the', 2, 75, 119–21, 184
  'Blue Carbuncle, The Adventure of the', 15–19, 83
  'Boscombe Valley Mystery, The', 30, 44–5, 73, 75
  'Brazilian Cat, The', 148–9
  Brigadier Gerard stories, 166–7
  British Campaign in France and Flanders, The, 166, 179–80
  'Bruce-Partington Plans, The Adventure of the', 6, 51, 195–200
  'Cardboard Box, The Adventure of the', 8, 42, 83, 159–67
  Case-Book of Sherlock Holmes, The, 63, 119, 219, 224, 234

'Case of Identity, A', 1–2, 8, 73, 81, 83, 91–2
'Charles Augustus Milverton, The Adventure of', 8, 61, 103–11
'Copper Beeches, The Adventure of the', 15, 21, 23, 73, 81, 92–3, 150, 160, 207
'Creeping Man, The Adventure of the', 219, 221–3, 225
'Crooked Man, The Adventure of the', 20, 45, 130, 136
Crown Diamond, The, 224–5
'Dancing Men, The Adventure of the', 26–8, 31, 49n, 51, 206, 207
'Danger!', 166, 185–7, 197
'Devil's Foot, The Adventure of the', 84, 86, 220
Doings of Raffles Haw, The, 185
'Dying Detective, The Adventure of the', 49n
'Empty House, The Adventure of the', 8, 20, 49n, 51, 63–9, 200, 206
'Engineer's Thumb, The Adventure of the', 15, 30, 206
'Final Problem, The Adventure of the', 3, 5, 63, 165, 206, 229, 230, 231–5
'Five Orange Pips, The', 67, 104, 144, 206, 207–8
German War, The, 181–2, 183
'Gloria Scott, The Adventure of the', 3, 224
'Golden Pince-Nez, The Adventure of the', 84, 206
Great Boer War, The, 174–6
'Greek Interpreter, The Adventure of the', 4, 51, 200, 206
'Green Flag, The', 165
His Last Bow, 112, 159, 234
'His Last Bow', 159, 179–91, 197, 215–16
Hound of the Baskervilles, The, 2, 23, 30, 46, 63, 67, 75–6, 83–4, 88, 148–9, 151, 165, 169–77, 230, 231
'Illustrious Client, The Adventure of the', 62–3, 221, 233
'J. Habakuk Jephson's Statement', 225
'Lion's Mane, The Adventure of the', 2, 6, 184, 225
Lost World, The, 29n, 142, 147, 174
'Man with the Twisted Lip, The', 30
'Mazarin Stone, The Adventure of the', 184, 224–5
Memoirs of Sherlock Holmes, The, 30, 45, 159–60
Memories and Adventures, 50, 55, 106, 145, 174, 181, 186–7, 230
Micah Clarke, 134
'Mr Stevenson's Methods in Fiction', 74, 76
'Musgrave Ritual, The Adventure of the', 3, 23, 26, 51–9, 97, 224
Mystery of Cloomber, The, 21, 125–6, 130
'Naval Treaty, The Adventure of the', 49n, 51, 170, 201–3, 226–7
'Noble Bachelor, The Adventure of the', 27, 30, 69n, 73–5, 81, 221
'Norwood Builder, The Adventure of the', 7, 46–8, 84
'On the Slave Coast with a Camera', 140, 145
'Priory School, The Adventure of the', 5, 93–8
'Red Circle, The Adventure of the', 2, 206, 208–10, 211
'Red-Headed League, The', 14–15, 30, 206

Doyle, Arthur Conan (*cont.*)
  'Resident Patient, The Adventure of the', 159, 160–1, 206
  'Retired Colourman, The Adventure of the', 83, 84, 224
  Return of Sherlock Holmes, The, 30, 45
  'Scandal in Bohemia, A', 2–3, 11–14, 49n, 51, 61–2, 63, 73, 81, 229, 230
  'Second Stain, The Adventure of the', 51, 150, 202–4, 226–7, 234
  Sherlock Holmes (with William Gillette), 229–31, 235
  'Shoscombe Old Place, The Adventure of', 23
  Sign of Four, The, 1, 2, 6, 20, 21, 30, 42, 45, 49n, 51, 73–4, 118, 125–36, 160, 223, 234
  'Silver Blaze, The Adventure of', 7, 45, 69n, 227
  Sir Nigel, 166
  'Six Napoleons, The Adventure of the', 206
  'Solitary Cyclist, The Adventure of the', 78–81
  'Speckled Band, The Adventure of the', 3, 5, 6, 20–8, 51, 73, 81, 92, 97, 233
  'Stockbroker's Clerk, The Adventure of the', 31–4
  Story of British Prisoners, The, 182
  Story of Waterloo, The, 166
  Study in Scarlet, A, 2, 6, 39–45, 76–8, 81, 125, 161, 206, 223, 229
  'Sussex Vampire, The Adventure of the', 150–2, 154, 225–6
  'Thor Bridge, The Problem of', 5, 84, 98, 150–1, 152–6, 218–19, 226
  'Three Correspondents, The', 165
  'Three Gables, The Adventure of the', 2, 5, 23, 138–40, 145, 149–50, 151
  'Three Garridebs, The Adventure of the', 49n, 120, 200
  'Three Students, The Adventure of the', 61
  Through the Magic Door, 7, 50
  To Arms!, 182
  Tragedy of the Korosko, The, 165, 175–6
  Valley of Fear, The, 45–6, 49n, 206, 210–16
  'Veiled Lodger, The Adventure of the', 83, 84, 219, 220–1
  'Visit to Three Fronts, A', 182
  War in South Africa, The, 64, 166, 181, 183
  White Company, The, 55, 166
  'Wisteria Lodge, The Adventure of', 8, 23, 49n, 112–21
  World War Conspiracy, The, 182
  'Yellow Face, The Adventure of the', 142–5
Doyle, Charles Altamont, 88, 160, 184
Doyle, Lady *see* Leckie, Jean
Doyle, Louise *see* Hawkins, Louise
Doyle, Mary (née Foley), 88
Duncan, Isadora, 220

Eagleton, Terry, 5
Easter Rising (1916), 215–16
Edalji, George, 48, 104, 141
Edmonds, James, 196
Edward VII, 5, 62–9, 181, 229
Edwards, Owen Dudley, 145, 209, 210, 212
Egypt, 67, 165, 175
Eliot, George, 91
Eliot, T. S., 'Macavity: the Mystery Cat', 233

Ellis, Henry Havelock and John Addington Symonds, *Sexual Inversion*, 117
Entente Cordiale, 184, 195, 203, 204
Epicurus, 163
espionage, 184–9, 195–204

Fanon, Frantz, 135
Fenian violence, 209, 213
First Anglo-Afghan War (1839–42), 126
First War of Indian Independence *see* Indian Mutiny
First World War, 179–91
Fitzgerald, Admiral Penrose, 186
Fourth Anglo-Mysore War (1798–9), 125
France, 195, 198, 203
freemasonry, 209, 212–13
Frohman, Charles, 229–30
future-war fiction *see* invasion-scare fiction

Gaboriau, Émile, 7
  Blackmailers, The (also known as *Le Dossier No. 113* and *File No. 113*), 105
Gagnier, Regenia, 13
Galsworthy, John, 88, 182
Garnet, Henry Highland, 145
Garrick Theatre (New York), 229
Gatiss, Mark, 200
Germany, 181–2, 184–5, 187–90, 202–3
Gillette, William, 229–31
Gissing, George, *The Whirlpool*, 35
Godwin, William, *Caleb Williams*, 60n
Gordon, Charles (General), 8, 67, 160, 165–6
Gordon Relief Expedition, 165
Gordon-Cumming, Sir William, 67–9, 175–6

Government of Ireland Act 1914, 213
Gray, John, 235
Green, Richard Lancelyn, 44, 103
Gregg, Hilda ('Sydney C. Grier'), 126
Griffith, George, 185
Guenther, Louise, 147–50

Haggard, H. Rider, 25
Haig, Douglas (Field Marshal), 180
Hardy, Thomas, 182
Harmsworth, Alfred, 185, 202
Hawkins, Louise ('Touie'), 88
Hobson, J. A., 181
Holmes, Mycroft (fictional character), 8, 197–9
Holmes, Sherlock (fictional character)
  as narrator, 2–3, 119, 184
  sexuality, 119–20
  untold adventures, 218–27
  use of close reading, 5
  use of imagination, 7–8
  use of knowledge, 6
homosexuality, 104, 114–21
Hopkins, Stanley (fictional character), 34–6, 45
Hornung, E. W., 88
  The Amateur Cracksman, 106–7
Howell, Charles Augustus, 103
Hudson, Mrs (fictional character), 39, 49n
Huh, Jinny, 141, 143–4
Hunter, William W., *Imperial Gazetteer of India*, 133–4

India, 64–5, 125–36
Indian Mutiny (1857), 126–35
Indian Rebellion (1857) *see* Indian Mutiny
Inter-Departmental Committee on Physical Deterioration, 177

invasion-scare fiction, 184–8, 195–204
Irish Republican Brotherhood (IRB), 209
Irish republican violence, 209–16
Irving, Henry, 229

Jann, Rosemary, 75, 162
Jevons, William Stanley, 12

Kenny, Kevin, 211
Kent, Constance, 43
Kerr, Douglas, 41, 78, 166
Kestner, Joseph, 21, 76, 80, 81, 214
Khalifa Abdullahi, 165, 200
Kipling, Rudyard, 139, 182, 230
  Barrack-Room Ballads, 167
  Kim, 195–6
Kitchener, Herbert, 165, 175
Knight, Stephen, 46, 236
Knox, Ronald, 235
Krueger, Paul, 203
Krueger Telegram, 203, 204
Ku Klux Klan, 206, 207–8

Labouchere, Henry, 104, 117
Labour Party, 215
Lancet, 117
Lang, Andrew, 134–5
Le Queux, William, 185, 186, 190, 196
  Great War in England in 1897, The, 185, 202
  Invasion of 1910, The, 185
  Secrets of the Foreign Office, 197, 202
  Spies of the Kaiser, 196, 197, 198
  Whoso Findeth a Wife, 201
Leckie, Jean, 88
Leopold II, King of the Belgians, 141
Lesage, Alain-René, *Le Diable boiteux*, 91
Lestrade, Inspector (fictional character), 7, 39–48, 172

Libel Act 1843, 109
Liberal Party, 215
Liberal Unionist Party, 215
Lippincott's Magazine, 13, 46, 118
Lusitania, 186

Maiwand (battle), 166
marginal utility (economics), 12
Marie Celeste, 225
marriage, 8, 73–81
Married Women's Property Acts 1870 and 1882, 81
Marshall, Alfred, 12–13, 16, 17, 19
  Principles of Economics, 12–13, 18
Marx, Karl, 12, 16
Masefield, John, 182
Masterman, C. F. G., *Condition of England, The*, 26, 182
Matrimonial Causes Act 1857, 87–8
McBratney, John, 133–4
Metress, Christopher, 161–2, 204
Metropolitan Police, 42–4
Meyer, Nicholas, *Seven-Per-Cent Solution, The*, 234
Miller, Jane Eldridge, 83
Miller, Karl, 118
Milner, Alfred (Lord Milner), 64
miscarriages of justice, 47–8, 103–4
Moffat, Steven, 200
Molly Maguires, 210–12
Moretti, Franco, 15
Moriarty, Professor (fictional character), 3, 63–4, 206–7, 209, 213, 215, 230, 231–5
Mouat, F. J., 135
Murray, Charles Augustus, 104

Nana Sahib, 128–9
Napoleonic Wars, 182–3, 208, 209
Nayder, Lillian, 131
Nordau, Max, *Degeneration*, 172
Northcliffe, Lord *see* Harmsworth, Alfred

Official Secrets Act 1911, 199
Oppenheim, E. Philips, 196
   Maker of History, A, 201, 203
Orwell, George, 139

Paget, Sidney, 56, 148, 165, 205n
Parliament Act 1911, 213
Peel, Robert, 43
Pemberton, Max, 116
Perkin, Harold, 43
Persia, 200
Pinkerton, Allan, *Molly Maguires and the Detectives, The*, 211–12
Poe, Edgar Allan, 7, 50–1, 219
   'Cask of Amontillado, The', 60n
   'Fall of the House of Usher, The', 27, 51–6, 173
   'Gold Bug, The', 30, 51
   'Masque of the Red Death, The', 51
   'Murders in the Rue Morgue, The', 50, 51, 54, 160
   'Mystery of Marie Rogêt, The', 50
   'Purloined Letter, The', 50, 51, 105, 201–2
Ponsonby, Arthur, 98
professionalisation, 43–7
Puck, 63
Punch, 43
Pursuit to Algiers, 226

Quarterly Review, 134

racism, 131–6, 138–45
Rathbone, Basil, 181
Reade, Winwood, *Martyrdom of Man, The*, 128, 133
Reconstruction Era, 144
Ridley, Jane, 63
Roberts, (Lord) Frederick, Field Marshal, 167, 195
Robinson, B. Fletcher, 176

Robson, W. W., 139
Roden, Christopher, 160
Ruskin, John, 103

Sayers, Dorothy L., 235
Schreiner, Olive, 181
Second Afghan War (1878–80), 64–5, 126, 160, 166, 184
Secret Service Bureau, 196
securities (finance), 8, 30–6
Seitz, Steve, 226
servants, 56–9
Shakespeare, William, *Hamlet*, 91
share ownership *see* securities
Sherlock (BBC), 120, 200, 226
Sherlock Holmes and the Voice of Terror, 181
Sherlock Holmes Journal, 235
Showalter, Elaine, 118
Shpayer-Makov, Haia, 46
Sinn Fein, 216
Slander of Women Act 1891, 109
Slater, Oscar, 48, 104
Smith, Herbert Greenhough, 78, 212, 229
Sophocles, *Oedipus Rex*, 88
South Africa, 6, 30–1, 64, 174–7, 203
South America, 34–5, 112–13, 141–2, 147–56
Spiritualism, 88, 103
Star Theatre (Buffalo, NY), 229
Stead, W. T., 103–4, 181
Stevenson, Robert Louis, 7, 74, 76–7
   'Humble Remonstrance, A', 76
   More New Arabian Nights: The Dynamiter (with Fanny Van de Grift Stevenson), 43, 76–7
   'Pavilion on the Links, The', 125
   Strange Case of Dr Jekyll and Mr Hyde, The, 221–2
Stoddart, J. M., 13, 118
Stoker, Bram, 118
Stone, Lawrence, 88
Stowe, Harriet Beecher, 164

Strand Magazine, 11, 63, 98, 113, 116, 148, 159, 165, 167, 176, 179, 181, 185, 186, 195, 201, 208, 212, 215, 218, 225, 230, 231
strikes (1910–14), 214–15
submarine warfare, 185–7
Sudan, 67, 165, 175, 200
Swinburne, Algernon Charles, 103

Teleny (anonymous novel), 116
Thackeray, William Makepeace, 91
 Pendennis, 58
Thomas, Ronald R., 236
Tibet, 200
Times, The, 43, 182, 185
Todorov, Tzvetan, 3
Tonypandy riots, 214
Towheed, Shafquat, 135
Tracy, Louis, 185
trade unions, 214–16
Tranby Croft Affair, 66–9
Tree, Herbert Beerbohm, 229
Trodd, Anthea, 58, 92
Trollope, Anthony, *Way We Live Now, The*, 35

Ulster Volunteer Force, 213

Veblen, Thorstein, *Theory of the Leisure Class, The*, 11–12, 41
Venezuela, 31, 34
Vidocq, Eugène François, 50

War Propaganda Bureau *see* Wellington House
Watson, Dr John (fictional character), 1–2, 33–4, 43–4, 64–5, 73–5, 126, 183–4, 218
Weekly News, 196
Weeks, Jeffrey, 118
Wellington House, 182
Wells, H. G., 13, 182
 Tono-Bungay, 26
Westminster Gazette, 165, 175
Whicher, Jack, 43
Whistler, James McNeill, 103
White, Arnold, 176
Wilde, Oscar, 13, 103, 114, 116–18, 122n
 Importance of Being Earnest, The, 25–6
 Picture of Dorian Gray, The, 13, 46, 118
Wilder, Billy and I. A. L. Diamond, *Private Life of Sherlock Holmes, The*, 120, 200
Wilhelm II (Kaiser), 203
Wilson, Arthur, 67
Wilson, Edmund, 4
Wynne, Catherine, 21, 209, 210, 212, 213

Yeats, W. B., 215–16
Young, G. M., *Victorian England: Portrait of an Age*, 24
Younghusband, Francis, 200